D0147562

3
3,

3 Crucial
Questions
about
Spiritual Warfare

3 Crucial Questions
Grant R. Osborne and Richard J. Jones, Jr., editors

Other Books by Clinton E. Arnold

3 Crucial Questions
about
Spiritual Warfare

Clinton E. Arnold

Baker Books

A Division of Baker Book House Co
Grand Rapids, Michigan 49516

© 1997 by Clinton E. Arnold

Published by Baker Books
a division of Baker Publishing Group
P.O. Box 6287, Grand Rapids, MI 49516-6287
www.bakerbooks.com

Seventh printing, February 2007

Printed in the United States of America

All rights reserved. No part of this publication may be reproduced, stored in a retrieval system, or transmitted in any form or by any means—for example, electronic, photocopy, recording—without the prior written permission of the publisher. The only exception is brief quotations in printed reviews.

Library of Congress Cataloging-in-Publication Data
Arnold, Clinton E.
    3 crucial questions about spiritual warfare / Clinton E. Arnold.
        p   cm. — (3 crucial questions)
    Includes bibliographical references and indexes.
    ISBN 10: 0-8010-5784-1
    ISBN 978-0-8010-5784-7
    1. Spiritual warfare. 2. Spiritual warfare—Biblical teaching. I. Title. II. Series.
BT975.A76   1997
235′.4—dc21   97-8642

Unless otherwise indicated, Scripture is taken from the HOLY BIBLE, NEW INTERNATIONAL VERSION®. NIV®. Copyright © 1973, 1978, 1984 by International Bible Society. Used by permission of Zondervan. All rights reserved.

To Brandon

*May the good hand of our God be upon you
as you begin your walk with Him.*

Contents

❖

Illustrations

❖

Editors' Preface

The books in the 3 Crucial Questions series are the published form of the 3 Crucial Questions Seminars, which are sponsored by Bridge Ministries of Detroit, Michigan. The seminars and books are designed to greatly enhance your Christian walk. The following comments will help you appreciate the unique features of the book series.

The 3 Crucial Questions series is based on two fundamental observations. First, there are crucial questions related to the Christian faith for which imperfect Christians seem to have no final answers. Christians living in eternal glory may know fully even as they are known by God, but now we know only in part (1 Cor. 13:12). Therefore, we must ever return to such questions with the prayer that God the Holy Spirit will continue to lead us nearer to "the truth, the whole truth, and nothing but the truth." While recognizing their own frailty, the authors contributing to this series pray that they are thus led.

Second, each Christian generation partly affirms its solidarity with the Christian past by reaffirming "the faith which was once delivered unto the saints" (Jude 3 KJV). Such an affirmation is usually attempted by religious scholars who are notorious for talking only to themselves or by nonexperts whose grasp of the faith lacks depth of insight. Both situations are unfortunate, but we feel that our team of contributing authors is well prepared to avoid them. Each author is a competent Christian scholar able to share tremendous learning in down-to-earth language both laity and experts can appreciate. In a word, you have in hand a book that is part of a rare series, one that is neither pedantic nor pediatric.

The topics addressed in the series have been chosen for their timelessness, interest level, and importance to Christians everywhere. And the contributing authors are committed to discussing them in a manner that promotes Christian unity. Thus, they discuss not only areas of disagreement among Christians but significant areas of agreement as well. Seeking peace and pursuing it as the Bible commands (1 Peter 3:11), they stress common ground on which Christians with different views may meet for wholesome dialogue and reconciliation.

The books in the series consist not merely of printed words; they consist of words to live by. Their pages are filled not only with good information but with sound instruction in successful Christian living. For study is truly Christian only when, in addition to helping us understand our faith, it helps us to live our faith. We pray therefore that you will allow God to use the 3 Crucial Questions series to augment your growth in the grace and knowledge of our Lord and Savior Jesus Christ.

Grant R. Osborne
Richard J. Jones, Jr.

❖

Author's Preface

Ninety-seven books on the topic of "spiritual warfare" line one of the shelves in my office. All but a dozen of these have been published in the last ten years. Most of them present some form of "deliverance ministry" and are full of dramatic and triumphant stories. Others are sounding the alarm about "territorial spirits" and make suggestions about identifying them and praying against them. A handful of the books react to all the others, insisting that most of what is being said about spiritual warfare is faddish, nutty, and unhealthy for the church.

What are we to think? In spite of all that has been said about spiritual warfare over the past decade, many believers are still troubled by a set of unanswered questions. At the top of the list remains one of the most important questions of all, "What does the Bible teach about these issues?" Specifically, can a Christian be demon-possessed? Do we really have a responsibility to engage territorial spirits? And, even more foundational, what is spiritual warfare all about?

This book is an attempt to provide biblical, theological, and some church-historical perspectives to these three crucial questions about spiritual warfare. It does not purport to be the final word, but it does endeavor to probe these particular questions more deeply in the light of Scripture than many of the popular works have attempted to do.

My perspective on these issues has not only come out of significant personal study, but also from my participation in the cause of Christ—presenting the gospel, teaching new believers, and helping people to grow in their relationship with and obedience to the Lord. On many counts, my understanding has been deeply enriched by dear friends and colleagues. At the top of the list are Dr. Douglas Hayward, associate professor of anthropology and chair of the department of intercultural studies at Biola University, and Dr. John Kelley, professor of psychology at

Rosemead School of Psychology and director of the Biola University counseling center. We have met biweekly for the past three years to discuss the issues surrounding dissociative disorders and demonization and how we might help people gain spiritual health. Perhaps a word of thanks should also be extended to the El Pescador restaurant in La Mirada for keeping our discussions going with an endless supply of tortilla chips, salsa, and iced tea as we have met there over the years.

I also want to express my appreciation to the members of the Spiritual Warfare Network and, especially, to Dr. C. Peter Wagner. Pete and I have maintained an ongoing dialogue over the past six years that has been very helpful. I have been deeply inspired by Pete's evangelistic fervor and especially by his passion for those in the regions of the world missiologists refer to as the 10/40 Window who do not know Christ.

A few other people whom I must mention by name are Dr. Robert Saucy (Talbot School of Theology), Dr. A. Scott Moreau (Wheaton College), Jim Logan (International Center for Biblical Counseling), Dr. Gerry Breshears (Western Seminary), Dr. Ed Murphy (OC Ministries), and some very special people from my church—Debbie Schuster and Sandy Enyart. Certainly not least among those from whom I continue to learn is my most important ministry partner, my wife, Barbara. This list could be extended by two or three pages.

Thanks are also due to Biola University and Talbot School of Theology for extending a sabbatical leave to me during the fall 1995 semester, during which time I wrote a good portion of this book. I am also grateful to Richard Jones and Grant Osborne for creating this fine series and for their insightful contributions as editors.

❖

Abbreviations

CEV	Contemporary English Version
DID	Dissociative Identity Disorder
GNB/TEV	Good News Bible/Today's English Version
KJV	King James Version
Message	*The Message: The New Testament in Contemporary English*
MPD	Multiple Personality Disorder
NASB	New American Standard Bible
NEB	New English Bible
NIV	New International Version
NKJV	New King James Version
NLT	New Living Translation
NRSV	New Revised Standard Version
RSV	Revised Standard Version
SLSW	Strategic-Level Spiritual Warfare
SRA	Satanic Ritual Abuse
SWN	Spiritual Warfare Network

❖

What Is
Spiritual Warfare?

hat is spiritual warfare all about? Foundational to spiritual warfare is a belief in evil spirits and a desire to get the upper hand on them before they get it on us. For many people, this is all a little too weird to take seriously.

Are We Getting into Something Bizarre?

A variety of images come to mind when demons are mentioned. Some people immediately think of the strange practices they have heard about in other countries or even among immigrants in our own communities. Take, for instance, the city of Fresno in the center of California's agriculturally rich San Joaquin Valley. This city continues to experience an enormous influx of Hmong immigrants from Southeast Asia. The Hmongs are a people who have a vibrant belief in evil spirits. They also have a well-established set of rituals and traditions for dealing with demons. These practices, however, have brought them into conflict with Fresno city authorities. Recently a Hmong shaman tried to appease an angry spirit that he thought was vexing his wife's health. He burned paper money; he sacrificed a chicken and then a pig. When this did not work, he took a three-month-old German shepherd puppy out onto the front porch of his home and, as he chanted the appropriate ancient Laotian formulas, a relative beat the puppy over the head until it died. Before he buried the dog, police arrived in response to a neighbor's call and the man was arrested.[1]

Spiritual warfare also calls to mind images of macabre exorcism rituals. Those who saw the popular 1973 movie, *The Exorcist,* did not quickly forget the ghastly bodily contortions and sinister voices a thirteen-year-old girl exhibited as she was exorcised by two priests. But these kinds of scenes are not limited to the cinema. In March 1995, five Korean women were arrested and charged with murder for allegedly beating a young woman to death in their attempt to "cast demons out" of her.[2] During the summer of the same year, a man on a weekend fishing trip with his two teenage sons near Estancia, New Mexico, came to the conclusion that the boys were possessed by the devil. He pulled off to the side of the road and beheaded one of his sons while the other fled the scene. Investigators on the case said "he indicated he was trying to beat back the demons. He thought his child was the devil."[3]

Talk of demons and witches also reminds us of the shame of the Salem witch trials over three hundred years ago—an unrepeatable event from a bygone era. Or is it? The *Los Angeles Times* reports that in 1994 at least one hundred witches were incinerated or stoned to death in South Africa. Many more have been forced to flee their villages, some have had their homes burned, and a number have had their children chased out of school. Many of the displaced now live in "Witches Hill," a kind of refugee camp in a police-sponsored witches protection program.[4] Fortunately, no such hostilities have been reported in the United States, but the practices of witchcraft, sorcery, Satan worship, and various forms of occultic arts are rising dramatically. Although our country may not see witch trials (à la seventeenth-century New England) in the future, we have already witnessed personal hostilities acted out against those identified as witches or demon-possessed.

Will the current revival of belief in the things of the devil cause many to fall headlong into dangerous superstitions that lead, if not to violence, to a strange assortment of beliefs, rituals, practices, and even contact with spirits? This may very well be the case if we do not seek guidance from the one true Spirit, the God who has revealed himself to us in the Lord Jesus Christ and in the Scriptures. This book, therefore, appeals to the Bible for understanding and wisdom on this issue. Although the Bible may not directly answer every specific question we may have, it does provide us with an overall framework for understanding the nature and activities of the evil spiritual realm. It helps us distinguish between destructive superstitions and what is true about the unseen world. Most important, it gives us significant insight into how we are to respond to the evil spirit powers.

Can't We Just Ignore This Topic?

Some believers are too frightened even to talk about spiritual warfare and thus try earnestly to avoid the topic altogether. A couple of years ago my wife, Barbara, went to the weekly meeting of a group of ladies who pray for the children and teachers at our local public school. During the course of the meeting she mentioned that I was leading a seminar in the area on the topic of spiritual warfare. One of the ladies immediately spoke up and said that she would never attend a spiritual warfare seminar again. She claimed that the only time she had ever gone to such a seminar, some very strange things happened that really scared her. Her solution was to ignore it and thereby, she hoped, she would never be spooked or troubled by it again.

Avoiding the topic is a profoundly inadequate response. Spiritual warfare is not an isolatable compartment of church ministry or Christian experience. Spiritual warfare is an integral part of the entire Christian experience. It is a fact of life. To think that a Christian could avoid spiritual warfare is like imagining that a gardener could avoid dealing with weeds. Our goal should be rather to gain an accurate and sober-minded understanding of spiritual warfare—not a view tainted by frightening superstitions and odd practices.

The Christian Life as "Spiritual Warfare"

Many Christians have come to think of spiritual warfare as a specialized form of ministry—exorcism, deliverance ministry, or certain types of intercession. While these may represent one facet of the topic—indeed, one manifestation of the battle—spiritual warfare is much broader and all-encompassing than this.

A Foundational Understanding of Reality: Kingdoms in Conflict

I am writing this chapter during the Advent season. I am deeply moved every year at this time as I join with other Christians in singing Handel's *Messiah*. What a joyous experience to proclaim, "the kingdom of the world has become the kingdom of our Lord and of his Christ, and he will reign for ever and ever." This line of the famous "Hallelujah Chorus" is straight from the Bible—Revelation 11:15. This passage points triumphantly to a time when God will decisively intervene in human history and strike down "the kingdom of this world." The Lord Jesus Christ, portrayed as wielding a sharp double-edged sword, will be the agent of God in judgment and the final subjugation of evil. This will involve bringing about the ruin of the leader of the opposing kingdom, which the Book of Revelation refers to as "the dragon, that ancient serpent, who is the devil, or Satan" (20:2).

From the very beginning of his public ministry, Jesus both spoke of and demonstrated the nature of the conflict with the opposing kingdom. He was drawn into struggle from the moment he began proclaiming the kingdom of God in the synagogue at Capernaum (Mark 1:21–28). Mark reports that immediately after he taught, an evil spirit manifested in a man and challenged Jesus. Jesus responded not by ridiculing the worldview assumptions of the people in Capernaum, but by dealing directly and firmly with what he perceived the problem to be. There was an evil spirit entity speaking through the man. By his own authority Jesus commanded the spirit to depart. Dealing with these spirits became a customary part of Jesus' ministry. Mark tells us that "he traveled throughout Galilee, preaching in their synagogues and driving out demons" (Mark 1:39).

The kingdom of God was the central theme of Jesus' teaching. The redemptive reign of God was beginning in the person and mission of the Lord Jesus. His exorcisms were a sign of the presence of the kingdom of God. Jesus said, "If I drive out demons by the Spirit [*finger* in Luke] of God, then the kingdom of God has come upon you" (Matt. 12:28; Luke 11:20). Ethelbert Stauffer aptly comments, "the kingdom of God is present where the dominion of the adversary has been overthrown."[5]

All of this points to the reality of a hostile realm in conflict with the kingdom of God. John reveals in his first epistle that "the whole world is under the control of the evil one" (1 John 5:19). Jesus spoke of Satan as "the prince of this world" (John 12:31; 14:30; 16:11). There was, then, some substance to Satan's claim of dominion when he offered Jesus the kingdoms of the world (Matt. 4:8–9; Luke 4:6). Ultimately, God is the sovereign King over heaven and earth, but these passages reveal that Satan and his minions do indeed exercise significant influence over this world and its power structures.

Satan's reign is not only territorial but temporal. The apostle Paul described Satan as "the god of this age" (2 Cor. 4:4). This reflects the biblical understanding of history as divided into two eras: this present evil age and the age to come. Satan is the prince of this age, but the Lord Jesus Christ is the inaugurator and king of a new age and a reign of righteousness. Figure 1.1 depicts the biblical-theological understanding of the two ages.

The end of the present evil age. With all believers, we look forward to the second coming of Christ. This will be the time when our Lord judges

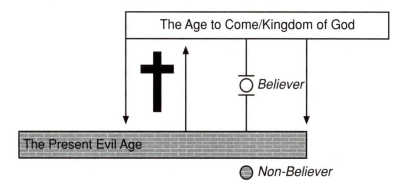

Fig. 1.1 The Two Ages

and eradicates evil, bringing an end to the present evil age. This will be a time when "there will be no more death or mourning or crying or pain, for the old order of things has passed away" (Rev. 21:4). We long for the full realization of the age to come. Unfortunately, we are not there yet. We live in a period when there is still death, mourning, crying, and pain. There is plenty of evil. Satan and his demons are just as active as ever.

The age to come. Our hope is rooted in God's kingdom and his promise of a new age. We eagerly anticipate eternal life with our Lord Jesus Christ. There is much more to our present experience, however, than finding a secure place to wait until Christ returns. The turn of the ages has already dawned with the coming of the Lord Jesus. The good news is that we can experience some of the blessings of the age to come right now. Eternal life is just as much a present experience as a future aspiration (cf. John 17:3). Some of these kingdom manifestations include the following:

- the empowering presence of the Holy Spirit in our lives
- union and close relationship with the Lord Jesus Christ
- reception and manifestation of the gifts of the Holy Spirit
- ability to break free from the bondage of sin
- authority over evil spirits

Tension between the ages. We live at a time when the present evil age overlaps the age to come. The kingdom of God coexists with the kingdom of darkness, but it is not a peaceful coexistence; there is tension. Entering a relationship with Christ means being supernaturally rescued from the kingdom of Satan and installed as a member of Christ's kingdom (Col. 1:13). Believers truly have a new citizenship in a heavenly kingdom (Phil. 3:20).

Our identity is wrapped up in Christ; our allegiance is to the kingdom of God; the eschatological reality is that we are now participants in the age to come and part of the new creation; we are joined to the people of God and we are indeed children of God.

Nevertheless, we still live in the world. Our existence is played out on the stage of the present evil age. Although we are spiritually renewed, our bodies are artifacts of this age and therefore subject to the greatest enemy, death. We continue to feel the impact of sin in profound ways all around us. Violence, bitterness, poverty, crime, terrorism, duplicity and betrayal, and brokenness all abound. Believers sometimes look no different than the unredeemed.

A time of struggle and conflict. Experience tells us that this is a time of strife. And this is precisely what the Scriptures teach us. The imagery of conflict and warfare is found throughout the New Testament.

Imagery of Warfare and Struggle in the New Testament

Image	Reference
The "strong man" (Satan) is fully *armed.*	Luke 11:21
"Someone stronger" (Jesus) *conquers* the "strong man" and takes his *armor.*	Luke 11:22
Jesus came to bring *the sword.*	Matt. 10:34
Jesus came to proclaim liberty to *captives.*	Luke 4:18
The demonized man had a *legion* of spirits.	Mark 5:9, 15
Jesus led the evil powers in a *triumphal procession.*	Col. 2:15
Jesus *stripped* the evil powers of their weapons.	Col. 2:15
Jesus took *captives.*	Eph. 4:8
The Christian life is a *struggle.*	Col. 1:29; 2:1; 1 Tim. 4:10
The Christian life is a *struggle* against evil forces.	Eph. 6:12
The Christian life is a *struggle* against sin.	Heb. 12:4
The desires of the flesh *wage war* against the soul.	1 Peter 2:11
Christians are called to *struggle* for the faith.	Jude 3
Paul *struggled* for the gospel.	Phil. 1:30
Paul "fought the good *fight.*"	2 Tim. 4:7
Christians are *soldiers.*	Phil. 2:25; Philem. 2; 2 Tim. 2:3–4
Christians need to wear *armor* (including *helmet, sword, shield,* and *breastplate*).	Eph. 6:12–17

Christians engage in *warfare*.	1 Tim. 1:18; 6:12; 2 Cor. 10:4
Christians wield *weapons* of warfare.	1 Tim. 1:18; 2 Cor. 10:4; Rom. 6:13; 13:12; 2 Cor. 6:7
Angelic *war* in heaven	Rev. 12:7
The beast and kings of the earth will make *war.*	Rev. 19:19
Satan gathers the nations for a final *battle.*	Rev. 20:8

Our conflict involves struggling against the profound and devastating implications of the spread of sin into the world. For Christians this involves resisting the tendency to commit moral evil. Peter spoke of "the desires of the flesh that wage war against the soul" (1 Peter 2:11 NRSV). This is only half the battle front. As Paul reveals, our struggle is also against spiritual forces of evil—the devil and his retinue of principalities, powers, authorities, thrones, unclean spirits, and demons (Eph. 6:12).

An uneven match. We are in the midst of a struggle that is far greater than us, but it is not bigger than our God. It involves two warring kingdoms, but the sides are not at all evenly matched. There is no cosmic dualism here, with two opposing gods of near-equal power. The testimony of Scripture from beginning to end is that Yahweh is sovereign. He created everything in heaven and on earth. All of the spiritual powers derive their life from him. He holds them in the palm of his hand and can do with them as he wills. In fact, he has already revealed the final outcome of the battle. Christians are on the winning side.

But there truly is a war. Satan and his forces fiercely pursue their objective of promulgating all forms of evil in the world. This includes, above all, deceiving people and hindering them from grasping the truth about God's revelation of himself in the Lord Jesus Christ. But it also includes working to bring about the demise of the church through inciting moral evils among its members. This understanding of the devil and his work was central to the Reformation. Heiko Oberman, Reformation scholar and biographer of Martin Luther, has observed that for Luther the precious truth that "God is for us" directly implies that "the devil is against us." He goes on to note that belief in the devil's opposition to Christ and the gospel "is such an integral part of the Reformation discovery that if the reality of the powers inimical to God is not grasped, the incarnation of Christ, as well as the justification and temptation of the sinner are reduced to ideas of the mind rather than experiences of faith."[6]

The decisive battle of the war was fought nearly two thousand years ago. Jesus Christ gave his life as a sacrifice and payment for sin. God then raised Jesus from the dead and exalted him to his right hand, "high above all rule, authority, power, and dominion." Believers are now joined to Christ in a very real solidarity with him. It is only on the basis of our union with him that we have victory over the enemy. The people of God overcome the adversary "by the blood of the Lamb" (Rev. 12:11). Recognizing this, Sabine Baring-Gould wrote a beautiful song in 1865 describing both the spiritual struggle of the church and its hope for victory in the Lord Jesus Christ:

> Onward, Christian soldiers, marching as to war,
>   With the cross of Jesus going on before.
> At the sign of triumph Satan's host doth flee;
>   On then, Christian soldiers, on to victory:
> Hell's foundations quiver at the sound of praise;
>   Brothers, lift your voices, loud your anthems raise.

Six Common Objections to Emphasizing Spiritual Warfare Today

Some people have dismissed the metaphor of spiritual warfare as an inappropriate way of describing the experience of the Christian today. I respond here to six of the most common objections.

1. *The concept of spiritual warfare reflects a primitive, prescientific worldview.* This modernist perspective on spiritual warfare has been deeply ingrained in American, British, and Continental educational institutions. Many people scoff that a belief in demons went out with a belief in dragons, elves, the tooth fairy, and the Easter Bunny. The issue is often framed as a choice between accepting a modern scientific worldview or devolving into a gullible, uncritical acceptance of a primitive, prescientific worldview. Of course, this is not an issue of being scientific or not. It is an issue of whether we accept the predominantly naturalistic assumptions of certain understandings of science. It is in no way incompatible with the scientific method to give credence to a belief in a personal God—or, conversely, to believe in the evil spiritual dimension. This issue is of such critical importance in our society that I devoted an entire chapter to it in my earlier book, *Powers of Darkness* (see chapter 13: "Reality or Myth").[7]

2. *Demons and evil spirits are not very prominent in the Bible.* Although this is not often stated as a formal argument, some people unwittingly believe that the Bible just doesn't have much to say about the evil supernatural realm. Yet the evidence of Scripture clearly points in the opposite direction. The conflict with Satan and the powers of evil is a major theme in

biblical theology. This has recently been researched in an important monograph by Sydney H. T. Page, professor of New Testament and academic dean at Edmonton Baptist Seminary, in a volume titled *Powers of Evil: A Biblical Study of Satan and Demons.*[8] Page offers the reader a comprehensive biblical analysis of each of the pertinent passages from Genesis to Revelation. Regardless of the number of times demons are mentioned in the Bible, what really matters is the fact that they are discussed and that they are presented as the enemies of Christ and his church.

3. *Experiences with the demonic realm happen only on the mission field, especially in the non-Western world.* I have heard a few people in a variety of churches suggest that demons are only operative in areas of the world where the gospel has not yet reached or where idolatry is still prevalent. They infer that Satan is just not as active in the Christian West. This position is both inaccurate and dangerous. First, there is no biblical support for the notion that demonic hostilities cease in a region where many people have become Christians and the influence of the gospel is felt. In fact, Scripture seeks to prepare believers for ongoing attacks from the realm of evil. Second, the Western world has become decreasingly "Christian" and increasingly open to diverse cults, non-Christian religions, and various occultic beliefs and practices over the past two generations. Third, there are vastly increasing reports of direct and explicit forms of demonic activity in recent years. There are a variety of reasons for this, some of which may be perceptual. I address this in more detail below.

4. *Demonic activity died out by the second century.* Some believers have argued that demonic activity was particularly acute during the ministry of Jesus, but progressively waned after that and eventually died out after the generation of the apostles. Church history illustrates just the opposite, however. Numerous accounts of demonization and exorcism as well as descriptions of the deceptive work of demons in pagan religions fill the writings of the church fathers. There is no hint of demonic activity dying out. The church fathers, rather, attempt to expose the malevolent activities and point people to the saving and keeping power of the Lord Jesus Christ. I provide a number of examples of their discussions in chapter 2.

5. *"Warfare" is not an appropriate metaphor for people who seek peace.* At a time when our nation is longing for peace in the streets of its cities and among warring factions in various countries of the world, it seems odd and somewhat inappropriate for Christians to be waving the banner of warfare. In a recent address, Harvard theologian Harvey Cox expressed his displeasure with the concept of spiritual warfare. He quipped, "I don't warm up to military metaphors and battle imagery."[9] When we talk about spiritual warfare, however, we are not envisioning armed con-

flict or the provocation of hostilities among people. We are taking the adjective *spiritual* quite seriously. We are suggesting that life is not just biology; there is a uniquely spiritual dimension to reality. There are unseen, personal forces that have an impact on day-to-day life. Not all of these spirits are positive and benevolent either. There are many that are evil and bent on destruction. The Bible calls Christians to be aware of this and to prepare for a struggle. The biblical metaphor of spiritual warfare, then, is a shorthand way of referring to our conflict with these spirit forces. They are the perpetrators of untold evil, in both the physical realm and the moral realm. The Bible describes these spirits as especially working to keep people from responding to the redemptive message of the Lord Jesus Christ and to bring about the demise of the people of God. The gospel of deliverance we bring to people is actually a message of peace and reconciliation that is precisely what the demonically inspired instigators of violence need.[10]

6. *Stressing spiritual warfare might lead to an unbalanced, experience-oriented theology centering on the spectacular.* Some conservative Christians shy away from talking much about spiritual warfare because they associate it with groups they perceive to be extreme or who focus too much attention on the spectacular. But, as we have already discussed and will develop even more, the theme of spiritual warfare is thoroughly biblical. For us to reassert an emphasis on spiritual warfare is to turn to the testimony of the Bible, not to a theology based on experience. This theology, however, should have an impact on experience as we see people set free from the captivity of the powers of darkness. And, in this sense, spiritual warfare is truly spectacular.

Although other objections may be raised, these six hold little compelling force to keep us from asserting that spiritual warfare is an important metaphor that needs to be emphasized in the church today. In fact, the weight of biblical importance given to the theme coupled with the struggle the church faces in following Christ would mandate that more attention be given to thinking through the nature of our conflict.

The Danger of Limiting Spiritual Warfare to One Form of Ministry

There is a tendency for people in some circles to think of spiritual warfare as a specialized form of ministry rather than as a descriptive phrase characterizing our common struggle as believers. Thus, for many people, to speak of spiritual warfare is to speak of exorcism, deliverance ministry, taking authority in the name of Jesus against the enemy, or special forms of authoritative prayer. Certainly these are all aspects of spiritual warfare, but no single ministry exhausts our understanding of spiritual warfare.

In the classic passage on spiritual warfare, Ephesians 6:10–20, Paul asserts that the devil uses a variety of methods in his hostilities against believers. He urges believers to "put on the full armor of God so that you can take your stand against the devil's schemes [*methodeiai*]" (v. 11). The verse implies that Satan and his companion spirits exercise their ungodly influence through a broad assortment of ways. Paul expressed this view of demonic activity in another context, where he tells the Corinthians that he is not unaware of Satan's "schemes" or "designs" (*noēmata*) (2 Cor. 2:11).

We need to begin thinking about spiritual warfare in a broader way. *Spiritual warfare is a way of characterizing our common struggle as Christians.* Whether we want to think about it or not, the truth is that we all face supernatural opposition as we set out to live the Christian life. We have an opponent who wants nothing more than to bring about our demise. We have an enemy who wants to blunt our every effort to share the good news of liberation with those still held in captivity.

Spiritual warfare is all-encompassing. It touches every area of our lives—our families, our relationships, our church, our neighborhoods, our communities, our places of employment. There is virtually no part of our existence over which the Evil One does not want to maintain or reassert his unhealthy and perverse influence. Conversely, Jesus longs to reign as Lord over every area of our lives. This is the locus of intense struggle for all believers. And it is a power struggle. To which kingdom—and source of power—do we yield?

This is not to say that the devil is the only form of evil influence against which we struggle and is therefore the only one to blame whenever we fall or lapse into sin. We explain below the nature of our two other enemies—the flesh and the world. Yet with all three, God has provided us with a way of escape and help. It is up to us to yield our lives to the one who can fight for us. We cannot succumb to the "devil made me do it" syndrome.

The metaphor of spiritual struggle helps us wake up to the fact that the Christian life is not just a matter of exertion of human effort. It is also a matter of suprahuman power, allegiance, relationship, and connectedness. Apart from Christ, the odds are clearly against us. We cannot live the lives Christ calls us to live. We need to learn to depend on the empowering presence of God himself through his Holy Spirit. Paul thus prayed for the Ephesians that God would "strengthen you with power through his Spirit in your inner being" (Eph. 3:16). Without the enabling power of God, Satan reasserts his rule.

Why the Upsurge of Interest in Spiritual Warfare?

At no time in the history of the church has more been written about the topic of spiritual warfare than in the past decade. It appears that more Christians are thinking about spiritual warfare now than they have for at least a couple of centuries. Why, all of a sudden, is there such tremendous interest in the unseen dimension of life?

Changing Worldview: The Inadequacy of Naturalism

Many people are beginning to question the dominant role that the naturalistic worldview has had on the way we think about every area of life. This is happening at a variety of levels in our society, among both Christians and non-Christians.

On the whole, atheism and agnosticism are on the way out in our society. Only 5 percent of the population would identify themselves by either of these categories. Ninety-four percent of Americans believe in God and 85 percent believe that religion is "fairly" or "very" important in their lives. On the other hand, half of the population believes in the devil, a quarter believes in ghosts, and a quarter believes in the tenets of astrology. As many as one out of six people thinks he or she has been in touch with someone who has died, and one in ten says he or she has actually talked with the devil.[11] Based on this Gallup study, it appears that religion and spirituality of various sorts have become quite important to Americans. Many believe that this change is a result of an overemphasis on a naturalistic worldview that dismissed spirituality as an artifact of a bygone age.

Harvard Professor Diana Eck recently stated that aspects of Eastern worldview have now become so deeply rooted in our country that it can be said that we are in the midst of a paradigm shift to a whole new worldview.[12] She observes that this new Eastern worldview is not in competition with Christianity and Judaism, but is reshaping them. At the root of this change is a new concept of God. The divine being is no longer transcendent, but completely immanent—"as salt infuses water." The body thus becomes an important object of investigation, not only for understanding ourselves, but also for finding god. We might summarize it in the following way:

- Spirituality is the highest level of consciousness.
- We all share in the divine nature, which we find in the highest level of consciousness.
- We find god by looking inward.
- Our goal is the linking (the "yoga") of our personalities with the inner divine spirit.

This is a worldview that, incidentally, gives no credence to the traditional Christian concept of sin, but rather views the root problem as inattention, distraction, and diversion. Neither, however, does it give serious attention to the notion that there are evil spirits bent on instigating moral evil and perpetrating misery and destruction in a variety of forms.

Much of what Eck refers to is integral to what is popularly known as the New Age Movement. New Age themes have permeated many aspects of American culture over the past twenty years. The New Age Movement is not an organized front that is strategically conspiring to tear down the moorings of Western civilization. It represents a dramatic change in our worldview assumptions influenced most strongly by Eastern thought. Paranormal beliefs and experiences are also integral to the New Age. A recent Gallup poll revealed that roughly half of all Americans now believe in extrasensory perception (ESP), about a third believe in telepathy, and 10 percent believe in channeling.[13]

Fortunately, not everyone who is rejecting philosophical naturalism is embracing Eastern thought or beliefs in the paranormal; some have turned to the Christianity of the Bible. Most notable in this regard is Philip Johnson, professor at the University of California–Berkeley and author of *Reason in the Balance*.[14] He eloquently points out the short-comings of the scientific naturalism of our modern era:

> Scientific naturalism is a story that reduces reality to physical particles and impersonal laws, portrays life as a meaningless competition among organisms that exist only to survive and reproduce, and sees the mind as no more than an emergent property of biochemical reactions.[15]

Rather than turning to a worldview that sees the universe as a living spiritual organism with some divine being that permeates everything, Johnson strongly contends that ultimate truth is found in the God who revealed himself to us in the Lord Jesus Christ. He is the one who has created the world, loves it, and has provided access to himself through the sacrifice of Jesus.

Many Christian leaders who are writing on spiritual warfare have described how they came to recognize that a Western naturalistic world-view had clouded their perception of the spiritual realm. For example, Charles Kraft, professor of anthropology at Fuller Theological Seminary, describes the confusion and discouragement he faced during his first term on the mission field serving among the Higi people of Nigeria. He laments, "we were totally unprepared to deal with the one area the Nigerians considered most important—their relationships with the spirit world."[16] This recognition, along with exposure to the effective ministries of some other Christians, led Kraft into a deeper experience of the manifestation of the power of God in the context of spiritual warfare. He credits that change, in part, to the shedding of the "technological mind-set" (or naturalistic worldview) he inherited by being raised in the United States.

Recognition of the Biblical Worldview

Many people who are talking and writing about spiritual warfare are doing so because they have come to recognize that it is an important part of the biblical perspective on reality. This is certainly my story.

I am frequently asked how I became interested in the topic of spiritual warfare. When people ask this, I think they expect to hear me tell a hair-raising story of how my mother led séances and my father was a satanic high priest before my conversion. Such was not the case. I began my doctoral studies in Aberdeen, Scotland, in 1983, investigating the theme of power in the New Testament against the historical/cultural background of the day. I soon realized that one cannot engage in a biblical study of the power of God without simultaneously exploring the opposing sphere of power—Satan and his principalities and powers. The Bible from beginning to end highlights this theme of conflict with the powers of evil. It is integral to the biblical worldview. Those of us who see the Bible as our authoritative and reliable guide to faith and practice need to take this aspect of the biblical message seriously. The biblical worldview, however, collides head-on with the modern worldview and its naturalistic assumptions. We often do not realize the extent to which naturalistic assumptions have permeated our thinking.

Recognition That the Biblical Worldview Corresponds to Reality

In an age when bacteria, viruses, and parasites can be identified as the causative agents of much physical illness and psychological diagnoses such as Dissociative Identity Disorder (DID) and Post-Traumatic Stress Disorder (PTSD) explain various forms of mental illness, what reason is there for recourse to demons or evil spirits? Precisely because certain manifestations of evil are consistent with the notion of powerful, personal, supernatural forces pushing people into destructive modes of behavior.

How can one explain why a mother would put her four-year-old child into an oven and burn her to death (Auburn, Maine, 1984)? Such an atrocity seems to go beyond the mere human capacity for destructiveness. Consideration of events such as this and the horrors of an Auschwitz are what has led scholar Jeffrey Burton Russell to affirm a belief in the real existence of a personal devil, a mighty being with intelligence and will whose energies are bent on creating human misery and death.[17]

Witnessing a person exhibit "possession behavior" also makes one wonder if there is merit to the biblical paradigm. Seeing a person suddenly change countenance and begin speaking with another voice, growling like a dog, uttering a murderous threat (like, "I'm gonna pin your head against that wall, you ————"), and having a totally different look in his or her eyes forces one to consider whether the biblical description of "demonization" may be appropriate in some instances. Granted, this kind of behavior could be feigned, or it may be a symptom of an organic brain disease or some form of dissociative disorder. Or, these signs might very well be a manifestation of a demonic presence in the person. In some instances I have been convinced that what I was seeing was all a charade. In other cases I think the primary problem was psychological (dissociation). There are yet other cases, however, where I am convinced that the odd behavior was best explained by an evil supernatural being manifesting itself to or through the person.

Frank Peretti

Few would have predicted the phenomenal impact of Frank Peretti's novel, *This Present Darkness*—a book that has enjoyed blockbuster sales.[18] He has followed this up with two more thriller novels, *Piercing the Darkness* and, most recently, *The Oath*. Peretti no doubt caught the crest of the wave of renewed interest in the topic of spiritual warfare, but his writing has also done much to stimulate that interest even further.

This Present Darkness is a suspenseful, action-packed account of the angels of God struggling with the forces of Satan for control of the rural town of Ashton. The plot does not unfold entirely in the heavens. These angels are deeply involved in the day-to-day life of the people in this college town. Peretti describes the workings of the demonic prince of the city down to the low-ranking demons of complacency, lust, murder, and jealousy. In all of the struggles between the angels of darkness and the angels of light, the prayer of God's people is what makes the difference. Peretti characterizes prayer as effectually charging up the angels to fight even more valiantly and powerfully.

The greatest criticism of Peretti's novel has been that numerous Christians have used it as a detailed manual on demonology and tactics for engaging in spiritual warfare. There is no disputing the fact that there are some Christians who have taken the book this way. Insofar as Peretti intended the book to reflect some modicum of reality (which I'm fairly confident he did), he may be open to criticism for the way he conceives of prayer working almost in a magical sense, his lack of emphasis on the ministry of the Holy Spirit, and the unhealthy reinforcement of popular worries of worldwide networked conspiracies.

Regardless of what one thinks of the novel and its sequels, the book has had a wide reading and a major impact in the Christian world. Perhaps its greatest positive impact has been in jarring many people into considering that there may be more to reality than germs, psychological disorders, and red-blooded sin. It forces one to take seriously the fact that the demonic may be far more pervasive in everyday life than ever previously considered.

Maintaining the Balance: Our Three Enemies

Many Christians are deeply concerned that they would ever be labeled extremists who "see the devil behind every bush." Beginning to recognize that the devil is a factor in our struggle against evil, however, certainly does not mean that we will ultimately go to the extreme.

The Bible teaches that there are three forms of evil influence that exert their power over the lives of people to lead them into transgression and away from God. These three enemies are simply described as the world, the flesh, and the devil. In some passages of the Bible, one of these sources of evil influence might be discussed more than the other two, but in general, the Bible maintains a balance among these three evil influences. The passage that brings out this balance most clearly is Ephesians 2:1–3:

> As for you, you were dead in your transgressions and sins, in which you
>   used to live when you followed
> [(1) The World] the ways of this world and of
> [(2) The Devil] the ruler of the kingdom of the air, the spirit who is now at work
>   in those who are disobedient. All of us also lived among them at one
>   time, gratifying
> [(3) The Flesh] the cravings of our sinful nature and following its desires and
>   thoughts. Like the rest, we were by nature objects of wrath.

This passage describes the nature of the believer's existence prior to entering a relationship of solidarity with the Lord Jesus Christ. Without Christ, a person lives in a state of "death," alienated from the one who gives life, and is subject to the judgment of God. This person is held in bondage by the world, the devil, and the flesh. The linking of these three categories can also be seen in James (see James 3:15) and John (see 1 John 2:15–17; 3:7–10). The only way of escape is entering by faith into a union with the Lord Jesus Christ, which results in God bestowing on us the gift of life (Eph. 2:4–10). These three powers continue to exert their influence on Christians, but now they are no longer compelling or irresistible. Because of the presence of the empowering Christ, the believer can say "no."

Holding these three in balance is the key. It is just as misguided to attribute every manifestation of evil to the human tendency to do wrong or to the influence of culture as it would be to attribute it to the devil. Figure 1.2 illustrates the common tendency to focus on the flesh and the world and to write the devil out of the picture.

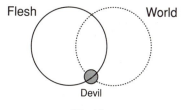

Flesh   World

Devil

"It's Me
and the World I Live In"

Fig. 1.2 Imbalanced View of Evil Influences:
Devil's Influence Ignored

Many Christians believe in the devil because his name is mentioned in the Bible, but the nature of his influence is not really taken seriously in the struggle against evil. They can easily discern the ungodly pressures from society and their own inclinations toward evil, but mere lip service is given to the idea that evil spirits may have anything to do with temptation and sin.

On the other hand, some Pentecostal, charismatic, and Third Wave believers point to the work of evil spirits in practically every aspect of life. If the unclean spirit causing this or that can be identified and cast out, then the problem is solved. Their worldview is depicted in figure 1.3.

Flesh   World

Devil

"The Devil Made Me Do It"

Fig. 1.3 Imbalanced View of Evil Influences:
Devil's Influence Exaggerated

Figure 1.3 depicts the categories of world and flesh as overwhelmed by the devil. The danger with this view, of course, is in not taking seriously the power and influence of the other two.

The Bible takes all three seriously. The inner inclination to think and do evil (the flesh) and the external pressure to conform to ungodly social standards (the world) are seen as just as important as the supernaturally powerful beings who are hostile to God and his people. I portray this balanced perspective in figure 1.4.

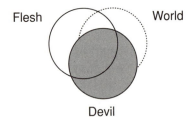

Fig. 1.4 Balanced View of Evil Influences:
Biblical Perspective

It is important to realize, however, that these three influences are not equal in what they are and in how they operate. Nevertheless, each needs to be taken into account in equal measure to the other two and the nature of their interconnectedness must be considered.

The flesh is the inner propensity or inclination to do evil. It is the part of our creatureliness tainted by the fall that remains with us until the day we die. It is our continuing connection to this present evil age, which is destined to perish but against which we must struggle now. As Christians, however, we are new creatures and the compelling influence of the flesh has been broken by Christ's death on the cross. Nevertheless, this inner compulsion continually seeks to reassert its claim and we can only resist it by the power of the Holy Spirit (see esp. Gal. 5:16–17).

The world is the unhealthy social environment in which we live. This includes the ungodly aspects of culture, peer pressure, values, traditions, "what is in," "what is uncool," customs, philosophies, and attitudes. The world represents the prevailing worldview assumptions of the day that stand contrary to the biblical understanding of reality and biblical values. Our culture has an incredibly profound influence on the way we think and act. It provides us with a complete script for how we conduct our lives—what we do when we get sick, how we act toward the opposite sex, how we spend our money, what we pursue in life, what we think about people who are different than us, and so on. Sherwood Lingenfelter, an anthropologist and the provost of Biola University, has characterized the evil dimension of culture as "a prison of disobedience" that holds us in bondage until we are freed by Jesus Christ.[19] Christians then embark on a lifelong task of discerning where these unhealthy influences are still operative in their lives, rooting them out, and adopting godly attitudes and values. As this transformation process continues in the life of a Christian, he or she then becomes an agent of cultural transformation in the community.

The devil is an intelligent, powerful spirit-being that is thoroughly evil and is directly involved in perpetrating evil in the lives of individuals as well as on a much larger scale. He is not an abstraction, either as a personification of the inner corrupt self or in the sense of a symbolic representation of organized social evil (e.g., Nazism). Paul describes him in Ephesians 2:2 as "the spirit who is at work in those who are disobedient." For the apostle, the disobedient are those who have not responded to God's revelation in the Lord Jesus Christ, non-Christians. The devil, or Satan, is portrayed as somehow powerfully at work in their lives, presumably not only inciting sin, but keeping them from responding to the message of mercy and grace in Christ. Paul also reveals that Satan is "the ruler of the kingdom of the air." This suggests his role as leader of a host of other powerful spirits who assist him in carrying out his designs.

The Bible therefore reveals that Christians not only continue to struggle with the inner propensity to evil and the powerful impact of worldview and culture, but also with a personal, supernatural being that is also bent toward doing evil. It is crucial to recognize that these three influences do not work separately but in concert. It is extraordinarily difficult, if not impossible, for us to make sharp distinctions among the three in trying to understand our own personal struggles and those of other people. As I have depicted in the diagram, there is a large area of overlap, where all three influences converge, working in harmony and with the same intent. There are times, however, when we might be able to detect that one of the influences is more prominent in a given situation with a person (as illustrated by the outer edges of the circles).

Another way of depicting the convergence of these three influences is by comparing them to three strands of a rope (see fig. 1.5).

There are three distinct strands, but they are braided together to make a strong rope. This three-stranded rope is what holds us in bondage prior to our coming to know Christ. As my former colleague, Neil Anderson, points out, the Lord Jesus Christ is "The Bondage Breaker."[20] Only through union with Jesus and experiencing his empowering presence do people have hope for escaping the compelling power of these influences.

World
Flesh
Devil

Fig. 1.5 The Nature of Evil Influences:
Three-Stranded Rope

Satan works in harmony with the flesh. For instance, if a person struggles with lustful thoughts, Satan will take advantage of this and exploit this tendency. As the tempter (1 Thess. 3:5), he will stimulate the natural inclination and introduce new thoughts and ideas. He will nudge the person into acting on the fantasies.

The activity of the devil is also closely connected to the world. His primary concern is people, but if he can focus his energies on people of status and power, he can thereby exert a significant impact on the course of culture.

This way of looking at the nature of evil influence has significant implications for life and ministry. Here are a few:

1. *It helps people realize that the deck is stacked against them.* We face supernatural odds in our efforts to live by the ethics and standards of Jesus Christ. We are not only bent the wrong way, but the world points us in the wrong direction, and, to top it off, we have a supernatural opponent pushing us down the wrong path on which we are already headed. We need Christ not only to free us from the irresistible pull of these forces, but then to help us on our Christian journey. We simply cannot live the Christian life by exerting more effort. Effort is needed, but effort assisted by the empowering Spirit of God.

2. *This perspective encourages a wholistic approach to Christian maturity.* It encourages us to consider all three influences simultaneously and not myopically attribute evil behavior to one source.

3. *The Christian life is a lifelong struggle, not a one-time fix.* One trip to someone who casts out demons will not make a person's problems go away. Neither will five visits to a therapist or three visits to a deliverance counselor. These interventions may help greatly and catapult a person to a new level of growth, but there will continue to be struggle over time.

4. *This perspective would encourage deliverance ministry in conjunction with sound therapy and a solid mentoring/discipleship relationship.* For people with deep, difficult issues to work through, a balanced approach is the best. If a person is troubled enough to see a deliverance counselor, it may also be advisable to have sound counsel from a Christian psychologist. At the

minimum, the person should be in a close mentoring relationship with a more mature Christian brother or sister who prays for this dear one in need and meets regularly with him or her.

We have now raised a number of issues that need to be treated in more detail. Chapter 2 continues our discussion by dealing with the devil and the flesh while chapter 3 treats the devil and the world.

The Classic Passage: Ephesians 6:10–20

In discussing the essence of spiritual warfare, it is imperative that we take a careful look at the classic spiritual warfare passage, Ephesians 6:10–20. I have commented on this passage in significant detail in other contexts.[21] I highlight here what I regard as its central message.

The passage is not about casting out evil spirits or dealing with territorial spirits. These verses describe the common struggle with evil in the day-to-day lives of Christians. Paul does this by underlining the role of demonic spirits as a source of evil influence. Although this passage does not mention the flesh or the world,[22] these other sources of evil influence are part of Paul's overall understanding of our struggle, as we have already seen.

The Christian Life as a Struggle

Paul uses the metaphor of battle to press the theme of conflict. The most popular verse of the passage, however, introduces the image of wrestling or struggle. When Paul says, "our struggle is not against flesh and blood [i.e., people]" (Eph. 6:12), he uses a term that all of his readers would have been intimately familiar with from the various athletic games held in Asia Minor and Olympia, Greece. The term *palē* was commonly used of the wrestling event, one of the main attractions in all the games. Notice the use of the term in an inscription that was found in Ephesus:

> The Council and the People honor Alexander, son of Menodorus, grandson of Dionysus, an Ephesian who won the wrestling [*palē*] at the Isthmian games, the Common Games of Asia at Ephesus, and at the great Epheseia. . . . [H]e also won the wrestling [*palē*] in the Common Games of Galatia . . . and he also won the wrestling [*palē*] in the Common Games of Asia in Sardis and at very many other games.[23]

Of course Paul emphasizes that it is not literal wrestling—"flesh and blood"—that he is referring to. He is speaking of a struggle with unseen

forces. The metaphor of wrestling highlights the immediacy of the struggle. It involves strenuous effort, stamina, and, especially, proper spiritual fitness.

The struggle is a daily affair. The wrestling event for the Christian is
not over in twelve minutes or even a half hour. Paul urged the Ephesians
to make the most of every opportunity, "because the days are evil" (Eph.
5:16). This was a reminder to his friends that they live in the present evil
age. This is not the time to settle down and relax. This is a time for mission and doing the work of the kingdom. Here Paul explicitly encourages
the Ephesians to prepare spiritually so they can resist their opponent
"when the day of evil comes" (Eph. 6:13). Yes, all days are evil in the sense
that we do not yet live in the fullness of the age to come. There are certain periods of time, however, when Christians face a flurry of terrible
difficulties or when temptation seems to comes with unusual power.

The Supernatural Opponents

The opponents Paul emphasizes here are demonic forces. Rather than
simply saying "demons," he uses a series of four terms to characterize
these forces:

archai	principalities
exousiai	authorities
kosmokratores	world rulers
pneumatika	spiritual forces

The first two terms are the most common way Paul speaks of demonic
spirits. They are normally found together in Paul's writings and appear
to be a summary way of referring to all sorts of evil powers (see 1 Cor.
15:24; Eph. 1:21; 3:10; 6:12; Col. 1:16; 2:10; 2:15). They were part of
the first-century parlance in Judaism for speaking of angelic beings.[24]

The term *kosmokratores* is much more rare. This is the only time it
appears in the entire Bible. It was a term that appears to have been used
in the first century by Jews when they spoke of hostile demonic powers.
It appears, for instance, in a Jewish document that describes the activities of thirty-six demonic spirits.[25]

The final term, *pneumatika,* is a very general reference to various
sorts of spirits. It is built on the common word for spirit, *pneuma.* It is
possible that Paul chose the neuter gender to grammatically associate
it with the neuter term *daimonia* ("demons"). More important, he
describes these spirit forces as evil *(poneria).* Here we are reminded of

the final line of the Lord's Prayer: "but deliver us from the evil one [*ponēros*]" (Matt. 6:13).

There has been much speculation about what is implied by the four terms Paul has chosen. With these in mind, I would make the following observations: (1) While the terms may imply a hierarchy within the demonic realm, we have no means of discerning the various ranks by the use of these terms. We cannot establish, for instance, that the *archai* have higher authority than the *exousiai,* and so on. (2) These terms probably do not represent the so-called territorial spirits that we find in Daniel—that is, a demonic prince with responsibility over a country or region (see Dan. 10:13, 20). The emphasis in the Ephesian passage is on the day-to-day struggle of every believer, a struggle that involves us as individuals and requires us to be individually prepared. (3) There is no special meaning to each of the terms that would give us further insight into the demonic realm. The terms appear to come from a large reservoir of terminology used in the first century when people spoke of demonic spirits.

Why, then, does Paul line up these four terms rather than just simply say, "our struggle is against evil spirits"? I think he does so for persuasive effect. He wants to wake believers up to the fact that the struggle is not over now that we are Christians. The struggle continues and there are all sorts of mighty demonic spirits intent on bringing about our demise.

Resources for the Struggle

God bestows on his people divine power for the struggle. Thus, Paul urges the Ephesians, "be strong *in the Lord and in his mighty power*" (Eph. 6:10). The letter to the Ephesians especially emphasizes the immediate access believers have to the power of God:

The Accessibility of Divine Power

Eph. 1:18–19	"I pray also that the eyes of your heart might be enlightened in order that you may know . . . his incomparably great power for us who believe."
Eph. 3:16	"I pray that out of his glorious riches he may strengthen you with power through his Spirit in your inner being.
Eph. 3:20–21	"Now to him who is able to do immeasurably more than all we ask or imagine, according to his power that is at work within us, to him be glory in the church and in Christ Jesus throughout all generations, for ever and ever! Amen."
Eph. 6:10	"Finally, be strong in the Lord and in his mighty power."

God imparts his power to his people in a personal way. It is not accessed through performing incantations, reciting formulas, or wearing magical charms. God empowers us through his indwelling Spirit and on the basis of our relationship with the Lord Jesus Christ. By entering into a relationship with Christ, we are linked to his work in the past. Therefore, on the basis of his blood shed on the cross, we have forgiveness of sins and freedom from the compelling grip of the principle of sin. Paul says in Romans 6:6 that "our old self was crucified *with* him." On this basis, we can say no to temptation because its power has been broken.

There is still more to our union with Christ. We have been linked with Christ not only in his death, but in his resurrection and his exaltation. Notice the repetition of "with" in Ephesians 2:5–6:

> New Life: "God . . . made us alive *with Christ* even when we were dead in transgressions"
> Resurrection: "God raised us up *with Christ*"
> Exaltation: "God . . . seated us *with him* in the heavenly realms in Christ Jesus"

Sharing with Christ in his exaltation is particularly important as we consider spiritual warfare because this entails sharing with Christ in his present authority over that realm. In Ephesians 1, Paul explained the meaning of Christ's exaltation with regard to Satan's domain:

> [God's] power is like the working of his mighty strength, which he exerted in Christ when he raised him from the dead and seated him at his right hand in the heavenly realms, *far above all rule and authority, power and dominion, and every title that can be given, not only in the present age but also in the one to come.* And God placed all things under his feet and appointed him to be head over everything for the church (vv. 19–22, italics mine).

Because Jesus was victorious over the powers of evil on the cross, he assumed a place of ruling prominence over them through his exaltation to the right hand of God. Believers are linked to this powerful and loving Lord in a vital and real relationship. We share in Jesus' authority over the demons and unclean spirits. Paul stressed the same point to the Colossians when he wrote,

> For in Christ all the fullness of the Deity lives in bodily form, and you have been given fullness in Christ, who is the head over every power and authority (Col. 2:9–10).

Paul qualifies the nature of our sharing in Christ's power by pointing out that it has to do with the demonic order. This is not a power theology in a human way of thinking. It is not power to influence the political process; it is not power to control people; it is not power to obtain whatever one desires; it is not power to contravene every form of physical evil, such as earthquakes, famines, or hurricanes.

We share in Christ's kingdom authority over the demonic realm. This means that we can now resist demonically inspired temptation. It means that we have power to command an evil spirit to flee if it manifests its presence to us at night. It also means that we can make known the gospel of the Lord Jesus Christ in a powerful way.

In the first chapter of Ephesians, Paul mentions the will of God seven times. God clearly has a plan and that plan involves us. He bestows his power on us to live according to his will and to fulfill the mission he has given to us. This involves above all

- getting rid of sinful thoughts and practices and acquiring virtue
- tangibly demonstrating love according to the ultimate pattern laid by Christ, who willingly sacrificed his own life for others
- coming alongside others and helping them grow in the Christian life
- using one's own giftedness to give to others in the Christian community
- creating and maintaining unity in the Christian community
- developing healthier family relationships
- spreading the good news of Christ to others

These seven items are unequivocally part of the will of God. There is no doubt that Satan and his wicked spirits will oppose these more than anything else. Satan is not just a perpetrator of evil; he is an opponent of the one true God. He seeks to thwart any momentum toward fulfilling God's will. We can expect opposition on each of these fronts. He endeavors to prevent each believer from fulfilling the will of God, and thus, to fall. It is little wonder that the overriding emphasis of the passage is on adequate spiritual preparation so believers can "stand." The term for standing, a military metaphor for those victorious in battle, appears four times in Ephesians 6:

- "Put on the full armor of God so that you can *take your stand* against the devil's schemes" (v. 11)
- "Therefore put on the full armor of God, so that when the day of evil comes, you may be able *to stand your ground*" (v. 13)

- "and after you have done everything, *to stand*" (v. 13)
- "*Stand firm,* then, with the belt of truth" (v. 14)

God has not left us without the resources for fulfilling his will. As Jesus said in John's Gospel, "I will not leave you as orphans; I will come to you" (14:18). He promises his own presence through the Holy Spirit: "But you know him, for he lives with you and will be in you" (John 14:17). Thus, Paul can encourage the Ephesians to "be filled with the Spirit" (Eph. 5:18). We find our strength in the presence of the indwelling Lord, who empowers us to stand against the devil's schemes.

As Paul continues discussing the nature of the struggle with the demonic in Ephesians 6:10–20, he also advises appropriating specific resources that we have in Christ and continuing to cultivate certain virtues. He presents these by elaborating on the metaphor of warfare, and specifically, armor that a soldier would be outfitted with for battle. He calls the spiritual counterparts "the full armor [*panoplia*] of God."

There is a tendency to overinterpret the metaphor and pull out of each specific weapon a meaning that is not made explicit by Paul. For instance, the belt of truth is so important because it holds up the pants, or the helmet is the most vital piece because it protects the brain. The purpose of this elaborate metaphor is to convey that the believer needs adequate protection because there is a dangerous struggle in the spiritual realm. What we need to focus on is not the belt, the breastplate, and the shield, but truth, righteousness, faith, and the rest. It is important not to overinterpret the various aspects of the metaphor, because some, such as prayer, which is not even attached to a piece of the armor, may be neglected.

Each of the weapons is crucial for preparing for the ongoing struggle, a struggle that is part and parcel of living the Christian life. The following list provides a concise summary interpretation of the armor of God:

Responding to the Powers of Darkness

You cannot succeed on your own. Draw on the strength that Christ promises to supply.

Realize that you cannot count on life to be a smooth, easy path. There are evil supernatural forces out to destroy you.

1. *Put On Your Trousers: Wear Truth*
   Know the truth of who you are in Christ (for the powers of darkness will try to deceive you).
   Practice honesty and live with moral integrity.

2. *Put On the Breastplate of Righteousness*
   Realize your status before God as one who has been acquitted of all guilt.
   Acquire personal holiness and develop good character.

3. *Put On Your Boots: Prepare to Share the Gospel of Peace*
   Prepare yourself for sharing the gospel wherever God calls you.

4. *Take the Shield of Faith*
   Do not doubt! Believe that God will help you overcome.

5. *Put On the Helmet of Salvation*
   Be secure in your identity in Christ—as one who has been saved, united
   with Christ, made alive, co-resurrected, and co-exalted.

6. *Take the Sword of the Spirit, the Word of God*
   Devote your life to aggressively spreading the gospel.
   Know Scripture and apply it to every difficult situation.

7. *The Bottom Line: Pray!*
   Ask God to strengthen you and other believers to resist temptation and
   share the gospel effectively.

The Primacy of Prayer

Prayer is the heart of spiritual warfare. Prayer is so vital because it is
the means of intimacy and communion with the almighty Lord. Prayer
is also an expression of faith. The very act of prayer is an admission that
"there is someone greater than I" and that "I am not able." The apostle Paul approached God with a tremendous sense of humility, which
he expressed even in his posture: "I kneel before the Father" (Eph.
3:14). Part of spiritual warfare is the recognition that you are not able
in your own strength; you need God to hold you by the hand and fight
on your behalf.

Peter recognized this when he wrote to believers in Asia Minor about
spiritual warfare. He prefaced his remarks by quoting Proverbs 3:34:
"God opposes the proud but gives grace to the humble" (1 Peter 5:5).
He continued by urging these dear believers to humility before God:
"Humble yourselves, therefore, under God's mighty hand, that he may
lift you up in due time. Cast all your anxiety on him because he cares
for you" (1 Peter 5:6–7). Peter then speaks of struggle against the unseen
forces of evil: "Be self-controlled and alert. Your enemy the devil prowls
around like a roaring lion looking for someone to devour. Resist him,
standing firm in the faith" (1 Peter 5:8–9).

The seventh weapon in the believer's arsenal listed by Paul is prayer
(Eph. 6:18). It is not seventh in importance, however. It is actually
foundational to deploying all of the other weapons. Prayer is the essence

and mode of spiritual warfare. Notice the ways Paul stresses prayer in this passage:

1. He mentions it last (as a way to emphasize it).
2. He does not link it to a physical weapon, such as a spear or a helmet (also as a way to emphasize it).
3. He uses the word *all* four times when he mentions it.
   And pray in the Spirit
     on *all* occasions
     with *all* kinds of prayers and requests.
   With this in mind, be alert and
     always keep on praying
     for *all* the saints.
4. He immediately asks for specific prayer for himself (Eph. 6:19–20).
5. He has twice previously reported his prayer for them (Eph. 1:15–23; 3:14–21).

Given the centrality of prayer to success in the struggle, a closer look at how we should pray is in order.

Arming Others for Spiritual Warfare: An Agenda for Small Group Prayer

Often when people think of putting on the armor of God for spiritual warfare, they conceive of it in individualistic terms. One finds a quiet place, reads and appropriates the Word, and asks the Lord to endue him or her with divine strength. This is certainly basic to the Christian disciplines and fundamental to making it through the struggle.

There is another dimension to "arming" that Paul may be stressing here that has significant potential for revolutionizing a common Christian experience—small group prayer. I have personally been involved in many small group prayer times where the major focus has been on listing everyone who is physically ill and then praying for them. In some instances it seems that this type of prayer request is the only thing people feel comfortable sharing. Although it is vitally important to pray for the sick, there are more dynamic possibilities for small group prayer.

Paul addressed his words to people who would have frequently met in groups to pray together. It is quite doubtful that there was one big church in Ephesus. The social reality was that Christians met in many homes scattered throughout the city. When they met, they not only had times of worship and instruction, but also times of group prayer. What did they pray for? What should they have prayed for? Paul here gives them an agenda for their times of group prayer. They should arm each other for spiritual warfare through prayer. Paul also asks them to arm him for his ongoing struggle for the sake of the gospel in Rome.

I have often referred to this form of prayer as "praying for the healthy." By this I mean praying specifically for individuals within the group to resist temptation in their personal areas of vulnerability; praying that "they might be able to stand on the evil day" (see Eph. 6:13). This includes "praying for the sick," since illness is an "evil day" trial that tempts people to turn away from God. This form of prayer also involves praying that the Lord would strengthen other believers to continue to strip off the characteristics of the old self and appropriate the virtues of the new self. It involves praying for the actualization of the will of God in every area of the lives of our brothers and sisters—with full knowledge that there is a supernatural opponent seeking to thwart every movement in the right direction.

All of this, of course, assumes a depth of relationship with other believers that goes beyond the superficial. As our intimacy with others grows, so should the specificity and depth of our prayer for them. This kind of praying makes for powerful times of small group prayer.

Paul prayed in this manner for the Ephesians. He tells them that in his times of prayer for them (which he often carried out with his missionary companions) that he has asked God to provide them with spiritual insight into the vastness of divine power working on their behalf and for God to strengthen them with this power (Eph. 1:15–23; 3:14–19). Paul's two prayers thus model the content of how he expects believers to pray for each other. We even have a glimpse of how the Lord Jesus himself prayed in this sort of way as he became aware of demonic hostility. He told Peter, "Simon, Simon, Satan has asked to sift you as wheat. But I have prayed for you, Simon, that your faith may not fail" (Luke 22:31–32). Our Lord understood the true nature of the battle and that Peter would face "an evil day" when he would be severely tested.[26] He knew that this testing would be inspired and energized by the unseen realm. Jesus responded by praying for Peter, specifically that Peter's faith would not falter during the testing. Our Lord's prayer was answered—in spite of Peter's momentary lapse when he denied knowing his Lord—in his commissioning of Peter to "feed my sheep" (John 21:15–21) and in the incredible ways the Spirit used Peter in the establishment of the apostolic church.

Forms of Prayer in Spiritual Warfare

There is not one form of prayer that is spiritual warfare prayer and another kind of prayer that is not. All prayer is related to spiritual warfare. Prayer is communication with the commander-in-chief during the battle. Our awareness of the battle heightens our sense of need to stay in constant touch with our superior officer, who can resupply us and provide us with our orders.

Paul stresses praying "in the Spirit" at the end of the spiritual warfare passage (Eph. 6:18). This refers to the Holy Spirit's work of guiding and directing us to pray for specific things. Paul calls us to cultivate a sensitivity to what the Spirit may be prompting us to pray for and then how we should pray about it. Prayer is more than just vocalizing a list of needs to God. Prayer involves asking God how we should pray and then acting on the promptings and impressions the Spirit places on our minds.

I clearly remember gathering with a group of thirty people to pray one Tuesday evening. The leader reminded us of a number of needs and items to pray about. But as we prayed, the Spirit clearly burdened the entire group to pray specifically for one individual who was going through a very difficult trial. First one person prayed for the individual, then another, and then another until the end of our time together. We normally each prayed for a different request, but that night, without any instruction to do so from the leader, we all prayed for this one troubled friend. As it turned out, there was a very dramatic change in the condition of the person that night. We all had a clear sense not only that the Spirit had led us to pray, but that God had marvelously answered our prayers.

The four "alls" of Ephesians 6:18 stress praying at a variety of times and occasions. Maintaining a readiness to pray on all occasions is very important. God is near. We have the privilege of entering his presence regularly as his children. As individuals, a good starting point is spending some focused time in prayer the first thing in the morning (committing the day and all of its contingencies to the Lord) and at the end of the day (thanking him for his faithfulness and asking for rest). As we grow in the recognition that he is with us throughout the day, we can appeal to him and render praise to him hour by hour. I have outlined some other times and circumstances for prayer below. Of course, the possibilities for various other forms of small group prayer go far beyond this.

Prayer: The Essential Weapon of Spiritual Warfare

Settings
Private

> Worship, confess, thank God, and ask him to supply your needs and to strengthen you to resist.
>
> Cast all your anxieties on him (because he cares for you).

Small Group

> Meet in a small group to pray and intercede for other believers.
>
> Share intimately with this group and ask them to arm you through prayer.

Subjects
Individuals in Need

> Be willing to meet with people and pray with them during their times of trial.

Your Pastor and Church Leadership

> Meet with others early on Sunday morning to pray for the pastor and other leaders in the church.

Your Children and Their School

> Women with school-age children can join a "Moms in Touch" group or start one.[27]

Your City: Community-Wide Prayer Initiatives

> Meet with a group of people and "prayer walk" through the neighborhoods in your city.
>
> Groups of churches in various cities sometimes plan and hold special prayer gatherings for the community (as, for example, "Lift L.A." in 1995[28] and David Bryant's "Concerts of Prayer").[29] Participate with other believers in these times of focused prayer.

Unbelieving Acquaintances

> Meet with a small group to pray specifically for those who do not know Christ.
>
> Talk to people in your neighborhood and ask them how you can pray for them.[30]

The Nation

> Pray for local, state, and national leaders. Pray for key issues facing these leaders.[31]

The World

> Join or form a prayer support team for one of the missionaries of your church.
>
> Personally commit yourself to pray for the countries and cities of the 10/40 Window.[32]
>
> Encourage your church or a group in your church to adopt a city in the 10/40 Window and commit yourself to pray for these people.

The first two areas—private devotion and regular small group prayer meetings—are vital and indispensable to the Christian life and success in spiritual warfare. The Christian life was not designed to be a private affair; we are joined to a body of people. We need people to pray for us and arm us for successful resistance.

Specially Called Intercessors

All Christians are called to make intercession for others, but there are a few people whom God appears to be using in mighty ways for the task of intercessory prayer. The Bible does not speak of a special gift of "intercessory prayer," but there are instances when certain individuals prayed earnestly on behalf of others. We think especially of people like Nehemiah and Daniel. We also have an image of persistent intercession in the story of Aaron and Hur holding up Moses' hands when Joshua led the Israelites in war against the Amalekites (Exod. 17:8–13). We discover that "as long as Moses held up his hands, the Israelites were winning, but whenever he lowered his hands, the Amalekites were winning" (Exod. 17:11). At the end of the narrative, Moses says that his hands were "lifted up to the throne of the LORD" (Exod. 17:16)—a beautiful symbol of prayer. As Paul makes clear in Ephesians 6:12, our warfare is not against physical armies, but against supernatural forces. Interceding for others in prayer is vital to successful outcome in war.

As I have spoken on the topic of spiritual warfare over the past few years, I have become convinced that God places a special burden of engaging in fervent prayer for others on the hearts of certain individuals within the church. It seems that there are many women who have especially heard this call. The Spirit has impressed on their hearts people that he wants these dear prayer warriors to intercede for. Sometimes they wake up during the night with a sense of urgency to pray for particular people or situations—and they pray until the burden is lifted.

In a recent book titled *Prayer Shield,* C. Peter Wagner has observed that as part of the great prayer movement now sweeping across our nation, an increasing number of congregations are taking intercessory prayer more seriously than in the past. He points out that while all Christians are called to the role of interceding for other Christians, some have a special calling to devote more time and energy to intercession.[33]

I am particularly grateful for the people whom God has led to pray for me in this way. Some of these have asked that I keep them regularly informed about key events and issues in my life. When I have neglected to keep one of these people informed, she reminds me of how important it was for Moses to allow Aaron and Hur to support him during the battle. How right she is!

All Christians need intercessory prayer on their behalf. Pastors and Christian leaders are no exception. In light of the unbelievable epidemic of Christian leaders succumbing to "moral failure," it is time for pastors, seminary teachers, and other Christian leaders to recognize their vulnerability and solicit prayer partners and prayer support teams.

Keeping the Mission Foremost

Spiritual warfare is not just defensive; it is offensive. We have a mission to accomplish. It is best summed up by Jesus' final words as recorded in Matthew's Gospel (28:18–20):

> All authority in heaven and on earth has been given to me. Therefore go and make disciples of all nations, baptizing them in the name of the Father and of the Son and of the Holy Spirit, and teaching them to obey everything I have commanded you. And surely I am with you always, to the very end of the age.

The heart of the mission is to "make disciples." This involves both making the gospel of the Lord Jesus Christ known to those who have not heard (or heard it properly) and incorporating them into the church as viable and growing members. The mission is thus both extensive and intensive; it involves reaching out and building up. Jesus was fully aware that there was a supernatural enemy who would organize his malevolent forces to powerfully oppose the carrying out of this mission. With this in mind, Jesus assured his followers of his presence with them and that he possessed "all authority" over this realm.

"Plundering the Strong Man's Possessions": The Redemptive Mission

During his earthly ministry, Jesus was outrageously accused by a group of scribal teachers of being possessed by "Beelzebub" and of driving out demons under the authority of the prince of demons himself (Mark 3:22). One of the ways Jesus responded to this blasphemous charge was by uttering a brief parable:

> No one can enter a strong man's house and carry off his possessions unless he first ties up the strong man. Then he can rob his house (Mark 3:27=Matt. 12:29=Luke 11:22).

This is a pivotal passage for understanding the work of Jesus and the mission he has entrusted to his church. It also points to Jesus' struggle with Satan and the implications of his work on the cross for our task.

The strong man in the passage is Satan. He is indeed supernaturally powerful and not to be taken lightly. His possessions are not personal property or personal effects, but people—people whom he has blinded to the truth about God's plan of salvation. The person who binds the strong man is the Lord Jesus Christ. Although some interpreters think that this tying up occurred when Jesus successfully resisted Satan's temptations or performed his many exorcisms, the binding is best explained by what Christ accomplished on the cross. It was there that Christ shed his blood and made satisfaction for the sins of the world. Satan thereby lost his ability to justly accuse people because God could extend forgiveness and bring them into a relationship with himself. Paul speaks of this defeat of the powers of darkness in eloquent terms in Colossians 2:15: "And having disarmed the powers and authorities, he made a public spectacle of them, triumphing over them by the cross." Satan has thus been bound, not absolutely, but with respect to those who have entered into a relationship with Jesus Christ. Satan no longer holds these children of God in bondage; they have the power to resist him and undertake the work of the mission.

The church carries out the last part of the parable. We are the ones who rob Satan's house. We do this by presenting the gospel of Christ in the power of the Spirit. We extend to our family, friends, people in our community, and those to whom we are sent the opportunity to hear and respond to the good news of salvation in Jesus Christ. As people turn to Christ and enter the kingdom of God, Satan loses his possessions.

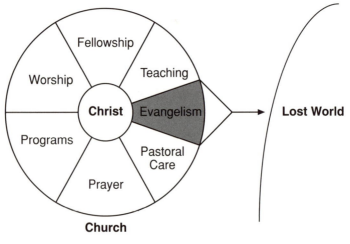

Fig. 1.6 Church's Mission: Popular View

The church thus has a mandate to grow—by conversion. A major portion of our time, resources, and energies should be devoted to serving effectively as Christ's ambassadors and communicating his message of reconciliation (2 Cor. 5:18–20). This is not the responsibility of a select few within the church who may be especially gifted in evangelism or impassioned for doing it. This is the task of the whole church. This is the mission that Christ extended to us all. Figures 1.6 and 1.7 show the contrast between the popular view of evangelism and the biblical view. As figure 1.7 makes clear, it is not just one spoke in the wheel that engages in outreach; it is the whole wheel.

What the diagrams do not illustrate is the fact that there will be opposition along the way. When Jesus sent out the Seventy, he "saw Satan fall like lightning from heaven" (Luke 10:18). Satan was furious. He was determined to stop this threat to his kingdom. There would be struggle. The Seventy returned from their mission to Jesus with joy, saying, "Lord, even the demons submit to us in your name" (Luke 10:17). In Christ, we too have authority over the demons. We can present the gospel and people will respond, as they have for the past nearly two thousand years. We are not to be overly awed by the fact that we have authority over demons, but rejoice that we are part of the people of God and earnestly endeavor to extend that opportunity to others.

Telling others the good news of Christ was the driving passion of Christians in the early church. But they faced all sorts of opposition. Without

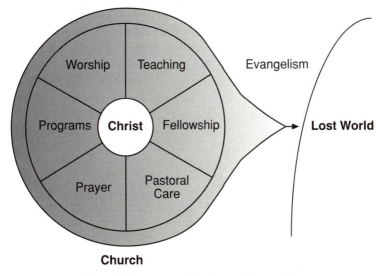

Fig. 1.7 Church's Mission: Biblical View

a doubt, Satan thundered in anger at what Christ was accomplishing through his people and unleashed all the devices in his power to thwart the spread of the gospel.

Intimidation was just one of his methods. After reading the glorious accounts of the apostle Paul spreading the gospel in the Book of Acts, I used to think he was never intimidated by opposition. One of his own letters reveals his human side, however. As he concludes his discussion about spiritual warfare to believers in Ephesus, he asks these dear believers to unite in praying for him (Eph. 6:19–20). He twice asked the Ephesians to pray that the Lord would strengthen him to make known the gospel boldly *(parrēsia)* during his incarceration in Rome. Apparently Satan's efforts at intimidating this great apostle were working. Paul realized, however, that the battle was spiritual and his strength must come from the Lord. He therefore asks the Ephesians to arm him for spiritual warfare.

Satan tried intimidating the apostles Peter and John together with all the believers in Jerusalem during the infancy of the church. Peter and John were arrested after the Lord used them to heal a paralyzed man outside the Jerusalem temple. They appeared before the Sanhedrin (the Jewish ruling council); the rulers repeatedly threatened them and "commanded them not to speak or teach at all in the name of Jesus" (Acts 4:18). When they were released, Peter and John met with the other believers and reported all that had happened. Intimidated, yet committed to the mission entrusted to them by their resurrected Lord, they joined in prayer and asked, "Lord, consider their threats and enable your servants to speak your word with great boldness [*parrēsia*]" (Acts 4:29). God immediately responded to their prayer, and "they were all filled with the Holy Spirit and spoke the word of God boldly [*parrēsia*]" (Acts 4:31).

Although Christians in the West have enjoyed the freedom of sharing their faith without the threat of corporal punishment or persecution, Satan has employed a different set of strategies for blunting our commitment to the redemptive mission. Some of these include

- making Christians think how extremist or obnoxious they might appear to friends by "forcing their faith" on others
- making Christians think that everyone has already heard the gospel
- inciting so many problems in the church that efforts to resolve conflict sap all of our energy and attention
- causing Christians to believe that only missionaries and evangelists should be concerned with outreach
- convincing Christians that there is a fair chance that everyone will be saved ultimately anyway, given such a loving God

Evangelism represents a frontal assault on the kingdom of Satan, yet our Lord has called us to this task. It is an integral part of our mission. We can expect spiritual warfare to occur quite intensely and in a variety of ways on this battlefront.

Helping People Mature in Christ (Col. 1:28)

The intensive growth of the church is the other key part of our mission. Jesus calls us to "make disciples" and to "teach them to obey everything I have commanded you." In our zeal to evangelize, we cannot neglect the crucial part of building community, teaching the Word, and facilitating spiritual growth. I have been particularly inspired by the apostle Paul's example of holding together both evangelism and nurture as two parts of the same mission. Paul did not just preach the gospel. He preached the gospel *and* formed communities of Christians. He worked diligently with these groups of people over the long term to insure their growth and stability. His ambition is well summarized in Colossians 1:28: "We proclaim him, admonishing and teaching everyone with all wisdom, so that we may present everyone perfect in Christ." This verse well illustrates Paul's actualization of Jesus' Great Commission. For Paul, making disciples includes a commitment to helping people mature in Christ right up to the end. The apostle recognized that this was a deep spiritual struggle with powerful opposition. In the very next verse, he clarifies his dependence on the power of God: "To this end I labor, struggling with all his energy, which so powerfully works in me" (Col. 1:29).

If the redemptive mission of the church amounts to robbing the strong man of his possessions, we can count on the fact that the strong man will attempt to get back what has been stolen from him. Satan therefore mobilizes his forces to reassert his dominion in the lives of individuals and corporately in church communities. He wants to re-enslave people with the bonds of sinful desires and lifestyles. He also seeks to turn people's attention away from Christ and onto other things. He often accomplishes this by presenting Christians with another Jesus to follow.

Watch Out for a "Different Jesus"!

One of Satan's key strategies is corrupting and distorting an understanding of who Jesus really is, what he came to do, and what he is about to do. Lamentably, this is also the most overlooked aspect of what spiritual warfare is all about in the deluge of books and articles on the topic in recent years. From Paul's adversaries in Corinth to the rise of Gnosticism in the early centuries of Christianity to the dispensing of salvation through indulgences in the Middle Ages to the prosperity gospel of today, Satan works with all his might to pervert how people understand Christ.

"Tearing Down Strongholds" (2 Cor. 10:1–3)

Paul warned the Corinthians not to be deceived into giving credence to "a Jesus other than the Jesus we preached" (2 Cor. 11:4). There were, in fact, people who had come to Corinth, claiming not only to be Christians but apostles. They were teaching something that sounded like Christianity, but it was a form of Christianity that had a distorted image of Christ. In responding to the situation, Paul spoke in the language of spiritual warfare.

First, he pointed out that Satan not only works in blatantly evil ways, but he also works in ways that appear right and good. He can masquerade as "an angel of light" (2 Cor. 11:14). Of course, Satan often accomplishes his aims by working through other people. This is precisely what he did in Corinth. Paul unmasks the recently arrived "apostles" as masquerading as servants of Christ while actually inspired by Satan (2 Cor. 10:13–15).

Second, he emphasizes Satan's work of deceiving believers about the Christ they have entered into a relationship with. He tells them, "I am afraid that just as Eve was deceived by the serpent's cunning, your minds may somehow be led astray from your sincere and pure devotion to Christ" (2 Cor. 11:3). Some in the Corinthian church had already followed after this different Christ, a mere chimera, an invention of Satan.

Finally, Paul speaks of full-scale warfare. He says,

> For though we live in the world, we do not wage war as the world does. The weapons we fight with are not the weapons of the world. On the contrary, they have divine power to demolish strongholds. We demolish arguments and every pretension that sets itself up against the knowledge of God, and we take captive every thought to make it obedient to Christ (2 Cor. 10:3–5).

These verses are widely quoted in all of the spiritual warfare literature and are most commonly used to refer to sinful habits over which a person has not been able to gain victory. Some use the word *stronghold* to speak of a city, region, or country where there is very little response to the gospel.

These uses of the term may very well be a correct application of the passage by extension, but they fail to recognize that the critical thrust of the passage is directed against christological heresy. Some of the Corinthians had been duped into believing dangerous and erroneous ideas about Jesus and his gospel. Paul traces these ideas to the false "apostles" who were really servants of Satan. It is against these arguments and ideas that have settled into the minds of some of the Corinthians as "strongholds" that Paul utilizes divine weapons to demolish.[34] His objective is to purify their understanding of Christ. Therefore, in its original context, *demolishing strongholds refers to changing wrong ideas about Christ in the minds of believers who have been influenced by demonically inspired teaching.* This amounts to something more than psychologically-informed cognitive restructuring. It does involve counseling, but of a special kind with specific content and drawing on the power of God.

Paul does not elaborate in 2 Corinthians 10 on what the weapons are and how he plans to use them. Assuredly, they would include what he taught the Ephesians (Eph. 6:14–18). Each of these weapons do play a part in the spiritual warfare Paul engages in as he handles the Corinthian problem. By looking at the letter as a whole, we can see more clearly how these weapons operate in this specific situation.

1. *Truth.* Paul confronts the distorted gospel by writing to the Corinthians, reminding them of the truth and appealing to them to accept it. He assures them that he speaks "the truth of Christ" in contrast to the other interloper "apostles," who are false and deceitful (2 Cor. 6:7; 11:10; 12:6; 13:8).

2. *Righteousness.* The apostle reminds the Corinthians that their righteousness is found in Christ, who became sin, suffered, and died for them (2 Cor. 5:21). This is the Jesus they are called to follow and give their devotion to; this is the true Jesus they have entered into a relationship with. Paul assures the Corinthians of his own righteous behavior toward them, which should serve to commend his teaching to them (2 Cor. 7:2). Because he is Christ's ambassador of the righteousness of God, Paul wields "weapons of righteousness in the right hand and in the left" (2 Cor. 6:7).

3. *Gospel.* The rivals spread a "different gospel" that was causing division and dissension in the Corinthian community (2 Cor. 11:4). Paul points them back to the true gospel of peace that he had originally brought to them (2 Cor. 10:14; 11:17) and that they were now called to proclaim (2 Cor. 5:18–20).

4. *Faith.* In spite of the discouraging situation in Corinth and Paul's numerous personal trials (see 2 Cor. 6:4–10; 11:23–33), he had learned to trust God. He tells the Corinthians, "we live by faith, not by sight" (2 Cor. 5:7). His faith in the God who is so powerfully at work in him and among the Corinthians gave him confidence that many of the flaming arrows of the Evil One would be extinguished.

5. *Salvation.* To refresh their understanding, Paul lays out God's plan of salvation for the Corinthians (2 Cor. 5:18–21). At the heart of his presentation is the realization that believers have been reconciled to God through the work of Christ. There will be difficulties and sufferings in this present world, but salvation has come (2 Cor. 6:2) and we have a secure relationship with God.

6. *The Holy Spirit and the Word of God.* In his appeal to the Corinthians, Paul turns to the Old Testament at many points, but especially to a proper understanding of Christ and his work (which had not yet been written up into the Gospels we now have). He warns the Corinthians, "the letter kills, but the Spirit gives life" (2 Cor. 3:6). By this he is not contradicting the importance of the Word of God, but emphasizing that it needs to be properly understood and not misused as the false apostles were doing. They proclaimed a "different spirit." He repeatedly assures them of their connection to the Holy Spirit (2 Cor. 1:22; 3:3, 8, 17, 18; 5:5; 13:14).

7. *Prayer.* We can be certain that Paul and Timothy would have engaged in passionate intercessory prayer for the Corinthians. Paul, in fact, tells us that he did and even some of what he prayed for. As he anticipates their response to his appeal, he says, "now we pray to God that you will not do anything wrong" (2 Cor. 13:7) and "our prayer is for your perfection" (2 Cor. 13:9). He concludes the letter by praying for them: "May the grace of the Lord Jesus Christ, and the love of God, and the fellowship of the Holy Spirit be with you all" (2 Cor. 13:14).

Foundational to Paul's work among the Corinthians was a heart full of love for them and a commitment to be with them and assist them in their growth and maturity in Christ. He had visited them once about this problem ("a painful visit"; 2 Cor. 2:1), addressed this problem in a previous letter that we do not possess ("For I wrote you out of great distress and anguish of heart and with many tears, not to grieve you but to let you know the depth of my love for you"; 2 Cor. 2:4), writes them now, and plans to visit them again shortly (2 Cor. 13:10). Emotion, tears, love, anguish, and prayer are all part of spiritual warfare.

Demonic Strongholds in the Early Church: Distorted Images of Christ

As the apostle Paul approached the end of his life, he warned of continuing demonic activity focused on inspiring twisted images of Christ to deceive people. Paul tells his co-worker, Timothy, that "the Spirit clearly says that in later times some will abandon the faith and follow deceiving spirits and things taught by demons" (1 Tim. 4:1). For Paul, these "later times" were now. These are the endtimes of the present evil age. Although deluded teachers would propagate a raft of incorrect and unhealthy ideas, Paul is most concerned about those who teach false doctrine not agreeing with the sound instruction about the Lord Jesus Christ (1 Tim. 6:3). A proper understanding of Christ is central to the Christian faith. It is worth dying for at the hands of persecutors. Paul was on his way to die for the sake of Christ. He urges Timothy, "Remember Jesus Christ, raised from the dead, descended from David. This is my gospel, for which I am suffering" (2 Tim. 2:8–9).

Among the Christian communities Timothy was working in, some had already turned away from a pure understanding of Christ and his work. Paul essentially says that they have been recaptured by the strong man. He tells Timothy not to give up on them, but to gently instruct them "in the hope that God will grant them repentance leading them to a knowledge of the truth, and that they will come to their senses and escape from the trap of the devil, who has taken them captive to do his will" (2 Tim. 2:25–26).

Satan inspired all kinds of deviant notions about Christ in the early church. Many of these wrong teachings denied that Jesus was fully man or fully God or claimed that Jesus was not sufficient.

Jesus Was Not a Real Man

As the apostle John ministered in Ephesus near the end of the first century, he cautioned Christian leaders to "test the spirits" (1 John 4:1–3). Some Christian ministers today see the primary application of this text in deliverance ministry, that is, one queries the spirit that manifests by asking it to acknowledge that "Jesus Christ has come in the flesh" (1 John 4:2). The original application of this verse had to do with discerning demonically inspired teaching in the context of the churches in Asia Minor. Schismatic groups had surfaced, with teachers contending that Jesus was a divine being but that he had not really taken on literal flesh and blood. It only appeared that he had. The early church came to describe this errant teaching as "Docetism" (from the Greek word *dokeō*, "it seems [that he had flesh]"). For John, such teaching was opposed to a right understanding of Christ and the purveyors of this teaching could aptly be termed "antichrists" (1 John 2:18; 2 John 7). It was inspired by a spirit of falsehood (1 John 4:6).

This teaching contributed to what was to become the greatest christological heresy in the early church, Gnosticism. For over three centuries, many Christian leaders, including Irenaeus, Hippolytus, and Origen, put on the armor of God and waged spiritual warfare with the influence of the unseen forces over the impact of Gnostic ideas on the church. Gnosticism was a grand mixture of all kinds of religious ideas, including Christianity, Judaism, Platonism, Egyptian religion, mystery cult theology, magic, astrology, and more. The redeemer figure of Gnosticism was not God in the flesh who came to give his blood as a sacrifice for sin. Jesus was merely a spirit who came to bring the knowledge *(gnō-sis)* that people are trapped in their evil physical bodies. The hope of salvation is the possibility of escape from matter on the day of death, when the immaterial separates from the material.

Jesus Was Not God

Satan also sought to inspire precisely the opposite—that Jesus was not God. This was of course a temptation for many Jews who became Christians. This truth about Christ was an enormous obstacle that prevented many Jews from turning their hearts to the Lord Jesus. Some who became Christians could never completely accept Jesus as fully God. These Jewish Christians, known as Ebionites, denied the deity of Christ and held on to many of their culturally distinct practices. Although Gnosticism repudiated Jesus' humanity, it also never really conceived of Jesus as God. In most Gnostic systems, the Christ figure is understood as a divine emanation, a being on roughly the same level as angels and principalities and powers.

The church continued to struggle with teachers who denied the true deity of Christ. One such teacher, Arius (A.D. 250–336), who ministered in Alexandria, Egypt, attracted a significant following. The church took a united stand against Arianism when leaders from churches all over—Italy, Greece, North Africa, Egypt, Asia Minor, Syria, Palestine, and Gaul—met at Nicaea, Asia Minor, to deal with this dangerous teaching. This group forged a statement reflecting the common belief of the church since its inception that Jesus is not only truly God, but also fully human. They described Jesus as one in substance or essence *(homoousios)* with the Father in a statement they drafted clarifying a proper understanding of Christ. This statement became known as the Nicene Creed (A.D. 325; revised at Constantinople, A.D. 381), part of which appears below.

Statement about Christ: We believe in one Lord Jesus Christ, the only-begotten Son of God, begotten from the Father before all time, Light from Light, true God from true God, begotten not created, of the same essence *(homoousion)* as the Father, through whom all things came into being, who for us men and because of our salvation came down from heaven, and was incarnate by the Holy Spirit and the Virgin Mary and became human. He was crucified for us under Pontius Pilate, and suffered and was buried, and rose on the third day, according to the Scriptures, and ascended to heaven, and sits on the right hand of the Father, and will come again with glory to judge the living and dead. His Kingdom shall have no end.[35]

The creed also corrects the wrong understanding of Gnosticism, which denies the true humanity of Jesus Christ. The Nicene Creed was written to serve not as a substitute for Scripture, but as a concise summary of the testimony of Scripture as to the identity and work of Christ.

JESUS IS NOT ENOUGH

Satan not only struck at the identity of Jesus, but also at understandings of the efficacy of his work and the nature of his relationship with his people. In other words, the devil attempts to convince people that what Jesus did was not enough, nor is he present or powerful enough to help us.

Throughout his ministry, Paul was continually dogged by a faction that is often referred to as the Judaizers. These were Jews who had accepted Jesus as Messiah, but argued tenaciously that believers also needed to undergo the Jewish rite of circumcision in order to be saved. They also advocated conformity to Jewish purity regulations and the observance of various sacred festivals. Paul argued strongly against them, saying that turning to circumcision and legal observances was tantamount to returning to slavery, a slavery to principalities and powers (*stoicheia,* Gal. 4:3, 9).[36]

In a different way, the spiritual health of the church at Colossae was threatened by a schismatic group teaching that Christ was not sufficient. For this group, Christ was not the exalted Son of God, but a divine mediator figure on par with the angels and as such could not provide protection to the Colossians from the evil principalities and powers. The faction insisted that the Colossian believers needed special spiritual insight that only came from ritual initiation into a mystery cult, they needed to invoke angels for protection from demons, and they needed to engage in various kinds of ritual observances and fasts. Paul does not sit by quietly when he hears of the teachings of this group. He writes an incisive letter to the Colossian Christians and exposes this teaching as demonically inspired deception (Col. 2:8). He argues that these people had an inferior view of Christ, which he attempts to correct (see Col. 1:15–20), and that they were not in a solid relationship with Christ as the leading and providing head of the church (Col. 2:19).[37]

Numerous forms of "Jesus is not enough" teaching plagued the church throughout the early centuries and on throughout its history. They have ranged from various kinds of legalisms ("you must also do this, this, and this to be saved") to divergent brands of syncretism (Christianity plus this belief and that belief).

One of Satan's key ploys has been deception. If he can't prevent people from turning to Christianity, he can alter the Christianity to which they turn and make it into something that is not Christianity at all. The chart below catalogs the opinions of a few of the early church fathers on the role of Satan and his powers in inspiring false teaching.

Ancient Sources on Demonic Strongholds

Epistle of Barnabas (2nd century A.D.): "We ought to give very careful attention to our salvation, lest the evil one should cause some error to slip into our midst and thereby hurl us away from our life" (2.10).

Shepherd of Hermas (2nd century A.D.): "The devil fills him [the false prophet] with his own spirit, to see if he will be able to break down any of the righteous. So, those who are strong in the faith of the Lord, having clothed themselves with the truth, do not associate with such spirits" (Mandate 11.3–4).

Ignatius (2nd century A.D.): "I urge you . . . keep away from every strange plant, which is heresy. These people, while pretending to be trustworthy, mix Jesus Christ with poison. . . . I am guarding you in advance because you are very dear to me and I foresee the snares of the devil" (*Letter to the Trallians* 6–8).

Justin Martyr (2nd century A.D.):
"They who are called devils [demons] attempt nothing else than to seduce men from God who made them, and from Christ His first-begotten" (*Apology* 58).
"The devils put forward Marcion of Pontus [a Gnostic teacher], who is even now teaching men to deny that God is the maker of all things in heaven and on earth, and that the Christ predicted by the prophets is His Son, and preaches another god besides the Creator of all, and likewise another son" (*Apology* 58).
"And a man, Maeander, a Samaritan . . . and inspired by devils [demons], we know to have deceived many while he was in Antioch by his magical art" (*Apology* 26).

Irenaeus (2nd century A.D.):
"But there is another among these heretics, Marcus by name. . . . It appears probable enough that this man possesses a demon as his familiar spirit, by means of whom he seems able to prophesy. . . . But such spirits as are commanded by these men, and speak when they desire it, are earthly and weak, audacious and impudent, sent forth by Satan for the seduction and perdition of those who do not hold fast that well-compacted faith which they received at first through the church" (*Against Heresies* 1.13.1, 3, 4).

"Let those persons, therefore, who blaspheme the Creator, either by openly expressed words, such as the disciples of Marcion, or by a perversion of the sense of Scripture, as those of Valentinus and all the Gnostics falsely so called, be recognised as agents of Satan by all those who worship God; through whose agency Satan now, and not before, has been seen to speak against God. . . . In like manner do those men, filled with a satanic spirit, bring innumerable accusations against our creator" (*Against Heresies* 5.26.2).

Tertullian (2nd–3rd centuries A.D.): "No one ought to doubt 'spiritual wickednesses,' from which also heresies come, have been introduced by the devil, or that there is any real difference between heresies and idolatry, seeing that they appertain both to the same author and to the same work that idolatry does" (*Prescription against Heretics* 40).

Cyprian (3rd century A.D.): "Beloved brethren, not only must we beware of what is open and manifest, but also of what deceives by the craft of subtle fraud. And what can be more crafty, or what more subtle, than for this enemy, detected and cast down by the advent of Christ . . . —seeing his idols forsaken, and his fanes and his temples deserted by the numerous concourse of believers—to devise a new fraud, and under the very title of the Christian name to deceive the incautious? He has invented heresies and schisms, whereby he might subvert the faith, might corrupt the truth, might divide the unity. Those whom he cannot keep in the darkness of the old way, he circumvents and deceives by the error of a new way. He snatches men from the Church itself; and while they seem to themselves to have already approached to the light, and to have escaped the night of the world, he pours over them again, in their unconsciousness, new darkness; so that, although they do not stand firm with the Gospel of Christ, and with the observation and law of Christ, they still call themselves Christians, and, walking in darkness, they think that they have the light, while the adversary is flattering and deceiving, who, according to the apostle's word, transforms himself into an angel of light, and equips his ministers as if they were the ministers of righteousness" (*Treatise* 1.3).

Numerous additional citations could be added to this list, illustrating Satan's strategy of attempting to deceive the church throughout history. God raised up many faithful leaders whom he used to effectively demolish these demonic strongholds. They did this by employing spiritual weapons. Following the example of Paul, they took the sword of the Spirit (the Word of God) and the belt of truth and exposed the lies, pretensions, deceit, and faulty notions of these erring teachers. They admonished individuals and groups of Christians, they taught in their churches, and they wrote for the benefit of many. Above all, they pointed the way back to

Christ. Cyprian said that these demonic strongholds become established "so long as we do not return to the source of truth, as we do not seek the head nor keep the teaching of the heavenly Master" (*Treatise* 1.3).

Demonic Strongholds Today: Distorted Images of Christ in "Christianity"

None of the demonic deceptions about Christ present in the early church are strangers to Christianity today. Satan continues his work of deceit, attempting to pervert a true and proper understanding of Christ. Of course there are a wide variety of opinions held about Christ in society at large. But more distressing is the multitude of perverted understandings of Christ among people who identify themselves as Christians.

Groups such as the Mormons, Jehovah's Witnesses, and Christian Scientists all teach a different Jesus than the one revealed in the Bible and confessed by the church throughout the centuries.[38] Mormons believe that Jesus was born as a spirit child to heavenly parents, the Father and his wife. He came to the earth when Mary conceived him through physical intercourse with God the Father. After enjoying marriage to at least three wives and fathering many children, Jesus was killed. His atoning death, however, only covered the transgression of Adam, not of those who would come to believe in him. The salvation of each individual is a matter of human works. Jehovah's Witnesses are well known for their denial that Jesus was God. They attempt to argue on the basis of John 1:1 that Jesus was "*a god*"— a real but nevertheless lesser god than God the Father. As such, Jesus is a spirit-being in the same sense as angels and should not be identified with the Almighty Creator God. Christian Science likewise denies the deity of Jesus Christ. Mary Baker Eddy taught that Jesus was merely the "way-shower" to God. Hence, Jesus was merely a human man, he did not die on the cross, he did not rise from the dead, and he did not pay for our sins on the cross. All three groups would claim to be "Christian," but all three distort the image of Christ as revealed to us in the Scriptures.

With the increasing influence of cultural and religious pluralism in our society, it has become fashionable for some Christians to explore other religious traditions while staying plugged into their local church. I sat next to a young executive on a plane trip from Akron to Los Angeles a couple of years ago. As the topic of our conversation turned toward spiritual things, this lady happily informed me that she, too, was a Christian and attended an American Baptist church. As we continued talking, she said that as an Asian, she had begun exploring her Buddhist roots about ten years ago and had reembraced much of what she had formerly been taught. In the past five years, however, she had also become deeply attracted to many aspects of Native American Indian spiritual beliefs. She claimed that the combination of these three was the ideal blend for her and had been spiritually enlightening and refreshing.

This form of religious syncretism that combines Christianity with Eastern beliefs is what many are calling the New Age Movement.[39] Although some have suggested that the New Age Movement is a tightly organized worldwide conspiracy, it is rather a loosely networked group of people holding a diverse set of beliefs but generally subscribing to a common worldview. At the core of their understanding of reality is that god, the world, and humanity are an organic unity (monism). God is in everything and in everyone (pantheism). For most New Agers, Jesus is an "enlightened master" who helps others see the true nature of reality. Jesus was truly a historical person, but not God in the flesh who came to shed his blood for the forgiveness of sin. The real Jesus was one of a line of spiritual teachers who went to the East as a child and studied with Hindu gurus before embarking on his ministry of bringing spiritual enlightenment.

Profound distortions of a true understanding of Christ are not only present in cults and the New Age Movement, but also in academia and in the halls of the universities. Almost every semester since I have taught at Talbot School of Theology, I have had one or more students approach me during the course of a semester and relate to me a struggle they experienced during their undergraduate education. The stories are generally something like this:

> I came to know Christ during my sophomore year at ———— University through the outreach of a campus ministry. Christ made a tremendous difference and for the first time I felt a sense of purpose and meaning to life. Through his grace, I was also able to get rid of some very ugly things in my life that I always knew were wrong but could never seem to control. My spiritual mentor was wonderful. We met weekly and this person prayed faithfully for me. I also learned a lot about the Bible in a weekly small group meeting in the dorms and through the teaching of a pastor at a church I started to attend. Toward the end of the year I even began to think that God might be leading me to be involved in ministry.
>
> As I was looking through the registration booklet for the fall semester, I noticed that the university was offering a class on "The Historical Jesus." As a new Christian, I felt this was an incredible opportunity to learn more about the Bible and the person that now meant more to me than anything in the world. The class, however, turned out very different from what I expected. For one thing, the professor started the class by informing us that scientific analysis of the Gospels in their first-century historical contexts has demonstrated that there is really not much about

the life of the historical Jesus that we can know with certainty. We also learned that the Gospels were written much later than I had originally thought and that they were based on legends and stories about Jesus that were actually created by the romantic notions of people in the early churches. Only some of the things that Jesus was reported to say, he actually said. But even these sayings have been reshaped and edited by writers much more concerned to address issues in the churches of their own day than to get down accurately what Jesus had originally said.

I was amazed by all of this. At first, I totally rejected what the professor had to say and didn't believe a word of it. But his arguments made a lot of sense and all of the books we were reading basically said the same thing. I didn't know what to make of the historical Jesus. The ideas of a virgin birth and a physical resurrection as well as the whole concept of "God in the flesh" now began to seem absurd to me. It became clear to me that even Mark 10:45, "The Son of Man did not come to be served, but to serve, and to give his life as a ransom for many," was probably what some people in the early church thought and not what Jesus actually said.

My Christian friends were sympathetic with what I was going through, but they were not able to give solid or credible answers to the tough questions I asked. I now felt like I was duped by this campus ministry into believing a big fairy tale. I was ashamed I had taken the Bible so literally. I thought about breaking off all contact with the group, but the friendships I had established with a few of them meant too much to me.

The semester finished and my faith was shipwrecked. My friends stuck by me though, prayed for me, and gave me some books and resources that began to answer some of my questions. The intensity of the crisis passed—I am still a Christian, still believe in Jesus, and once again want to be involved in ministry. That is why I am now in seminary. But the fact is, I still have some big questions and a lot of doubts and sometimes wonder if I am not living a lie.

Whether they realized it or not, the individuals I have alluded to in this account were in the midst of spiritual warfare. The enemy of their souls was seeking to reclaim them for himself. His mode of operation was through hollow and deceptive teaching, distortions of the truth about Jesus Christ. The demonic strongholds that had settled into their minds needed to be demolished by spiritual weapons, which include confrontation with the truth and fervent prayer.

This sort of teaching about Christ is nothing new. It has been deeply rooted in the religion departments of our universities for a century or longer. It represents the bankrupt spiritual legacy of the Enlightenment era, which sought to free thinking people from the shackles of the church. The influence of well-known continental scholars such as Albert

Schweitzer, Wilhelm Wrede, and Rudolf Bultmann is still strongly felt throughout the world.[40]

This radical skepticism, philosophical naturalism, and antipathy to all things orthodox and evangelical has surfaced in a more organized and popularized form in recent years in the work of the so-called Jesus Seminar. The seminar consists of a self-appointed group of about seventy-five scholars who sought to reach some concrete conclusions about the teachings and life of the historical Jesus. They are well known for their highly publicized method of voting on the authenticity of the sayings of Jesus by using colored beads: a red bead means he surely said this, a pink one indicates that he probably did, a gray one suggests that it is doubtful that he said this, and a black one means that he certainly did not. At the end of their deliberations, the seminar concluded that Jesus only said about 18 percent of the sayings attributed to him by the Gospel writers; the Gospel of John contains nothing "red," or historically accurate; and the Gnostic Gospel of Thomas should now be reckoned as the fifth Gospel. The results of their work were published in their color-coded edition of the Gospels titled *The Five Gospels.*[41] In a recent critique of the methodology and results of the Jesus Seminar, Ben Witherington suggests that the benign, witty, and humorous Jesus they end up with seems a much better candidate for a late-night visit with David Letterman or Jay Leno.[42]

Should we be surprised by these recent developments? No. Throughout the history of the church, the adversary has inspired every shade of false teaching about Jesus in an effort to lead people astray. His strategy does not change.

Just as our spiritual predecessors did in the earliest church—luminaries like Ignatius, Irenaeus, Cyprian, and Hippolytus—we need to take up the armor of God and, in the words of the apostle Paul, "demolish arguments and every pretension that sets itself up against the knowledge of God, and we take captive every thought to make it obedient to Christ" (2 Cor. 10:5). This involves

- research and writing, as my colleagues Michael J. Wilkins and J. P. Moreland did in pulling together a team of scholars to respond to the outlandish claims of the Jesus Seminar (published in *Jesus under Fire*).[43]
- teaching and proclaiming the truth. Christian leaders are responsible for rooting their people deeply in the truth through a steady diet of solid biblical teaching. The modern evangelical church has

lost sight of giving new Christians extensive and rigorous training in the Christian faith.

- meeting with those who are struggling and gently leading them back to Christ. This involves helping them apprehend the truthfulness of the gospel and the reality of their connectedness to the risen Christ.
- stimulating the faith of the believers. This involves enabling them to exercise faith in the true Christ, the sure foundation for faith.
- dependence on the Holy Spirit for every facet of life and ministry.
- intercessory prayer for all believers, that Satan would not gain any sort of foothold and that they would be strengthened with the power of God in their innermost beings.

Christological Heresy in Our Churches?

Far more times than I would like to remember over the past ten years I have heard evangelical pastors and teachers suggest that we do not have doctrinal problems in the church today; our problems are with interpersonal relationships, moral compromise, management styles, and differences in philosophy of ministry. Often the implication is that less time should be spent studying theology, and more time should be devoted to learning better church administration, developing management skills, and the like.

Very little of what we do is disconnected from how we think. Our worldview is the script by which we live and theology is an integral part of worldview. In other words, the kinds of notions we hold about Christ will have a direct impact on how we live. Perhaps we do not deny the deity of Christ, the virgin birth, or the incarnation, but are there other ways that we may have been influenced by demonically inspired distortions of a proper view of Christ? I am convinced that there are numerous christological heresies—demonic strongholds—in the minds and hearts of people in our churches. Many people subscribe to these heresies without even realizing it, fully convinced that they are conservative to the core. Some are more dangerous distortions than others, but all have a negative impact on the spiritual well-being of believers.

The Jesus without a body: there are plenty of Christian individualists who feel no need to be connected to or accountable to the body of Christ. These are people who are "fingers" or "eyeballs" and prefer floating about doing their thing in a disembodied state.

The Jesus who is far, far away: this is the view held by Christians who practically conceive of Christ as so remote from their life issues that they focus only on sharing their griefs and discussing their problems without any meaningful attempt to draw on Christ's strength.

The Jesus superseded by angels: Jesus is so austere, demanding, and inaccessible that it is better to get in contact with our guardian angels. They watch out for us and are right there to help us if we should call on them.

The Rambo Jesus (or the Judge Dredd Jesus): Jesus is blowing away the devil all over the place right now through his victorious church. All we have to do is use his name to tear down anything that gets in our way. This "commando Christology" sees the devil behind every bush.

The healthy, wealthy Jesus: Jesus wants us all to kick back and enjoy all this life has to offer. With enough faith, we can claim for ourselves enormous wealth and freedom from illness. I will never forget when my wife was becoming acquainted with a new co-worker at the time I was finishing seminary. When my wife mentioned to this lady that I was preparing for ministry, the young lady retorted, "Wow, you guys are gonna be rich. My pastor has two Mercedes and. . . ."

The Jesus who is my pal: Jesus is a cool friend who makes me feel real good about myself. This view ignores the fact that the Spirit of Jesus comes to bring conviction about patterns of sinful behavior and to promote holiness and integrity in our lives. It also minimizes Jesus' identity as the transcendent God, Creator of heaven and earth, worthy of worship, honor, and profound respect.

The Jesus who did not suffer: although the New Testament says that "since Christ suffered, arm yourselves also with the same attitude" (1 Peter 4:1), there is a segment of Christianity that thinks all suffering is from the devil. We must remember that we live in the present evil age. Suffering and evil are awful facts of life until Christ returns and once for all deals decisively with the problem of evil and brings his people into the full experience of the kingdom of God. Until then, we do not seek suffering. Yet when we do encounter hardships, we have access to the strength, peace, and joy Christ can give even in the midst of suffering.

The Jesus with no mission: this is the view of Jesus that holds that he entrusted his people with no task around which to unite themselves, commit their resources, and work. Jesus essentially came to provide forgiveness of sin, for which we are to be grateful and get on with our lives.

The Jesus with no heart: Jesus had no social conscience and was unmoved by the plight of the poor, the oppressed, and the outcasts of society.

The Jesus who did not die for all *our sins:* there are some Christians who believe that they will definitely pay for some of the bad things they have done. I have had more than one person tell me, "Clint, you just don't know some of the things I've done. Jesus could not possibly forgive me for that. I know I'll pay for it." Satan wants nothing more than to make Christians believe this lie. Unfortunately, I am convinced that many Christians do secretly believe it. This awful stronghold needs to be torn down with the truth of Colossians 2:14: "He forgave us all our sins."

The unforgiving Jesus: Jesus is so stern and severe that he does not easily forgive. When he looks at me, he recoils at the sight of my filth.

The Jesus who does not discipline: at the other end of the spectrum are those who believe they can entangle themselves in sin with minimal consequences. They emphasize the love and grace of the Lord Jesus to the exclusion of his discipline of believers who err and fall into sin. Jesus counseled the mediocre church of Laodicea, "Those whom I love I rebuke and discipline. So be earnest, and repent" (Rev. 3:19).

These demonic strongholds need to be discerned, rooted out, and replaced by the truth. Most of these are not doctrinal heresies in the traditional sense of the term, but they are nevertheless faulty theological notions that have a powerful, adverse impact on the way we live. Many of these ideas are held unwittingly—believers have little or no idea how wrong and dangerous their thinking is.

We need to ask the Lord to grant us a special measure of discernment to detect these demonic strongholds in our lives and in our churches. Then we need to don the armor of God to demolish these faulty notions and bring every idea into conformity with a proper understanding of who Jesus is, what he has accomplished, and who I am in relationship to him. Satan works very hard to cause us to believe a lie. He wants to hide the truth or distort it in such a way that it is detrimental to following in the steps of Jesus on the path of discipleship.

Why Even Think about the Enemy?

By now it should be abundantly obvious why we need to give some thought to the nature and workings of our adversary, the devil. It may be helpful, however, to make this more explicit.

Awareness of the Opponent Is Helpful

"How much should we think about the enemy?" A listener posed this question to me during a "Live on LA" radio broadcast with Warren Duffy in 1995. After my response, Duffy gave a better reply by using the example of a quarterback playing football. If the quarterback keeps his eye on the linebackers and the defensive backs, he will never connect with his receiver. The quarterback must focus primarily on his wide receiver, but at the same time he must be aware of the defensive players and anticipate their moves or his throw will be intercepted.

It is also important in football to study the game strategies of the opposing teams. Analyzing the opponents is so important that a high school coach recently lost his job and his league-championship team forfeited their spot in the playoffs when officials discovered that he had given an edited videotape of his team to the coaches of the team he was about to face. He did not want his opponents to know all of his plays.

Paul told the Corinthians that he was "not unaware of [Satan's] schemes" (2 Cor. 2:11). Because of this, Satan will not outwit us. Clearly some knowledge of what Satan is up to and how he goes about his business is important for all Christians. This does not mean that we become enamored with him and grant him a dangerously inordinate amount of our time and attention. It simply means that we become aware.

It Wakes Us Up to the Reality of Supernaturally Powerful Opposition

Awareness of the demonic realm jolts us into recognizing that the deck is stacked against us. The Christian life is more than just notching up the level of our effort. There are evil supernatural forces seeking our moral and spiritual demise. We also begin to realize that evangelism is not just a matter of finding an effective strategy for reaching our community; evangelism represents an aggressive assault on territory held by a supernaturally powerful enemy.

It Prompts Us to Depend on God

"Rugged individualism" has almost served as a national motto for our country. Most of us were taught self-sufficiency, self-reliance, and personal responsibility from an early age. Any form of dependence is looked down on. This philosophy of life may serve us well in certain forms of business or track and field, but it does not work well in the Christian life. God did not bring us into his family to be loners or to live without reliance on him. One of the most important lessons we must learn is our need to depend on God and other believers in the body of Christ.

Paul therefore begins his discussion of the believers' struggle with a reminder of just this fact. He urges Christians to "be strong *in the Lord* and in *his* mighty power" (Eph. 6:10). He also reminds believers in the same book that they have been incorporated into one body and that the body is only growing and healthy when each part does its work (Eph. 4:16). In practical terms, this means that God not only bestows his power on us as we directly depend on him, but also through the lives of other believers. As we begin to recognize our vulnerability to the forces of evil when we live independently of God and other believers, we are thrust back into the arms of our loving heavenly Father, who wants to manifest his power in our lives.

The Danger of Thinking Too Much about Demons

During the summer of 1995, I received a call from a man in our neighborhood who desperately wanted my counsel on a spiritual warfare issue. He was convinced that his house was loaded with demons. He was obviously very frightened and wondered what he should do. He claimed that he was a Christian and said he was involved in a local church from time to time. He also said that he had an ongoing drinking problem. I asked him if he had done anything about the demons he perceived to be plaguing his home. He then explained that a group of people had come on three separate occasions and prayed through the house, anointing it with oil. They had in fact poured so much oil on the windows that it was impossible to see through them. His landlord was not too happy about all of the oil on the house and had insisted that it all be cleaned off within a few days. The man was now deeply worried that without the oil on the windows and around the doorframes the problem would worsen.

This man was too fixated on demons. He clearly needed to get his focus off the demons and onto Christ. The church he had been attending most recently was a solid church that had a reputation for offering a loving, caring ministry to people. A group from the church came, met with the man, and began working with him. For this man, I am convinced that more oil on the windows would not have solved the problem. Nor would a special one-time focused prayer session. He needed to be enfolded in a caring group of people who would meet with him on a regular basis, help him grow in his understanding and appropriation of the Word, hold him accountable for dealing with his problem with alcohol and other issues, pray for him, and generally care for him.

On another occasion a lady called me from a large metropolitan city in the Midwest. She had read one of my books and thought I might be able to offer some help. She began to relate to me her tremendous fear that she was being stalked by members of a cult group. She said that she could sense them watching her at almost all times of the day and night. Most troubling of all, she said, was their ability to read her thoughts. She claimed that she could tell whenever they would access her mind. She could sense the spirits like electricity traveling through her spinal cord and into her brain. Since I lived a great distance away from her, there was little I could do except listen, pray for her, and refer her to other Christians who could help. I strongly encouraged her to pay a visit to an acquaintance of mine in her area who had experience in deliverance ministry. She immediately reacted to this referral, stating that she knew of this person and was convinced that he was part of the cult. I then urged her to attach herself to a group of believers in a good church in her area. Knowing two outstanding churches in the city, I recommended them to her. She recoiled at the mention of both of these churches. She claimed that she was familiar with them and knew that they were filled with demonized people from the cult. She could never trust anyone there. Tragically, this lady was so paralyzed by fear, so suspicious of everyone around her, that she was blocked from seeking out the very avenues of help she needed most.

There are clearly dangers in thinking too much about demons, evil spirits, and what they are doing in the world today. The roaring lion wants to instill as much fear as possible into believers and create paralyzing anxiety. Our gaze needs to be fixed on Christ, our warrior.

Recommended Reading

Arnold, Clinton E. *Powers of Darkness: Principalities and Powers in Paul's Letters.* Downers Grove, Ill.: InterVarsity, 1992. This is a focused study on the theme of spiritual warfare as presented by the apostle Paul in his thirteen letters. The book not only describes Paul's teaching on principalities and powers, but presents much historical background information as well as implications for the contemporary church.

Kraft, Charles H., and others, eds. *Behind Enemy Lines: An Advanced Guide to Spiritual Warfare.* Ann Arbor: Servant, Vine Books, 1994. This is a collection of essays on various facets of spiritual warfare by missionaries, evangelists, seminary professors, and even a recent convert from the New Age Movement. The contributors include Kraft, Ed Murphy, Tom White, Edgardo Silvoso, and others. You may not agree with everything that is said in this book, but it is an excellent sampling of current discussion on the theme.

Moreau, A. Scott. *Equipped for Battle: Essentials of Spiritual Warfare.* Wheaton,

Ill.: Harold Shaw, forthcoming. Moreau served for ten years as a missionary in Africa and is now a professor of missions at Wheaton College. This is an excellent introduction to spiritual warfare that is well rooted in Scripture and well balanced in its approach.

Page, Sydney H. T. *Powers of Evil: A Biblical Study of Satan and Demons.* Grand Rapids: Baker, 1995. The only comprehensive biblical study of this theme on the market. Page is a biblical scholar who completed his doctoral study at the University of Manchester under F. F. Bruce. This is an outstanding analysis of all the pertinent biblical texts.

Can a Christian Be Demon-Possessed?

Janet felt the presence late at night, a few hours after she had drifted off to sleep. Her heart beating wildly, she would sense someone in her bedroom, someone vile and menacing. Visibly no one was there, but there had to be. Every part of her knew it. She felt herself pinned down to the bed. She couldn't move her arms or her legs. She tried to scream, but nothing would come out. At times, she had the sickening feeling that whatever was there was violating her sexually. Finally, after five or ten minutes, the presence would lift and be gone. What an incredibly awful dream! Or was it a dream? It seemed so real. Janet would then turn on the light and pull her Bible off the nightstand. Reading the Book of Psalms brought her deep consolation.

Rin had been a Christian for three years. How grateful he was that missionaries had come to translate the Bible into his tribal language! He was exultant when one of the translators asked him to become a language consultant. Rin worked hard at helping them understand the various nuances of his tribal tongue. For many years he had been hearing voices in his head. But now that he was helping the missionary, the voices had become louder and often suggested hostile ideas to him. As the translator was sitting at his desk, he would hear a voice speak to his mind, "Pick up the hatchet—kill him." *No, no!* he exclaimed to himself. Where did this voice come from? This was the last thing he would want to do. He tried to ignore the voices, but they did not go away. They kept telling him to "get the hatchet, get the hatchet." The voices tormented him daily, but he kept trying to suppress them, and told no one. On Thursday, they were in the office once again working. Rin rose from his chair to get a drink. One of the voices came loudly and with such authority: "Grab the hatchet and strike him." Rin picked up the hatchet. The voices came with fury: "Hit him! Hit him!" Rin did. The missionary was found three hours later, slumped over his desk. Rin was detained and accused of murder.

Mark had a reason to be angry. No one should have treated an innocent child the way his father had treated him. Prone to violent outbursts, Mark resented the fact that he was becoming just like his dad. Coming to Christ had made a big difference. He not only appreciated God's forgiveness, but the Lord had saved his marriage from certain doom two years earlier. But now things were falling apart again. Why couldn't he get a handle on his anger? Why did he cross the line and fly into a rage virtually every time he had an argument with his wife? He was always filled with regret when he cooled down and thought about what had happened. He knew that it was inevitable for two people to have an occasional disagreement, and he could maintain control of his emotions up to a certain point. But then it was like he would experience a sudden rush of a "crazy-making" drug and he would totally lose it. It felt like something took over and drove him into these rages.[1]

Nighttime visitations, hearing voices, driving rage—what is going on? Are these symptoms of the typical struggle believers have with the flesh? Or is it possible that they reflect evil of a different sort, the influence of actual spirit-beings intent on corrupting, hurting, and destroying?

Some earnest believers would say that God protects genuine Christians from such experiences with evil spirits. As temples of the Holy Spirit, believers are immune to demonic spirits messing with their minds in these kinds of ways. Episodes like these are either explained by the fact that the three people were not truly in a relationship with Christ or there are some other natural factors that need to be considered. Perhaps Janet is prone to nightmares, Rin was superstitious, and Mark just needed to get a handle on his anger and unlearn some bad behavior patterns.

However, an increasing number of Christian leaders have been saying that there is more to situations like these than hyperimaginations and inflamed emotions. They suggest that there may actually be demonic spirits planting images, speaking to people's minds, manifesting their presence in fear-inducing ways, and exploiting flesh-oriented sinful tendencies. They are insisting that believers like Janet, Rin, and Mark need to recognize their authority in Christ and deal directly with these foul spirits.

But to what degree can *Christians* be afflicted and troubled by evil spirits? Is it even possible for a Christian to be "demon-possessed"?

Background Perspective

For much of Christianity in North America, Great Britain, and the Continent over the past two hundred years, the belief in "demon possession" and the consequent practice of exorcism have existed only on the fringes. Advances in medicine and the behavioral sciences have helped us see a variety of alternative explanations for outlandish behavior and altered states of consciousness (especially when people perceive themselves to be under the influence of an intruding spirit). Medication and psychotherapy have virtually replaced exorcism. This is true even of Roman Catholicism and the Orthodox traditions, which still have rituals of exorcism but seldom practice them in the West.

Nevertheless, Scripture contains stories about evil spirits and even portrays Jesus casting out demons from people on various occasions. This has created somewhat of a dilemma for those of us who appreciate the scientific advancements of our era but also view the Bible as the foundational revelation for our faith and practice. Christians have tended to respond to this dilemma in one of three ways: (1) *Dismiss the stories about demons altogether.* This was the "demythologizing" approach of the twentieth century associated particularly with Rudolf Bultmann, a Bible scholar and Lutheran minister. He debunked these tales as reflecting a primitive worldview. (2) *Reinterpret the stories about demons.* Some are suggesting that there is value to the exorcism stories in spite of the fact that they are relics of an outdated worldview. These narratives have contemporary value when we get behind their surface to discover their deeper messages. Some, for instance, have suggested that "demons" is a code word for the Pharisaical religious establishment or that an "unclean spirit" should be seen as a psychological projection of our inner self. Both of these approaches, in my opinion, show signs of allowing a set of naturalistic worldview assumptions to unduly color how one interprets the Bible.

Another option is to (3) *accept the stories as what really happened.* This is the response of most evangelicals and Bible-believing Christians. This does not necessarily mean that all Christians will find what is said in the Bible about demons relevant for today. Some, for instance, are still convinced that demonization only happened back in the first century. This is easily countered, however, by taking even a cursory glance at church history. There are numerous accounts of demonization and exorcism in every century of the history of the church.[2] We are now left with the option of not only accepting what the Scriptures say but also finding out how these accounts correspond to life as we know it today and what we can learn from the example of Jesus.

There is a significant segment of Western Christianity that has seen Jesus' ministry of exorcism as normative and follow his example. This has been particularly true of Pentecostalism and those who became involved in the charismatic renewal of the 1970s.[3] They have confidently called on the name of Jesus to drive out evil spirits from non-Christians as they have engaged in evangelism and missions. Some groups, however, such as the Assemblies of God, reached the conclusion that Christians could not be demon-possessed; this was something that only could happen to nonbelievers. Christians could be influenced, afflicted, or oppressed by demons, but not possessed.

The bulk of conservative evangelicalism also tended to be convinced that genuine Christians could not be demon-possessed. There was a strong assumption that demon possession was a phenomenon normally associated with the lands where idolatry flourished, but God had shown his favor on the United States because of the widespread Christian influence. Satan only used this tactic in places like Africa, India, Asia, and Latin America. It created little difficulty, then, to hear missionaries on furlough tell incredible stories of demon possession among the tribal people they worked with.

Many evangelicals found confirmation of their assumption that Christians could not be demon-possessed in the 1952 book written by the respected biblical scholar, Merrill Unger. In *Biblical Demonology,* Unger reached the comforting conclusion that the believer "is not liable to demon inhabitation."[4] The fact that a believer is indwelt by the Holy Spirit necessarily precludes demonic invasion. Because Unger was the author of numerous Bible reference books, including the immensely popular *Unger's Bible Dictionary,* his view received a wide hearing and broad acceptance. Nearly twenty years later, Unger wrote that he had changed his mind on this issue. He was now quite convinced that believers could be demon-possessed. His change of perspective came as a result of numerous letters from missionaries all over the world claiming that they had witnessed cases of true believers manifesting possession behavior. Unger himself visited and ministered in a variety of cross-cultural contexts, where he witnessed the phenomena firsthand. He also began ministering to people in the United States whom he considered to be genuine believers but who showed clear symptoms of demonic inhabitation. All of this forced Unger back to the Scriptures to reevaluate the incongruities between his experience and what the Bible teaches. Unger came to the conclusion that he had clearly overstated his case in the 1952 volume. He revised his position by arguing that demons assert their influence over Christians in a variety of ways, one of which could be inhabitation or possession. He defended his new position in his two books, *Demons in the World Today* (1971) and *What Demons Can Do to Saints* (1977).[5]

Unger's reversal met with mixed reactions, but his later teaching clearly paved the way for the broader acceptability of what has become known as modern deliverance ministry. From the early 1970s until now, there has been a steady stream of popular books written by evangelical pastors, counselors, and teachers explaining how Christians can effectively deal with demonic influence in their lives. People like Kurt Koch, Mark Bubeck, Neil Anderson, Tom White, Tim Warner, and Ed Murphy have written extensively on this theme. All of them are convinced that Christians can be inhabited by demons. Most of them, however, prefer not to use the expression *demon possession;* they speak rather of *demonization* (a transliteration of the Greek word often translated "demon possession"). For them, the expression *demon possession* is less appropriate because people often associate it with gruesome scenes like those portrayed in *The Exorcist* (which is not representative of how they would conduct a ministry session) and it carries a lot of other misleading overtones (such as ownership). This view received significant support when the chairman of the theology department at Moody Bible Institute, C. Fred Dickason, published his 350-page book, *Demon Possession and the Christian* (1987).[6] He not only set forth a biblical and theological case for the possibility that Christians could be demonized, but he claimed to have counseled at least four hundred genuine believers from 1975 to 1987 who were actually inhabited by demons.[7]

During this same period a new movement was springing up led by evangelist and pastor John Wimber. Described by Fuller Seminary professor C. Peter Wagner as the "Third Wave of the Holy Spirit" (assuming the Pentecostal movement and the charismatic renewal as the first and second), Wimber was stressing not only backing up the proclamation of the gospel with a demonstration of its power with signs and wonders, but also the Spirit's power to heal when God's people were assembled. Wimber taught that when the people of God gathered to worship and a context was given for a time of ministry, the Holy Spirit would come and sovereignly distribute gifts to individuals within the body to minister to one another in various ways. This involved the discerning of spirits and casting them out of believers who were in need of deliverance and healing.[8]

In general, over the past twenty years there has been a strong reaction within evangelicalism to the foundational assumption that a Christian can be inhabited by a demon. A variety of books, articles, and pamphlets have been published denouncing the notion of the demon possession of a Christian as unbiblical and dangerous. Many arguments have been put forth, but there are two that surface in all of the writings. The first insists that *a Christian cannot be demon-possessed because his or her body is a temple of the Holy Spirit.* The Spirit of God cannot dwell in the same space as a demonic spirit. The second asserts that *a Christian cannot be demon-possessed because he or she is already owned by God.* An evil spirit cannot come and take ownership of what God has bought with the price of his beloved Son.

This brings us back to the primary focus of this chapter. Can a Christian be demon-possessed? Can a demon inhabit the same body as the Holy Spirit? And can a Christian be owned by Satan?

The Tragic Confusion Surrounding the Word "Possession"

What most people think of when they hear the word *possession* is the idea of ownership—I own some kind of property and thereby have the right to use it as I choose. This is the natural way for people to think about possession. We use the term this way all the time. The Ford Aerostar van that I own, for instance, is just one of my possessions. I can choose to leave it in the garage, or I can take it out and drive it whenever I want. It is up to me whether I maintain it properly or decide never to change the oil. When I am behind the wheel, I have total control of the vehicle. The van has no ability to disagree with me and apply the brakes when I press on the accelerator or to turn on the windshield wipers when I press the turn directional. Once I sign the title, however, and hand the van over to someone else, I no longer retain ownership of the vehicle and have no say in when it is used, how it is maintained, or how it is driven. That will be the prerogative of the new owner.

English speakers have used the term *possession* in this way for many years. The idea of ownership and control has also been the legal understanding of the term. The *Oxford English Dictionary* reports that in the context of law, possession means "the visible possibility of exercising over a thing such control as attaches to lawful ownership."[9] The dictionary continues by explaining that the control over the person or property is exclusive. No one else has the right to come and dictate how the possessed entity is to be used.

Most people believe, then, that the ideas of ownership and control attach to the expression *demon possession*. To be possessed by the devil is to be owned by the devil and to be totally under his control. It means that the person is incapacitated and no longer able to act on the basis of his or her own volition. Demon possession is like being hijacked; a hostile intruder has taken over and the unsuspecting victim has no ability to regain control.

Many earnest Christians have thus rightly denied that possession is something that could ever happen to a believer. Demon possession of a follower of Christ is inconsistent with biblical teaching about what it means to be a Christian. How could a person who has become a possession of the living God be snatched away by the devil or any demon? God is our new owner, not Satan. We belong to the Father and we are his children. It is inconceivable that a true Christian could ever belong to an evil spirit. The logical conclusion to reach, therefore, is that a Christian cannot be demon-possessed.

I wholeheartedly agree with this conclusion. *A Christian cannot be owned and controlled by a demon.*

What many people do not realize, however, is that the word *possession* never even appears in the Bible in the passages where Jesus or the apostles cast evil spirits out of an individual. The expression *demon-possessed* or *demon possession* does occur in some English translations of the Greek text, but there is never a Greek word for "possession" that stands behind it. "Demon possession" is always the translation of a single Greek word, *daimonizomai*. Words for ownership or possession (e.g., *huparchō, echō, katechō, ktaomai,* or *peripoieō*) are absent in the original text.[10] The idea of possession is the interpretation of the Greek term by Bible translators. This translation of the word became standard because the most popular English Bible translation for over three centuries—the King James Version—used "demon possession" or "possessed with the devil" to render the Greek.[11] Today, the most popular English translations continue to use "demon possession," as seen in the following translations of Matthew 8:16:

KJV: "They brought unto him many that were possessed with devils."
NKJV: "They brought to him many who were demon-possessed."
NASB: "They brought to him many who were demon-possessed."
NRSV: "They brought to him many who were possessed with demons."
NIV: "Many who were demon-possessed were brought to him."
NLT: "Many demon-possessed people were brought to Jesus."

Some Bible translations—usually those following more of a dynamic translation philosophy—varied from the fixed rendering, *demon possession:*

CEV: "Many people with demons in them were brought to Jesus."
GNB/TEV: "People brought to Jesus many who had demons in them."
Message: "A lot of demon-afflicted people were brought to him."

In other occurrences of *daimonizomai,* these and other versions have employed expressions such as "tormented," "vexed," or "troubled" to translate the term.

Nevertheless, the terms of the current debate have been set by the longstanding tradition of translating the expression *demon-possessed.* Where did English Bible translators get the idea of translating *daimonizomai* as "demon possession"? The translation was most likely influenced by the Latin church's tradition of using the term *possessio* to describe a person deeply troubled by a demonic spirit. Interestingly, the Latin Vulgate, however, does not use the term *possessio* to translate *daimonizomai,* but the simple expression *to have a demon* (*habeo* with *daemonia*). But it is also important to realize that the English term *possess* has a long history of usage where the emphasis could fall on control or occupancy as opposed to ownership.[12] This is significant because it is by no means certain that the translators of the King James Version intended to convey the notion of ownership by using the term *possession.*

The obstacle for us is that in popular contemporary usage we have a difficult time disentangling possession from the concept of ownership. To avoid this confusion, some Christian leaders have suggested that we begin transliterating the term *daimonizomai* by the expression *demonized.* This has the advantage of providing us with a new term to use without the baggage that comes with "demon possession." It might also be advisable to use other common translations of *daimonizomai* that we noted earlier.

I am convinced that there would be far greater agreement among Christians on this issue if we framed the question differently, leaving out the word *possession.* We might ask, "Can Christians come under a high degree of influence by a demonic spirit?" or, "Is it possible for Christians to yield control of their bodies to a demonic spirit in the same way that they yield to the power of sin?"

Christians Cannot Be Owned by Satan

For a Christian, the issue of ownership is settled once and for all when a person turns to Christ. At that time, Satan loses any legal claim to ownership on the basis of the blood of Christ shed on the cross. We are legally acquitted by God from our guilt due to sin (Rom. 5:1) and transferred from the domain of Satan into the kingdom of God (Col. 1:13). In his recent book, *Possessed by God,* David Peterson says, "By his saving work in Christ, *God takes possession of us* and renews us through the operation of his word and his Spirit."[13]

Jesus told a brief parable about people who were possessed, or owned, by Satan:

> How can anyone enter a strong man's house and carry off his possessions unless he first ties up the strong man? Then he can rob his house (Matt. 12:29=Mark 3:27=Luke 11:21).

The "strong man" in this parable represents Satan, and those who have not experienced God's redemptive activity are Satan's "possessions" (*ta skeuē* in Matthew and Mark; *ta huparchonta* in Luke). But the result of Christ's defeat of Satan by the cross is that people can be set free from this evil overlord and brought into a relationship with a loving master. They are no longer the possessions of Satan, but the property of Christ; Satan is no longer their master, but they belong to the one Lord—Jesus Christ.

It is therefore inappropriate to speak of a Christian's coming under the ownership of Satan.[14] Demons cannot come and take away a person's new identity as a child of God and a saint. Believers are now "in Christ" in a relational solidarity that cannot be shattered. Christians properly are owned by God. The Father views us as his own precious inheritance (Eph. 1:18).

When a person becomes a Christian, he or she is sealed with the Holy Spirit (Eph. 1:13). The Spirit indwells our lives and is God's mark on us, indicating that we belong to him. The Spirit brings us into the family of God, bestowing on us the irrevocable status of being "children of God" (Rom. 8:16–17). Try as he may, there is nothing Satan can do to change any of this. Paul celebrates this fact at the end of the eighth chapter of Romans:

> For I am convinced that neither death nor life neither angels nor demons, neither the present nor the future nor any powers neither height nor depth, nor anything else in all creation, will be able to separate us from the love of God that is in Christ Jesus our Lord (vv. 38–39).

A Temple of God, but a Dwelling for Demons?

There is a popular misconception that since the Bible refers to the believer's body as a temple of the Holy Spirit (1 Cor. 6:19), a demon cannot occupy the same space as the Spirit of God. Some contend on this basis that a Christian cannot be demonized or show symptoms of being profoundly influenced by demons. Demons can influence Christians, they say, but only from the outside, not from the inside.

In spite of our eternal status, it is clear that demonic spirits attack and endeavor to create all kinds of problems for Christians. But can they invade the life of a believer?

First, if the power of sin can inhabit a Christian's body and exert such a significant influence that Paul could say it "reigns" (Rom. 6:12–13), why do we suppose that another form of evil influence cannot dwell there? After conversion the "flesh"—the evil inclination (the *yetser harah*), a structure of the present evil age—continues to be present with the believer. This is the locus of much of the struggle for the believer. It is an evil, a part of us and within us, resident in the same body as the Holy Spirit of God.

Second, Paul uses spatial language to refer to the devil securing inhabitable space in the life of a believer when he warns, "do not give the devil a foothold" (Eph. 4:27). This directly contradicts the view that the two cannot coexist in the same body.

Third, the Old Testament temple imagery actually lends itself to supporting the idea of the potential demonization of Christians. Often in the history of Israel, this dwelling place of God was inhabited by other gods and goddesses. This often came about because God's people brought in idols, set them up, and worshiped them—right in the temple! It is important to remember that these idols represented demonic spirits (Deut. 32:17). One illustrious example is the condition of the temple at the beginning of the reign of King Josiah. When he renewed the covenant with God, he found an amazing assortment of vile impurities in the temple, including religious paraphernalia used in the worship of Baal, Asherah, and the host of heaven. He also discovered an Asherah pole, rooms for the male cult prostitutes operating in the temple, horses and chariots dedicated to the sun, and altars dedicated to other gods (2 Kings 23). In an inspiring act of fidelity to God, he removed all of these unholy trappings piece by piece.

In a similar way, demons will take as much room as we will give to them. Merrill Unger put it well when he said, "Certainly by permitting heinous sin or indulging in occultism or occult religion or yielding to some other transgression, a believer limits the protection that is his in Christ. . . . Dare we be so naive as Christians to believe that demonic powers will not press their claims to the limit!"[15] The questions for all believers are: What are we *bringing in* to this holy temple? What are we *allowing to remain* in the temple?

It is extremely disquieting for many Christians to think that they may be invaded by a demonic spirit. To conceive of the Holy Spirit as resident in the same body as a demonic spirit could lead to excessive feelings of anxiety, insecurity, and fear for some people. We need to ask, then, in what sense a believer is a "new creation" with "the old" (including the demonic) having passed away (2 Cor. 5:17).

The Bible does envision a radical change happening within people when they turn to Christ. This is well illustrated by Paul's language of "the old self" and "the new self" (Eph. 4:22–24; Col. 3:9–10).

Prior to becoming a Christian, the core of a person's identity is corrupt, that is, it is not directed to God but to self and to evil. This does not mean that a person is thoroughly evil in all of his or her actions; each individual is created in the image of God and has the capacity to do good things. Nevertheless, the image of God within the person is tarnished by the presence of sin.[16] The individual's way of thinking, feeling, and choosing is fundamentally out of harmony with what God desires. In practice, everyone has engaged in sinful activities and everyone has set up "idols" in place of God.

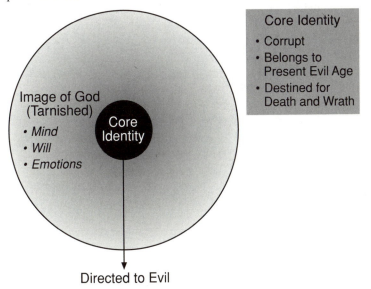

Fig. 2.1 The Old Self

The larger circle in figure 2.1 represents "the old self," the person prior to conversion. Sin adheres to the person, even to the very center of his or her being. The presence of the power of sin is manifested in what Paul calls "the flesh"—an impulse to do evil that is a part of our earthly existence. Demonic spirits work in conjunction with this evil inclination and incite a person to sin. These evil agents may also work directly to tempt or afflict the individual. They can attach themselves to the individual (the larger circle) and take up residence at the very core of the person (the smaller circle).

When a person becomes a Christian, however, Paul explains that he or she has become a new person. He exclaims, "Therefore, if anyone is in Christ, he is a new creation; the old has gone, the new has come!" (2 Cor. 5:17). Although a person may think that he or she is simply making a decision to follow Christ, in the spiritual realm a supernatural transformation and change have occurred. Figure 2.2 portrays this transformation.

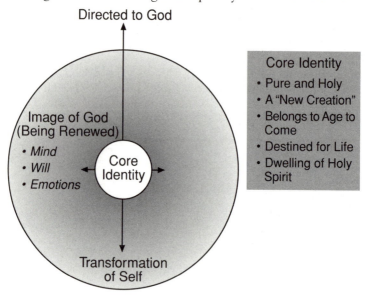

Fig. 2.2 The New Self

A fundamental change has taken place at the core of this person's being. The person's identity is no longer corrupt, but is now pure and holy. The Christian is identified by his or her connection to Christ, the age to come, and the kingdom of God. At the center of this person's being now lies a desire for God and a passion to please him in every respect. This is the place of the Holy Spirit's dwelling. No evil spirit can enter here or cause the Holy Spirit to flee. To extend the image of the temple, we might say that this is the inviolable "holy of holies." Some theologians and many popular-level writers on deliverance ministry have referred to this as the human spirit, which has now been made alive unto God. But biblical theology does not support the notion of a clear distinction between soul (*psychē*) and spirit (*pneuma*) in the Scriptures.[17] It is perhaps best simply to refer to this as the core of the person, the center of his or her being, his or her ultimate nature and identity.

In spite of the fact that this core transformation has occurred, the continued impact of the presence of sin is still felt. The person lives in a decaying and dying body, a structure of this present evil age. In practical experience, the new believer continues to have corrupt thoughts and desires that seem to come from within. These are more than just ingrained habits that need to be overcome; they are manifestations of the presence of the evil inclination, or "the flesh."[18] In other words, the "old self" is still present and continues to experience corruption (Eph. 4:22), but it is in the process of being overcome and subdued by the core of the new self, energized by the Spirit of God.

The believer does indeed have a new identity as a child of God, a citizen of heaven, and a saint. Yet the Christian still retains a structure of the present evil age: his or her body and the power of sin presenting itself as an inner propensity to do evil.

Demonic spirits seek to exert their influence in the same way and in the same places that the evil impulse does. They attempt to reassert their control over the mind, will, and emotions of the individual in a variety of insidious ways. Because of the inextricable nexus between mind and body, their influence can even be manifest in the body through physical symptoms and actions.

The difference between a believer and a nonbeliever is at the core of their being. The believer has an entirely new nature because he or she has been brought into a relationship with Jesus Christ and endowed with the Holy Spirit.[19] Demonic spirits cannot penetrate to the core of this person's being and snatch away what belongs to God. A believer may yield to the evil impulse or to a demonic spirit, allowing it to assert a dominating influence over mind, will, emotions, and even the body. But the person's new identity as a child of God cannot be erased or stolen. Nor do demonic spirits have the ability to evict the Holy Spirit of God.

On the contrary, because of the presence of the Spirit, the believer is no longer under the compelling sway of sin and the powers. He or she is energized by the dynamic and empowering presence of God to defeat these unholy influences at every turn. Nor is this struggle a battle of equals. God's power is incomparably greater than the power of sin or the power of Satan.

The Holy Spirit does not manifest his divinely powerful presence in such a way as to obliterate every trace of evil influence in a person's life when he or she becomes a Christian. A believer can choose to embrace sensual desires and succumb to the flesh. The Holy Spirit appeals to every Christian to pursue purity and supernaturally enables every believer to defeat temptation in every instance, but he does not overpower the person's will and prevent him or her from giving in to this evil. When a person succumbs to evil influence and sins, the Holy Spirit temple then becomes defiled and the Spirit grieves (Eph. 4:30). Habitual and protracted sinful behavior then makes the believer vulnerable to a deeper level of demonic influence—a concept the apostle Paul explains with the spatial language of inhabitation (Eph. 4:27).

Figures 2.1 and 2.2 depict biblical teaching, and especially Paul's theology, on this issue. Of course any diagram can only point to the truth without exhausting it since the Bible uses a wide variety of metaphors and images to present spiritual realities. A perspective from a slightly different angle may be useful.

A number of years ago, Robert Munger wrote a very helpful booklet entitled *My Heart–Christ's Home.*[20] In it he attempts to portray the meaning of Paul's prayer for believers in Asia Minor, "that Christ may dwell in your hearts through faith" (Eph. 3:17). He creatively elaborates on the spatial metaphor of Christ taking up residence in a home as a means of describing the Christian experience of growth to maturity in Christ. He portrays conversion as the time when Christ initially enters the home. The time after conversion then involves allowing Christ to successively enter and assert his influence over every room in the house. Munger depicts Christ entering the library ("the control room of the house"), the dining room ("the room of appetites and desires"), the drawing room (an "intimate and comfortable" room for visiting), the workshop (where the homeowner applied his skills for productive labor), and the rumpus room (a place for activities and amusements). Room by room Jesus goes in and takes control of the decorating and activities occurring in these places. He transforms each of the rooms and brings into them purity, happiness, laughter, and real friendship. Finally, Jesus asks permission to enter the hall closet after noticing a putrid stench coming from the small room. Jesus takes the key, opens the closet door, and cleans out "the one or two little personal things that I did not want anybody to know about."

This little book is a vivid representation of what it means to surrender our lives to Jesus' lordship. In the context of Ephesians, Paul is clearly addressing Christians, calling for them to yield more and more of their lives to Jesus' control. He is not praying that Christ would take up residence in their hearts for the first time in the sense of conversion. The spatial metaphor of surrendering control room by room effectively depicts the increasing levels of influence Christ seeks to have over our lives.

Munger never touches on the role evil spirit intruders can have in attempting to maintain a claim over each of the rooms. Yet this would also be an appropriate elaboration of the metaphor because of the prominent role they play in the overall context of the Book of Ephesians. They want to remain hidden in the hall closet and pollute the house. They certainly do not want Christ to get into the dining room or the rumpus room; they want the appetites to remain unrestrained and pleasures to prevail.

Varying slightly from Munger's depiction, we could say that although a spirit may not be residing in the living room, it might be hiding in the bedroom or bathroom. As long as the pornographic literature remains hidden on the bathroom shelf, the spirit feels that it has every right to remain. All the while the illicit relationship continues in the bedroom, another evil denizen is determined to stay. We might depict the "house" as in figure 2.3.

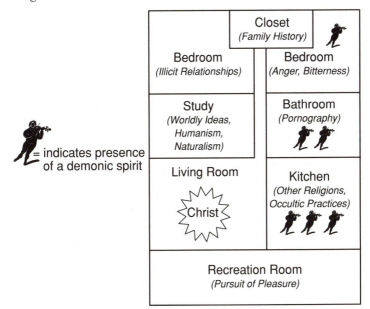

Fig. 2.3 Heart Home

When a person becomes a Christian, Christ dwells in his or her heart, but sin is still present. The point is that Christ wants to assert his lordship over every room of the house. He wants to dwell in all the rooms and be the most important influence in each. Believers need to open the door of each room to him and allow him to clean out the defilements, chase out any illegal occupants, and rebuild and redecorate the rooms.

In ancient Israel, the temple of the Lord remained the Lord's house in spite of various kings bringing in defiling and impure objects. Our bodies and our very beings belong to the Lord regardless of the compromises we make and the defilements we yield to and allow into our lives. Like the godly kings of Israel, we need to clean the garbage out of the temple and break the unholy allegiances. The apostle John assures us that Jesus keeps the believer safe "and the evil one cannot harm him" (1 John 5:18). No one, including Satan or any of his host, can separate us from the love of God and steal from us our precious salvation. But we can allow demons a significant amount of turf, which they are all too happy to take, and they can exercise a high degree of influence and control.

Christians Can Be Inhabited and Controlled by Demons

The biblical, theological, and historical evidence suggests that Christians can be profoundly influenced by evil spirits—even to the extent that it can be said that they are inhabited and controlled by demons.

Giving Turf to the Devil

The one passage in the Epistles that comes closest to the language of demonization is Ephesians 4:26–27: "In your anger do not sin; Do not let the sun go down while you are still angry, *and do not give the devil a foothold.*"

The term translated "foothold" is the Greek word *topos,* an expression that was commonly used for inhabited space. Scripture tells us that Mary and Joseph laid Jesus in a manger because there was no room *(topos)* for them in the inn (Luke 2:7); a seat at the dinner table could be referred to as a *topos* (Luke 14:9); a city or village in a region could be spoken of as a *topos* (Luke 4:37); and, Jesus said that he has gone to prepare a *topos* for us in heaven (John 14:2–3).

Even more to the point are passages that illustrate the use of *topos* to refer to the inhabiting space of an evil spirit. Jesus said in proverbial form that "when an evil spirit comes out of a man, it goes through arid places [*topos*] seeking rest and does not find it. Then it says, 'I will return to the house [*oikos*] I left' " (Luke 11:24). In the Book of Revelation, after Satan and his forces are defeated in the war in heaven, there is no longer any place *(topos)* for them there (Rev. 12:7–8).

The most natural way to interpret the use of *topos* in Ephesians 4:27 is the idea of inhabitable space. Paul is thus calling these believers to vigilance and moral purity so that they do not relinquish a base of operations to demonic spirits.

It is possible, on the other hand, to interpret *topos* as "chance" or "opportunity." There are a couple of passages where the term is used in this sense (e.g., Rom. 12:19; Heb. 12:17). But the idea of inhabitable space is more appropriate to the context of Ephesians and to the discussion of the workings of spirit powers. Paul uses spatial language extensively in Ephesians to describe spiritual realities. He speaks of the believer as a vessel capable of being "filled" with God (3:19). Similarly, he describes the church as a temple that is in the process of being built "to become a dwelling in which God lives by his Spirit" (2:22). More important, he speaks of Christ dwelling *(katoikeō)* in the hearts of believers through faith (3:17). What is surprising about this text is that it is an intercessory prayer *for believers* that Christ would dwell in their hearts. The assumption is that he is already there, but they need to allow Christ to completely fill them—room by room. They should not allow any portion of their dwellings to be occupied by a demonic spirit.

All of this spatial terminology is metaphorical language. It provides us with a glimpse into reality without literally explaining it. We miss the intent of a metaphor if we take the language too literally. I remember well a discussion with one of my sons when he was three years old. He wondered if a doctor cut him open and took out his heart, if there would be a little Jesus figure in the organ. A couple of years later he had a better grasp of the metaphor. He exclaimed to me one time that since Jesus had entered his heart, he had taken the key, locked the door, and threw the key away. This was a vivid way for him to express the nature of his commitment to the Lord.

One of the principal ideas expressed by the spatial language of indwelling is the concept of authority and control. When Paul prays for a more extensive indwelling of Christ, he is praying for a greater realization of the lordship of Christ in the lives of these dear believers. He wants them to allow Christ to assert a more invasive reign among them in such a way that they exhibit an increasing amount of Christian virtue. Conversely, when he cautions them about surrendering space to the devil, he is warning them against allowing the devil (or a demonic spirit) to exert a domineering influence in an area of their lives. For a Christian to nurture anger, for example, may grant a demonic spirit inhabitable space.

Allowing Evil to Reign

The Bible clearly conceives of the possibility that a Christian may allow an evil force to have a controlling and dominating influence in his or her life. The apostle Paul admonished the believers in Rome, "Do not let sin *reign* in your mortal body so that you obey its evil desires" (Rom. 6:12, italics mine). Paul viewed sin as an incredibly powerful evil force that once held believers in slavery and apart from God. This evil power does not vanish when one becomes a Christian. It repeatedly attempts to reassert its control. In fact, the term Paul uses for "reign"—*basileuō*—is strong language. It is from the same set of terms describing what Jesus is setting out to do, that is, establish his kingdom (*basileia* is "kingdom") and exercise his reign (*basileus* is "king").

Paul is not making this plea just for the sake of argument. He knows that Christians still have a strong impulse to do evil. He is fully aware that Christians sometimes give in to this impulse and commit sin. He is painfully aware of the fact that, on occasion, Christians can blow it "big time" and get involved in a sinful pattern of life over an extended period of time. It is this that he wants believers to avoid. And the promise is that there is a way out now through understanding who we are in Christ and by appropriating the resources of this new life.

In the biblical perspective, evil asserts its influence in three different, but related, ways (as we discussed in the previous chapter): through the "flesh" (the inner inclination to evil), through the "world" (the unhealthy social and cultural environment), and directly through Satan and his demons. These three evil influences most commonly work in concert to lead people astray from God and his purposes (see fig. 2.4).

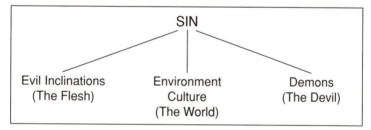

Fig. 2.4 Sin's Power Points

Therefore, when Paul urges believers not to allow sin to have dominion, he is thinking of every possible form of evil influence. He is saying, "Don't give in to the evil desires that well up from within you; don't succumb to the ungodly pressures put on you by acquaintances and by society, demanding that you conform to 'what's in.'" But he is also saying, "Resist evil spirits in the multitudinous ways they will come after you to bring you down."

The key implication of this passage is that all three of these evil influences—representing the personified power of sin—conspire against believers to rule and dominate their lives. The main point for our purposes here is that demons are one of these three evil influences that can "reign" in the life of a Christian. They can dominate and they can control. They will take as much governing power as we will allow them to take.

Their authority and control, however, are not absolute. By virtue of our union with Christ, we now have the ability to offer every aspect of our lives to God and allow him to reign over us. As Peterson puts it, Christians "must revolt in the name of God, their rightful ruler."[21]

A Possible Example of the Exorcism of Christians

During Paul's three-year ministry in Ephesus, God performed extraordinary miracles through him (Acts 19:11). These manifestations of God's power included healings and exorcisms. Luke makes this clear when he notes that "even handkerchiefs and aprons that had touched him [Paul] were taken to the sick, and their illnesses were cured and the evil spirits left them" (Acts 19:12).

We often and too quickly assume that this illustrates "power evangelism"—the authentication of the gospel in the context of proclamation. Undoubtedly, this is part of the story, but is it all of it?

Luke tells us of the exorcism ministry of Paul immediately after explaining that "all the Jews and Greeks who lived in the province of Asia heard the word of the Lord" (Acts 19:10). There was a massive turning to Christ during Paul's extensive ministry in this city. Many house churches were formed and Ephesus was well on its way to becoming one of the most important centers of early Christianity.[22]

As I have documented and illustrated elsewhere, Ephesus was famous in antiquity for being a center for the practice of magic, witchcraft, and sorcery.[23] It was out of this context of darkness that a great number of people had turned to Christ. Unfortunately, many of these new believers did not immediately renounce their involvement in the occultic arts (beliefs and practices involving the use of supernatural forces and beings).[24] God directly intervened, however, in a dramatic way to bring conviction on them through the notorious failed exorcism attempt by a Jewish exorcist named Sceva (Acts 19:13–16). Luke then tells us that "many of those *who believed* now came and openly confessed their evil deeds" (Acts 19:18, italics mine). The result was a massive ceremony of renunciation involving the burning of 50,000 days' wages worth of magical papyri. These were Christians burning their occultic texts! They had received Christ and were worshiping him every Lord's Day but had continued to practice the occultic arts.

It is quite likely that many of the new believers would have experienced a ministry of exorcism by Paul prior to this time (and even subsequent to it). The kind of magic they were involved in—indeed, what was typical of the day—often consisted of specific invitations to gods, goddesses, and assistant spirits to come, take residence, and manifest their presence in a variety of ways.

For instance, one magical text explains how to perform a ritual in which "a daimōn comes as an assistant who will reveal everything to you clearly and will be your companion and will eat and sleep with you."[25] This being is then described as "a god; he is an aerial spirit which you have seen." Once the door is opened, others invade the life of the person: "He will quickly bring daimons [for a banquet], and for you he will adorn these servants with sashes. These things he does quickly." Of course, the person using this kind of magic assumes that he or she is obtaining good spirits who will help and protect. Thus, the magical text assures, "as soon as you order him to perform a service, he will do so, and you will see him excelling on other things. . . . [H]e stops very many evil daimons."

If prior to, and even subsequent to, their conversion, believers in Ephesus were engaging in this sort of magic—summoning spirits and inviting them into their lives—how would the apostle Paul have responded? Surely he was not blind to this phenomenon. Was providing these people with instruction in the Scriptures enough, or was more direct intervention required on occasion?

Because of the background of the people becoming Christians in Ephesus, I am convinced that at least part of Paul's ministry of exorcism in that city was to new believers. As we will see later, exorcism of new believers became the common practice of the church throughout the Mediterranean world.

Proper instruction was also of paramount importance. These people needed to know that Jesus was not just another helper spirit. He was far more than this and was seeking their exclusive allegiance. Someone had to break the news to them that the spirits they had previously received and thought helpful were actually wicked spirits aligned with the prince of darkness. They also needed teaching about the nature of spiritual power. God tolerated for a time their substance notions of power—that it was like an electrical current that could charge up a handkerchief. But they needed to grow in the understanding that the power of God is different. It is imparted through an intimate relationship with the exalted Lord Jesus, who enables them to share in his authority over the unseen evil realm.

Conclusion

Although the Epistles do not use the terms demonization or have a demon to describe the experience of a Christian, the concept is nevertheless present. The ideas of demonic inhabitation and control are clearly a part of the biblical teaching on what demons can do to saints. To limit our-selves to the same Greek words that the Gospels use to describe the phe-nomena of demonic influence could cause us to miss the same concept expressed in different terms. No one, for instance, questions the valid-ity of making disciples as part of the church's mission. Yet the term *dis-ciple (mathētēs)* never appears in the New Testament after the Book of Acts. It would be quite erroneous to conclude that the concept of dis-cipleship died out early in the history of the church. What has happened is that Paul, Peter, John, and other New Testament authors have made use of a variety of other terms to describe the same reality.

Biblical Examples of Extreme Demonic Influence on Christians

There are a number of additional passages in the Epistles illustrating that demonic spirits can have an extensive influence on believers.

Following Deceiving Spirits (1 Tim. 4:1)

Paul warns Timothy that "the Spirit clearly says that in later times some will abandon the faith and follow deceiving spirits and things taught by demons." Paul is not looking into the distant future, thinking only of the series of events just before the return of Christ. He is speaking by the Spirit to the situation facing the believers in Ephesus, where Timothy was ministering.[26]

The folks in Ephesus were being allured by a faction identifying them-selves as Christians. These people were in the churches and involved in ministry, but they taught ideas inconsistent with the gospel. Whatever the precise nature of their doctrinal beliefs, the implications involved significant lifestyle matters. They advocated celibacy and a rigid form of asceticism (including taboos about eating certain kinds of food). Undoubtedly they wanted to be seen as a spiritual elite among the churches and were appealing to others to join them.

Paul saw these factional leaders as the agents of deceiving spirits *(plana pneumata)* and demons *(daimonia)* (1 Tim. 4:1–2). In light of this, would it be appropriate for us to surmise that these leaders also manifested extreme or dramatic symptoms of demonization, such as writhing, foam-ing at the mouth, seizures, and so on? It seems to me that this would be doubtful. How could they entice Christians to join them if they were so obviously controlled by demonic entities?

On the other hand, they may have been experiencing behaviors con-sistent with common cultural understandings of what it meant to have a spirit come upon them. Perhaps they heard voices in their heads that they interpreted to be the teaching and counseling voice of the Spirit of God. Perhaps they went into trance states (an altered state of consciousness) and experienced dreams and visions, which they mistook as divine revelation. Religious experience of this nature was quite common at this time.

The issue would then be one of discerning whose voice they were hearing. Quite assuredly, they did not style themselves as teaching demonic doctrines. Paul, however, was able to discern quite a different source for their teaching. How he was able to make this determination appears to come both from Spirit-guided insight as well as from a sober analysis of the situation.

He begins his warning to Timothy by expressing, "The Spirit clearly says . . ." (1 Tim. 4:1). This indicates that the Holy Spirit directly imparted to him special insight about the character of these factional teachers and about others who would be surfacing. Yet Paul also sees the gross inconsistencies between their teaching and both Old Testament revelation and early Christian confession. He therefore encourages Timothy to pay careful attention to doctrine, that is, to the common confession of the churches about Christ and the kingdom of God (1 Tim. 4:16; see the confession Paul himself cites in 1 Tim. 3:16). We also see, for example, Paul rejecting the dietary rules of these people on the basis of an Old Testament understanding of the creation (1 Tim. 4:4–5).

The danger for believers in Ephesus when Paul wrote was that they, like their deceived teachers, might be swept away by this new teaching and come under the dominating influence of evil spirits.

Taking Christians Captive to Do His Will (2 Tim. 2:25–26)

In another passage, Paul advises Timothy on how to minister effectively to a believer whom Satan has "taken captive": "Those who oppose him [the Lord's servant] he must gently instruct, in the hope that God will grant them repentance leading them to a knowledge of the truth, and that they will come to their senses and escape from the trap of the devil, who has taken them captive to do his will" (2 Tim. 2:25–26).

Paul continues to be concerned about false teachers in the midst of the churches. He is not speaking of wolves among the sheep, but of sheep who have been led astray and threaten to lead others astray. Since Paul advises Timothy on how to minister in a way that effects restoration, these opponents are Christians who have fallen off the rails. They have become ensnared in a trap *(pagis)* set by the devil, and the result is quite severe—they are now captives of Satan. George Knight aptly comments that the phrase *being captured alive (ezōgrēmenoi)* "conveys the sense of 'having been taken and held captive' and expresses the decisive hold that the devil has."[27]

It is quite possible that these false teachers were Christians who had never made a clean break with their occultic past and were continuing to be involved in magical practices. Paul compares their opposition to what Moses experienced when he faced Jannes and Jambres, the Egyptian sorcerers (2 Tim. 3:7–8; cf. Exod. 7:11–12, 22). These two men are not mentioned in the Old Testament, but are well known in Jewish writings. Paul probably mentions them here not simply because they are opponents of God's servants, but also because of a similar kind of opposition—involvement with magic and sorcery.

Looking for Someone to Devour (1 Peter 5:8)

The apostle Peter warns believers in Asia Minor to be strong in their faith because of the real possibility that they could be "devoured" *(katapinō)* by the devil. Peter compares Satan to a lion who paces back and forth and creates fear through his awful roar.

This passage clearly has believers in view and, at the minimum, envisions the potential for Satan to have extensive and dominating control over the life of a Christian. The term for devouring *(katapinō)* was commonly used for wild animals that tore apart their prey and swallowed all that was edible—a term quite appropriate for the hungry lion.[28] Because of the context of intense, localized persecution of Christians, J. Ramsey Michaels thinks that the imagery of the passage points to Satan working in the hearts of believers in such a way that they renounce their allegiance to Christ.[29] The fear and dread Satan creates by his roar—perhaps signifying the threats to family members, friends, and acquaintances by the persecutors—was one of the principal means he used to carry out his designs.

In this verse, the devouring does not suggest demonic control in the sense of dramatic manifestations of demonization, but it does convey the idea of near-total dominance.

Falling into the Trap of Elemental Spirits (Col. 2:8)

Paul's motive for writing his letter to the Colossians was to prevent these believers from falling captive to a demonically inspired teaching.[30] He warns them, "See to it that no one takes you captive through philosophy and empty deceit, according to human tradition, according to the elemental spirits of the universe, and not according to Christ" (Col. 2:8 NRSV).

Once again he sees Satan operating powerfully through inspiring a teaching that would keep believers away from the Lord Jesus Christ. On the surface, it would appear that the teaching of the faction in the church at Colossae could be explained strictly on a human level (it "depends on human tradition"), but ultimately it can be traced to demonic powers, which Paul here calls *stoicheia tou kosmou*. [31]

Paul's anxiety over the danger to the church is expressed by his choice of the rare term *sulagōgeō*, "to take as plunder" or "to take as captives." Paul sees the possibility that these Christians could be victimized by Satan through this factional teaching in a way that once again brings them under satanic bondage.

The group within the church advocating this variant theology and practice certainly would not have seen themselves as demonized or even demonically influenced. They thought they were living on a very high level of spiritual existence and experience. Paul sees things quite differently, however. He describes their teaching as deceitful (Col. 2:8) and insists that they are not walking in a close relationship with Christ (Col. 2:19).

The deluded Christians purveying this teaching did display many facets of overt demonic influence. They sought contact with spirit-beings, visions played a significant role in their experience, they may have engaged in ritual forms of initiation (modeled after the local mystery religions) (Col. 2:18), and their mode of worship may have bordered on the "ecstatic" (Col. 2:23).

Paul unmasks their deviant beliefs and practices as inspired by demonic spirits. They were already captives and threatened to lead others astray.

Becoming Re-enslaved to Elemental Spirits (Gal. 4:9)

Paul had a similar concern about the health of the churches in the nearby province of Galatia. Since he had planted churches in this region, a group of believers (presumably from Judea) had come on the scene with a dangerous teaching that Paul saw as demonically inspired. Thus he warns the Galatians, "Now, however, that you have come to know God, or rather to be known by God, how can you turn back again to the weak and beggarly elemental spirits? How can you want to be enslaved to them again?" (Gal. 4:9 NRSV). [32]

The language is strong. Just as these Gentile believers had been in bondage to Satan prior to their turning to Christ when they were in idolatry, Paul now fears that they will be re-enslaved. This time, however, not by returning to the false gods, but by embracing the law and a variety of Jewish sectarian practices (including circumcision, the food laws of the Torah, and the observance of festivals and sacred days). For Paul, this sort of law-centered approach to Christianity minimizes the person and work of the Lord Jesus Christ. Demonic spirits inspire and promote this works-oriented approach as a means of blinding people to Christ (see 2 Cor. 4:4).

The language of slavery once again points to the biblical understanding that believers can yield themselves to a very high degree of demonic influence and control in their lives.

Summary

1. Although these passages do not use the spatial language of inhabitation (except for the reverse notion of the believer inhabiting the stomach of the devil!), they do address the fundamental issue of demonic influence and control. Believers can come under a very high degree of domination by evil spirits, as portrayed by the images of "being devoured," "taken captive," "following evil spirits," "taken as plunder," and becoming "enslaved."

2. Because of the occultic nature of some of the deviant forms of teaching, it may be possible that a number of these deceived Christians were exhibiting aspects of overt forms of demonic influence—altered states of consciousness, trances, visions, and so on.

3. All of these passages hold out the hope of deliverance for these Christians. They still have the possibility of being restored and reestablishing a vital relationship with Christ.

How Demons Exert Their Influence on Christians

The New Testament Epistles show us a variety of ways that Satan often works to reassert his dominance over the lives of believers.[33] These operations of the Evil One discussed below are certainly not the only ways he attacks Christians, but they are very important to consider because of the prominence they are given in the Epistles.

Temptation

The classic way Satan operates is by enticing believers to sin, which has garnered him the title "the tempter" (1 Thess. 3:5). According to John, this has been one of the devil's primary modes of operation since the beginning (1 John 3:8). Thus, he put it in Cain's heart to murder Abel (1 John 3:12; cf. John 8:44). He is also blamed for influencing Ananias and Sapphira to sin. Luke says, "Satan has filled your heart [*eplērō-sen tēn kardian*] to lie to the Holy Spirit" (Acts 5:3). If this couple were believers, and we have no indications to the contrary, this passage says a great deal about the extent of influence Satan can have on individuals.

James, however, emphasizes the role of the evil inclination within each individual as the source of temptation. He says, "each one is tempted when, by his own evil desire, he is dragged away and enticed. Then, after desire has conceived, it gives birth to sin" (James 1:14–15). This is not the sole root of temptation though. James draws a close connection between the evil impulse and the work of the devil. He observes that the tongue is set on fire by Gehenna (James 3:6; a way of referring to Satan as the ultimate source). He similarly points out that certain forms of worldly wisdom are not only "earthly and unspiritual," but are "of the devil" (*daimoniōdēs,* James 3:15). James is therefore not only acutely aware of our own capacity to perform evil, but he sees the devil behind the evil impulse and operating in the world.

None of the biblical writers explicitly describes the process of temptation and precisely how demonic spirits are involved at each interval as the temptation unfolds. Neither do the biblical writers appear to be as concerned as we are about discerning when a temptation is from the inner evil impulse, from a cultural/societal influence, or directly from a demon. They seem to see all three involved in the process.

The example of the temptation of Jesus, however, would lead us to believe that there are times when an evil spirit might directly impress thoughts or images on our minds to entice us to act contrary to the will of God (Matt. 4:1–11). This was certainly the conviction of many of the church fathers. For instance, Tertullian says, "So, too, by an influence equally obscure, demons and angels breathe into the soul, and rouse up its corruptions with furious passions and vile excesses" (*Apology* 22).

To be tempted, however, is not to be dominated or controlled by Satan. Temptation is the experience of every Christian. To succumb to the temptation and fail to appropriate the power of the indwelling Spirit of God is to surrender space in one's heart for the devil to occupy and exercise control.

False Teaching

As we have seen in chapter 1 and in the passages discussed above (1 Tim. 4:1; 2 Tim. 2:26; 1 Peter 5:8; Col. 2:8; Gal. 4:9), another prominent way Satan attempts to re-enslave believers into his domain is through false teaching. He contrives to inspire teachings within the church that distort the person and work of the Lord Jesus Christ.

John therefore counsels the leaders of the churches in Ephesus and western Asia Minor to "test the spirits to see whether they are from God"

(1 John 4:1). In this case there were some who had once been affiliated with the church and were now teaching that Jesus had not assumed a bodily existence when he came to earth.

Many modern scholars reject the notion that there are dastardly little spirits that inspire false teaching. They contend that "satanic" and "demonic" were adjectives used by the sociologically dominant religious group to vilify the teachings of all those groups with whom they disagreed. This is essentially the conclusion Elaine Pagels reaches in her recent book, *The Origin of Satan.*[34] Her study, however, is predicated on the naturalistic assumption that God as well as Satan are not objective realities and that truth is something that we cannot apprehend with any degree of certainty. In contrast, we believe that the God of the universe has in fact revealed himself in an objective way throughout history and primarily through the earthly life, teaching, and work of Jesus Christ. Because of the life-and-death importance of the revelation of Christ, the adversary strikes as hard as he can to distort, diminish, and distract people away from this all-important truth.

Creating Feelings of Guilt, Doubt, and Fear

As "the Accuser," the Evil One brings indictments to God continuously against believers (Rev. 12:10). He likewise reminds believers of their shortcomings, unworthiness, and sin. By stimulating feelings of guilt, he hopes to keep Christians from feeling well-assured in their relationship to Christ and unworthy to receive his empowering grace. One writing in the Apostolic Fathers emphasized Satan's work of inspiring doubt and called it "a daughter of the devil" (*Shepherd of Hermas,* Mandate 9.9).

The image of Satan "as a roaring lion" (1 Peter 5:8) depicts his attempts to instill fear into believers. Anxiety, panic, and terror are feelings that Satan endeavors to arouse as a means of paralyzing Christians and preventing them from yielding to and experiencing the work of the Holy Spirit in their lives. The representation of Satan as a lion is not merely literary hyperbole, however. A more appropriate image would not be a defanged and declawed house cat. The Evil One does have the ability to devour; he still has his fangs and he is still a mighty being that one should respect. But Peter has already made it clear that the Lord Jesus Christ is mightier. He has "gone into heaven and is at God's right hand—with angels, authorities and powers in submission to him" (1 Peter 3:22). Christians are in close connection with this almighty God and can therefore resist Satan and stand firm in their faith (1 Peter 5:9). Christ can push all fear away and provide protection from the powerful foe.

Physical Attack

The Evil One can also induce physical illness in Christians. The apostle Paul himself experienced this. He writes, "To keep me from becoming conceited because of these surpassingly great revelations, there was given to me a thorn in my flesh, a messenger of Satan, to torment me" (2 Cor. 12:7).

We do not know precisely what this thorn in the flesh was, but it was most likely a physical affliction. Many suggestions have been put forth, including defective eyesight, recurring malarial fever, a nervous disorder, defective speech, and even epilepsy, but we have no way of knowing with any certainty. What is important for us to see is that Paul realized that he was afflicted by a messenger (literally, "an angel") of Satan.

It appears that Paul did not seek the help of other believers in terms of some form of deliverance ministry in spite of the fact that he had discerned the demonic origin of the problem. Rather, he petitioned God directly to make this spirit of infirmity flee from him. God made it clear to him, however, that he was permitting the spirit to afflict Paul so that he would continue to depend totally on God's grace and power for his life and ministry.

Persecution

The church has faced violent opposition and persecution since its inception. Peter perceived the devil behind the suffering the believers in Asia Minor were experiencing when he wrote to them (1 Peter 5:8–9). The stringent opposition that Christians in Smyrna and Philadelphia faced at the hands of the local Jewish populace led to each of their synagogues being dubbed "the synagogue of Satan" (Rev. 2:9; 3:9). The letter warns the church in Smyrna that "the devil will put some of you in prison to test you" (Rev. 2:10). Satan is even seen as behind the martyrdom of a Christian leader in Pergamum (Rev. 2:13).

The seething violence of Satan toward the people of God is symbolically depicted in Revelation 12–13. The red dragon persecutes the woman (Rev. 12:13) and wages war with her seed (Rev. 12:17). The beast of the sea is animated by Satan and goes to make war against the saints (Rev. 13:7).

One of the most well known apostolic fathers, Ignatius of Antioch, saw his own suffering and eventual martyrdom as incited by Satan. He describes "fire and cross and battles with wild beasts, mutilation, mangling, wrenching of bones, the hacking of limbs, the crushing of my whole body" as "cruel tortures of the devil" (*Letter to the Romans* 5.3). Yet at the same time he could victoriously exclaim, "Let these come upon me, only let me reach Jesus Christ!"

Conclusion

Most of the ways that demons work against believers would not be described as symptoms of "demonization" or inhabitation. Nevertheless, they fill out more of the picture of the immense variety of ways our enemy works to influence believers and thereby thwart the purposes of God in their lives.

Because of the multitudinous ways demons work to afflict Christians and reassert their influence, it is advisable for us to move away from the bipolar notion of "demon possession" or nothing. The most fruitful and accurate way of describing demonic influence is along a continuum (see fig. 2.5).

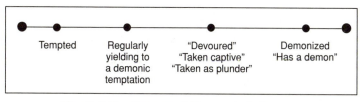

Fig. 2.5 Continuum of Demonic Influence

Every Christian experiences demonic temptation and suggestions, but not every Christian has taken the step of inviting a demonic spirit to reside within him or her and be a helper spirit (as may happen with Christians who dabble in the occultic arts). Some Christians may be enticed to exhibit rage, but not all Christians are overtaken by rage whenever they have a dispute with a spouse or a family member.

Can a Christian Exhibit an Altered State of Consciousness?

Central to the debate over whether a Christian can be "demon-possessed" is the question of whether it is possible for a believer to experience an altered state of consciousness, which may be attributed to the influence of a spirit entity. This is the means by which some medical doctors, psychologists, psychiatrists, and anthropologists determine whether a person is experiencing what they call "spirit possession."

An altered state of consciousness refers to any significant deviation from normal waking consciousness. Of course, we all experience altered states of consciousness when we sleep, day dream, or concentrate very intensely on something we are doing. But not all of us experience an unusual state of consciousness in which we identify ourselves as someone else and demonstrate behavior that is not typical of how we normally act.

In the complexity of their humanness, people have the capacity to take on a different identity. Psychologists refer to this phenomenon as dissociation. Children dissociate when they talk to an imaginary playmate. A little boy with a car in each hand may be "Joe" one minute and "Bud" the next. This is a perfectly natural and good use of the imaginative capabilities. It becomes unnatural and unhealthy when an adult switches among various "persons" in the interactions of daily life. Mary may become the professional "Janelle" to her colleagues at work and then turn into the swinging "Lisa" in the nightclubs. She may also become the seven-year-old frightened "Judy" as she talks with her counselor. "Dissociative Identity Disorder" (formerly known as "Multiple Personality Disorder") has been much discussed by mental health professionals in the past decade and has been portrayed in a number of television dramas.

Dissociative disorders, however, are not attributed by psychologists to inhabiting spirits. They are complex manifestations of the human personality. Many mental health professionals explain the onset of the disorder by postulating that it is often the result of serious chronic child abuse. As a way of coping, the victim creates a series of imaginary identities to help deal with the trauma. By imagining that the abuse is happening to someone else, a young victim may be able to survive the trauma.[35]

Many Christian psychologists today are working with patients who are genuine believers and are struggling with the difficulties of a dissociative disorder. The fact that Christians are not exempt from this kind of malady is amply attested by clinical evidence. Yet Christians have the benefit of the indwelling Holy Spirit and a community of caring believers to help them reach wholeness and health.

What happens, however, when someone visits a pastoral counselor or mental health professional and manifests an altered state of consciousness with the "personality" (or alter) claiming to be a demonic spirit? What if this is accompanied by significant behavioral changes—the patient begins to speak in a different voice and curse God in the foulest of language, the face grimaces and distorts, and the appearance of the person's eyes becomes hateful and evil? The fact is that these kinds of manifestations happen in clinics all across our country and around the world. Some of the people who show these symptoms are indeed professing Christians.

What are the options for the counselor as he or she assesses the situation and attempts to make a diagnosis? The person, of course, may be delusional as the result of taking a hallucinogenic drug. The person may be faking it for one reason or another. Most commonly, mental health professionals would interpret the behavior as some form of dissociative disorder. Perhaps the person created a demonic alter personality as a way of giving expression to the ugly and dark side of his or her being. Or perhaps the alter was a means for the person to give vent to seething anger over childhood experiences of abuse.

Normally, doctors or psychologists would not even consider the possibility that a real spirit entity might be manifesting its presence in the person's body.[36] The international community of mental health professionals, however, does officially consider this as a possibility and labels it "Trance and Possession Disorder" (TPD).[37] In fact, it has been described as "the most common dissociative disorder reported in non-Western cultures."[38]

Clinicians, pastoral counselors, lay counselors, and a variety of other Christian leaders encounter professing Christians who show these kinds of symptoms. The question we must raise here is this: Is it possible that a genuine Christian who manifests these symptoms is actually being influenced or controlled by an evil spirit?

This is a worldview question that cannot be answered strictly on the basis of clinical evidence. Yet based on the biblical, theological, and historical evidence we have assessed thus far, it would appear to be possible for a demon to manifest its influence in a Christian in this manner. There is certainly nothing inconsistent with this conclusion and the biblical data. The church historical evidence patently supports this conclusion. As we have seen, Scripture affirms that a spirit can inhabit a Christian who yields to it and from that basis exercise significant control over the life of a believer.

Once again, however, it is necessary to emphatically declare that the intruding spirit cannot come and take ownership. Neither is the believer a slave to the influence of the evil power with no means of escape. The child of God merely needs to yield himself or herself to the Holy Spirit and appropriate the power of God to be rid of these evil intruders (often with the help of prayer partners). Along with this comes a life of discipleship in which the human psychological aspects are dealt with over time in the context of belonging to a loving and caring group of believers.

Are the Exorcism Accounts in the Gospels Examples for Us?

This leads us to consider the instructional value of the exorcism accounts in the Synoptic Gospels. Are these written and preserved for us strictly as testimony to the remarkable power of the Lord Jesus

Christ in his earthly ministry? Or, do these accounts also model an approach for us as we minister to people who are severely afflicted by demonic spirits?

First of all, it is important for us to think of the Gospels not strictly as historical records, but also as manuals on what to believe and how to live and do ministry in following the example of our Lord Jesus Christ. This is how the Gospels functioned in the early church and how they have been used in succeeding generations. The Holy Spirit inspired Matthew, Mark, and Luke to record Jesus' life, death, and resurrection twenty-five to thirty-five years after his death to serve churches as they evangelized and helped people mature in Christ. Gentiles who became Christians in Rome during the 60s, for instance, were usually turning to Christ from a background of devotion to deities like Mithras, the Mother Goddess Cybele, Isis, or any number from the pantheon of Roman gods. Dealing with demonic issues related to their cultic involvements was a key part of their discipleship as new believers.

The accounts of Jesus' exorcisms would have had much instructional value, then, to the leaders of the churches as they ministered to people troubled by evil spirits. They would see the absolute authority Jesus had over the demonic spirits and how his method of dealing with them differed sharply from other "exorcists" of his (and their) day. They would learn the importance of faith, prayer, and reliance on the Holy Spirit in engaging in this form of ministry. They would also be impressed with the obedience of the demons when Jesus issued a stern, authoritative command to them. The evidence from the practices of the early church, which I present below, demonstrates that the exorcism accounts in the Gospels were important instructional and inspirational models for the leaders of this powerful movement.

The fact that Jesus was "God in the flesh" could make us feel incapable of ever ministering the way he ministered. We may think, "Well, of course Jesus could drive out demonic spirits—he was God! But who am I?" Yet the Gospels give evidence that most of Jesus' ministry was done in reliance on the power of the Holy Spirit—the very Spirit he has poured out into *our* hearts! Luke, for instance, points out that Jesus was "full of the Holy Spirit" when he successfully resisted the devil's temptations in the desert (Luke 4:1–13). As Jesus resisted Satan, so now we are called to resist the temptations of Satan by the power of the Holy Spirit. But our authority in the Spirit goes even further than this.

Matthew's Gospel records Jesus as teaching that he conducted his ministry of exorcism "by the Spirit of God" (12:28). We have dwelling in us the same Spirit that Jesus relied on to drive away evil spirits. We therefore share with him the same divine authority over the realm of the demonic. In the parallel passage, Luke highlights that Jesus' ability to cast out demons was also an indication that the kingdom of God was present (Luke 11:20). Jesus did indeed inaugurate the kingdom of God (in a partial, spiritual sense). We are citizens of the kingdom and now experience many of the benefits of the kingdom—union with Christ, righteousness, the presence of the Spirit. This is the basis for us to continue the redemptive work of Jesus by reaching out and ministering to those victimized by Satan and his demonic forces.

We may also point to the relevance of the mission of the Twelve to the present ministry of the church. Jesus gave the Twelve authority to cast out demons when he sent them out (Mark 6:6–13 = Matt. 10:1–9 = Luke 9:1–6). But of course not every aspect of the mission of the Twelve is something we are to emulate in continuing to fulfill the mission Christ has given us: our mission clearly extends beyond the borders of Israel; it is not for a limited time; we are not restricted from making adequate preparations and taking provisions;[39] and our message involves more than calling people to repentance. Nevertheless, this mission was a foundational experience for the Twelve in preparing them for their task after the day of Pentecost. As such, it was preparatory to the later mission of the church and therefore is instructive for our mission:[40] we are commissioned by Jesus; we have a message to proclaim; some will accept the message and some will reject it; we have been given power and authority by Jesus; this authority is to be used in our struggle with the demonic. This latter point is made abundantly clear by the apostle Paul, who teaches that we have been united with Christ who is the leading and empowering head of his body. We thereby share in Christ's authority over the realm of the demonic (see esp. Col. 2:9–10).

The mission of the Seventy also anticipates the mission of the church (Luke 10:1–11, 17–20).[41] As he did for the Twelve, Jesus gave the Seventy authority to cast out demons: "I have given you authority to trample on snakes and scorpions and to overcome all the power of the enemy" (Luke 10:19). They returned from their mission with excitement because "even the demons submit to us in your name" (Luke 10:17). The mission of the Seventy helps us see that the authority to cast out demons is not only an authority exercised by Jesus or the twelve foundational apostles, but is passed on to others whom Jesus sends out to perform the mission that he calls them to undertake. We, too, have been granted authority in fulfilling the mission that Jesus has called us to engage in. He prefaces his "Great Commission" with "all authority in heaven and on earth has been given to me" and then assures his people of his real presence with them until the end of the age (Matt. 28:18–20). Jesus therefore uses us as his agents not only to reach the lost, but to deliver them from bondage to demonic powers.

Jesus gives foundational teaching on this redemptive ministry of the church in his parable on the binding of the strong man (Mark 3:22–27=Matt. 12:22–30=Luke 11:14–23; cf. Col. 2:15). He taught that "the strong man" (Satan) must be defeated so that his house can be plundered. This parable anticipates the church's ministry of rescuing those victimized by Satan—a ministry that the church is able to carry out because of Jesus' defeat of "the strong man" by means of his death on the cross, his resurrection, and his exaltation (see Col. 2:15). We are therefore not called to bind the strong man ourselves; this has already been done by Christ. We are called to plunder the strong man's possessions by bringing to them the message of redemption and deliverance and helping free them from the enslaving grip of Satan and his forces. Satan no longer has a death grip on everyone. People can break free and be liberated through the message of the gospel. They can be delivered and freed from tormenting demonic spirits who have invaded their lives.

In the first generation of the church (following the ascension of Christ), the apostle Paul casts out demons as part of his ministry (Acts 16:16–18; 19:11–12). He appropriates the power of God in following the example of Jesus and in fulfilling the mission of the church. He calls all believers to follow his example, as he follows the example of Christ (1 Cor. 11:1). As we will see below, Christians throughout the second, third, and fourth centuries did indeed follow his example and the example left by Jesus by proclaiming the message of the gospel and casting out demons as part of their ministry.

Granting that there is normative value for Christians today in the exorcism accounts in the Gospels, some would still object that the application of this authority to drive out demons should only be directed to non-Christians since none of the demonized people in the Gospels were Christians when Jesus ministered to them. We need to remember, however, that no one was a Christian then (properly speaking). I have already attempted to show that it is quite possible that part of the apostle Paul's ministry of casting out spirits was done among new Christians. The subsequent history of the early church gives us the most valuable insight for responding to this question.

Exorcism of New Christians in the Early Church

Contrary to an erroneous popular tradition that the ministry of exorcism died out after the time of the apostles, there is abundant church historical evidence illustrating that it not only continued but was practiced widely in the early church. The apologists in the early church give eloquent testimony to the ability of Christians to cast out evil spirits in the name of Jesus Christ. Such accounts can be seen in the writings of Justin Martyr (c. 110–165), Tatian (c. 160), Tertullian (c. 160–225), Origen (c. 185–254), and Minucius Felix (2nd or 3rd century).[42] Demons were often cast out of people as the church evangelized, but it appears that the primary context for the casting out of evil spirits was in the classes for new Christians.

One important source informing us of early church practice is a document known as the *Apostolic Tradition*.[43] This set of traditions was preserved by Hippolytus of Rome (A.D. 170–235), "one of the most learned and eminent scholars and theologians of his time."[44] Hippolytus is well known as a bishop of the church in Rome and as the author of *Refutation of All Heresies*. The editor of the English edition of the *Apostolic Tradition* notes, "It is now generally recognized that the *Apostolic Tradition* of St. Hippolytus is the most illuminating single source of evidence extant on the inner life and religious polity of the early Christian church."[45] The value of this document is not so much that it came from the hand of an important church leader, but that it preserves many of the traditional ministry practices of the churches of the time. The editor comments, "We may safely take it that in outline and essentials the rites and customs to which the *Apostolic Tradition* bears witness were those practiced in the Roman Church in his own day, and in his own youth (c. A.D. 180). And it is also safe to say that this Roman tradition was, *mutatis mutandis,* typical of the practice of the Great Church everywhere in the second century."[46]

New converts were required to go through a period of extensive instruction in the Scriptures prior to baptism. These new believers were called *catechumens,* a Greek word meaning "pupils" and related to the verb *katēcheō,* "to instruct."[47]

These new believers were instructed not only in the Word but also in Christian ethics. They were challenged to leave behind various unhealthy trappings of their pre-Christian lives. For example, artists who worked on idols were enjoined to quit their occupation and gladiators were admonished to leave the arena. There was no compromise on the necessity of turning away from immoral practices and occupations. New Christians who were involved in the occultic arts were similarly admonished: "a charmer or an astrologer or an interpreter of dreams or . . . a maker of amulets, let them desist or let them be rejected" (16.22).

Just before their baptism, many of these new believers went through a time of "deliverance ministry," when a church leader would cast out any evil spirits present in their lives. This is well illustrated by two excerpts from the *Apostolic Tradition:*

> Moreover, from the day they are chosen, let a hand be laid on them and let them be exorcised [*exorkizein*] daily. And when the day draws near on which they are to be baptized, let the bishop himself exorcise each one of them, that he may be certain that he is purified (20.3).

> But if there is one who is not purified let him be put on one side because he did not hear the word of instruction with faith. For the evil and strange spirit remained with him (20.4).

As the new Christians were baptized, they were also instructed to make a verbal renunciation of Satan. "And when the presbyter takes hold of each one of those who are to be baptised, let him bid him renounce, saying, 'I renounce thee, Satan, and all thy service and all thy works' " (21.9). The church leader performing the baptism also performed an exorcism. The leader would anoint the person with oil and say, "Let all evil spirits depart far from thee" (21.10).

This period of training and preparation for baptism for people who had recently confessed Christ is attested all over the Mediterranean world—Italy, Egypt, North Africa, Palestine, Syria, Greece, and Asia Minor. It is also attested by many early church writers to the time of Augustine. Although there were minor variations in the way the cate-chumenate was carried out, the basic outline remains similar to what we have summarized in the *Apostolic Tradition:*

1. intensive instruction in the Scriptures
2. training in Christian lifestyle with admonitions to give up and renounce ungodly practices
3. deliverance ministry
4. baptism, including renunciation of Satan and confession of allegiance to Christ

Although we may quibble about the timing of the baptism—whether it should be performed soon after conversion or after there has been substantial preparation—we cannot lose sight of the fact that the early church took the discipleship and training of new believers very seriously. This was also the time that these new believers were led into the realization that demonic spirits were very much a part of the deception of their former belief systems. Thus, converts from the worship of the Mother Goddess, Dionysus, Mithras, Sarapis, Isis, and all the other deities as well as new believers who had a background in magical practices, astrology, and divination were taught to renounce their former beliefs and practices. Because of the omnipresence of idolatry, Tertullian asked rhetorically, "What man is there to whom an evil spirit does not adhere, even at the very gates of his birth, waiting to ensnare his soul?"[48] Another early Christian writer well illustrates this conviction:

> Everyone who has at any time worshiped idols and has adored those whom the pagans call gods, or has eaten of the things sacrificed to them, is not without an unclean spirit; for he has become a guest of demons, and has been partaker with that demon of which he has formed the image in his mind, either through fear or love.[49]

The logical time to deal with these unholy spirits was during the period subsequent to conversion. This was done, however, in a wholistic approach to discipleship that simultaneously involved in-depth study of the Scriptures and the cultivation of a distinctively Christian lifestyle.

The way the early church enfolded new believers presents a significant challenge to contemporary Christianity. Many churches have become strong on evangelism and seeker-orientation, but weak on follow-up and rooting these precious new believers in the faith.

How many new believers today desperately need a better foundation in the Scriptures, help in developing a Christian lifestyle, and encouragement to become disentangled from ungodly allegiances? And, more to the point of this chapter, how many new believers could use counsel and help in dealing with demonic spirits who want to maintain their claim?

It is clear that the early church believed that Christians could be demonized. This was a working assumption from the beginning, and leaders in the church dealt with it at the outset of a person's walk with the Lord.

Belief in the Demonization of Christians in the Early Church

In addition to the accounts of renunciation and casting out of spirits tied to the intensive discipleship of new Christians, there are numerous other accounts of ministry to Christians troubled by evil spirits throughout church history. A recounting of all of these would fill several volumes. A few illustrations should underscore the fact that it has been widely believed in the church that Christians can be inhabited and controlled by demons.

Perhaps the earliest testimony comes from Hermas (c. A.D. 100–150), whose writing reflects an early-second-century understanding in Roman Christianity. In one passage he gives perspective on demonic "oppression" in response to a defeated Christian's concern that no matter how hard believers try, "the devil is hard and oppresses [*katadunasteuō*] them." Hermas protests that it is not inevitable that Christians should be oppressed if they put their faith and hope in God and remain filled with the Spirit:

> He cannot oppress God's servants who hope in him with all their heart. *The devil can wrestle with them, but he cannot throw and pin them.* So, if you resist him, he will be defeated and flee from you in disgrace. But those who are empty fear the devil, as if he had power. . . . So also the devil comes to all God's servants to tempt them. All those who are full in the faith resist him mightily, and he leaves them alone, because he finds no place [*topos*] where he can gain entrance. So then he comes to those who are partially empty, *and finding a place he enters them, and then he does what he wants with them, and they become enslaved to him* (*Shepherd of Hermas,* Mandate 12.5, italics mine).

Hermas clearly conceived of the possibility that a Christian could be inhabited and controlled by a demon. The key for him was for the Christian to remain full of the Lord's grace so that when the time of temptation came, the believer could mightily resist. There is much in Hermas's presentation that is reminiscent of Ephesians 4–6. What makes Hermas's testimony especially significant is that his book was so highly respected in the early church that many Christians regarded it as Scripture.

Origen (c. A.D. 185–254), an important church leader in Alexandria (Egypt) and then later in Caesarea (Palestine), actually mentions the authority of believers to cast a demon out of themselves. He notes, "Anyone who vanquishes a demon in himself, e.g. the demon of lewdness, puts it out of action; the demon is cast into the abyss, and cannot do any harm to anyone."[50]

Cyprian (A.D. 200–258), bishop of the church in Carthage, North Africa, has much to say about the role of the demonic in his writings. In a letter he wrote to a church leader, Magnus, he reflects on the struggle the exorcists sometimes have in attempting to secure deliverance for new believers (the catechumens): "and although he [the demon] often says that he is going out, and will leave *the men of God,* yet in that which he says he deceives, and puts in practice what was before done by Pharaoh with the same obstinate and fraudulent deceit" (*Epistles* 75.15, italics mine). Cyprian puts much faith in the efficacy of baptism—more than I think is appropriate—for assisting in deliverance. Nevertheless, he teaches that Christians can be demonized even after baptism if they yield to sin: "some of those who are baptized in health, if subsequently they begin to sin, are shaken by the return of the unclean spirit, so that it is manifest that the devil is driven out in baptism by the faith of the believer, and returns if the faith afterwards shall fail" (*Epistles* 75.16).

Another ancient writer, often associated with Clement of Rome, admonishes healthy believers "to visit those who are harassed by evil spirits, and pray and pronounce exorcisms over them." The context makes it clear that the people who receive this ministry are other believers: "In this way let us approach a brother or a sister who is sick." The writer once again interjects the appeal, "Let this man cast out demons and God will help him."[51]

The Clementine literature has much to say about the workings of evil spirits. One text explicitly reveals a belief that a Christian not walking in faith may be inhabited by a demon:

> Therefore the demons themselves, knowing the amount of faith of those of whom they take possession, measure their stay proportionately. Wherefore they stay permanently with the unbelieving, tarry for a while with the weak in faith; but with those who thoroughly believe, and who do good, they cannot remain even for a moment. . . . The labor, therefore, of everyone is to be solicitous about the putting to flight of his own demon (*Clementine Homilies* 9.11; see also *Recognitions* 4.17).

The good news from the perspective of this writer is that there is sure deliverance through growing in faith in the power of God and appropriating righteousness.

The *Apostolic Constitutions* (c. 300s), a collection of church practices and regulations from Syria, reflects the deliverance practices performed during the time of training for new Christians, thus further illustrating the *Apostolic Tradition* that we discussed earlier: "Ye energumens, afflicted with unclean spirits, pray, and let us all earnestly pray for them, that God, the lover of mankind, will by Christ rebuke the unclean and wicked spirits and deliver His supplicants from the dominion of the adversary" (*Apostolic Constitutions* 8.6). For these people seeking baptism, the church insisted that they make a clean break with the past and renounce all occultic practices. This was particularly important for "a magician, an enchanter, an astrologer, a diviner, an user of magic verses, a juggler [trickster], a mountebank [dealer in spiritistic medicines], one that makes amulets, a charmer, a soothsayer, a fortune-teller, an observer of palmistry" (*Apostolic Constitutions* 8.32). There was an assumption that anyone engaging in these sorts of practices may be demonized: "if anyone hath a demon, let him indeed be taught piety, but not received into communion before he be cleansed" (*Apostolic Constitutions* 8.32). The document also prohibits a demonized Christian from becoming a leader in the church: "If anyone hath a demon, let him not be made one of the clergy. No, let him not pray with the faithful; but when he is cleansed, let him be received; and if he be worthy, let him be ordained" (*Apostolic Canons* 79).[52]

The ministry of deliverance was so important in the early church that Eusebius cites a Roman bishop named Cornelius (c. A.D. 250) who says that there were fifty-two exorcists serving in the church at his time (Eusebius, *History of the Church* 6.43). Cornelius tells us that these exorcists ministered to a convert named Novatus, a future presbyter in the Roman church, after a spirit "entered into him and stayed within him for a considerable time," causing him to become desperately ill. Eusebius gives similar testimony to the presence of exorcists in the churches of eastern Asia Minor and Syria during the time of the emperor Diocletian (c. A.D. 284–305) (Eusebius, *History of the Church* 8.6).

Certainly much more could be cited from the church leaders of the first three hundred years of the Christian movement. These illustrations are adequate to show that there was indeed a chronologically and geographically widespread assumption that Christians could be seriously afflicted by demons.

Numerous other accounts and excerpts could be given from Christian leaders throughout the post-Nicene age, the Byzantine Empire,[53] and from luminaries such as Thomas Aquinas, John Calvin,[54] Martin Luther, and the Puritans. A thorough treatment of this topic from the vantage point of church history would be very helpful and illuminating. They all took the realm of the demonic seriously and believed that Christians could be profoundly influenced by evil spirits. Yet they also were thoroughly convinced that believers had authority in the Lord Jesus Christ to send these spirits packing. As Martin Luther said regarding the devil in his famous hymn, "one little word shall fell him." That word is Jesus.

Who's Responsible?

Since comedian Flip Wilson gave us the guilt-absolving line, "the devil made me do it," there has been an increasing concern that Christians might truly begin blaming their actions on a demon and not take responsibility for what they do. A step closer to this becoming a reality has actually been taken in some places, with people blaming their criminal actions on alter personalities. If an evil spirit can actually inhabit and control a person, what is wrong with putting the blame for a sinful or criminal action squarely on the agent who inspired and prompted the action? How is it fair for God or even the courts to hold us accountable for an action committed under the influence of an alien spirit?

The answer to this question is quite clear in the Bible. From beginning to end, Scripture holds individuals personally responsible for the outcome of their actions. No special provision is ever made releasing a person from culpability for an evil action carried out while under the influence of an evil spirit. Satan filled the hearts of Ananias and Sapphira to lie, and they faced the deadly consequences (Acts 5:1–11). Satan entered Judas and prompted him to betray Jesus (Luke 22:3), yet Jesus exclaimed to Pontius Pilate, "The one who handed me over to you is guilty of a greater sin" (John 19:11).

One may object that this seems particularly unfair, especially when we think of children who are victimized by Satan. Two of the four exorcism accounts in the Gospels speak of the demonization of children. In one instance, Jesus asked a boy's father, "How long has he been like this?" and the father replied, "From childhood" (Mark 9:21). How can young people be held responsible for a condition they are in that they did not choose?

This question is in many ways parallel to the issue of the fairness of "original sin," that is, the biblical teaching that every person is counted as guilty before God and is born with a tendency to sin because of Adam's sin (see Rom. 5:12–21). Yet God does count every person as guilty and we all face the eternal consequences of that sin—death and the wrath of God.[55]

Freedom from guilt does not come from determining the degree of victimization. God has provided a way out for everyone. There is a means of escaping from the dominating influence of the presence of sin or from the controlling influence of a demonic spirit. People are given the opportunity to yield their lives to a sphere of power that is exceedingly greater than either the power of sin or the power of Satan. By coming to Christ, individuals are delivered from the compelling influence of evil; they now have the opportunity and the power to resist. A choice remains for Christians. They can yield themselves to the power of the evil domain, or they can yield themselves to the power of God (see Rom. 6:12–14).

Even in the most severe cases of demonization, God provides a way of escape. When Jesus arrived in the region of the Gerasenes, he encountered a man so severely afflicted by "a legion" of demons that he lived among tombs, engaged in self-mutilation, and had the power to break chains apart (Mark 5:1–20). Yet this man was able to run to Jesus and fall on his knees before him, an action that I think is best understood as a dramatic plea for help. Immediately the demons manifested in the man, never allowing the man himself to speak a word to Jesus. Nevertheless, Jesus understood the plea for help and responded by exerting his authority over the realm of darkness and commanding the demons to enter a herd of swine.

Is Contemporary "Deliverance Ministry" the Answer?

Contemporary deliverance ministry—as advocated in the ministries and books of people such as John Wimber, Charles Kraft, Neil Anderson, Ed Murphy, Fred Dickason, Tom White, Tim Warner, Jim Logan, and Mark Bubeck, to name just a few—has occasioned a high degree of controversy. Disagreement usually focuses primarily on their assumption that Christians can be inhabited by demons and their often aggressive response to those people victimized by demons (i.e., the evil spirits may need to be "cast out" or commanded to leave).

We have already demonstrated that there is sufficient biblical, theological, and historical evidence to assert that a Christian can be inhabited and controlled by a demonic spirit. The evidence also supports the appropriateness for an afflicted believer (or someone ministering to him or her) to exercise authority in the name of Jesus and firmly command a spirit to leave.

In a recent book titled *Power Encounters: Reclaiming Spiritual Warfare,* David Powlison has argued that this is not appropriate.[56] Although he believes in the reality of demons and the pervasive influence they can have on Christians, he would contend that the Bible teaches us not to cast out spirits. Rather, he suggests that troubled Christians simply need to repent, exercise faith, embrace the truth, obey God's Word, and pray. This "classic mode" of spiritual warfare is adequate for dealing with anything the devil can throw against a believer.

I would say "amen!" to the ministry approach Powlison affirms, but question why he is so concerned to deny the appropriateness of a believer taking authority in the name of Christ to deal with a demonic spirit. Ironically, the "classic mode" of spiritual warfare in the early history of the church would in fact include a power encounter type of approach (as I have briefly outlined in the discussion of the catechumenate). When he says, "occultists need repentance, not EMM"[57] (= "ekballistic mode of ministry," i.e., commanding a spirit to depart), this runs counter to the entire early history of the church. New believers were indeed required to renounce their allegiances to the gods and goddesses, but the Christian leaders working with them would also lay their hands on them and command foul spirits to depart.

I agree with Powlison that there are a number of serious shortcomings and problems with contemporary deliverance ministry. I address many of these in the final section of this chapter. Yet I question his critical insistence that believers should not exercise authority in Christ to exorcise a demon. I think he downplays the normative aspects of what Jesus modeled for us in his encounters with demons, the ministry of the Twelve, the ministry of the Seventy, and Paul's ministry in Acts, as well as virtually ignoring what we can learn from a very important stream of church history.

A Biblical Framework for Dealing with Demons

If Christians can be inhabited and controlled by demons, what can they do to avoid and rid themselves of these unwelcome intruders? What can we do to help other believers who are deeply struggling? The following summary, based on some vital biblical concepts, suggests ways for Christians to deal with various forms of evil influence in their lives, particularly the demonic.

A. Draw Near to God (James 4:7; Ps. 91:9)

The Book of James gives the most important way to deal with this problem: "Submit yourselves, then, to God. Resist the devil, and he will flee from you" (James 4:7). The most important first step for any struggling believers is to draw near to God. Thirty counseling sessions, five deliverance ministry times, and meeting others for Bible study twice a week are of no avail to a person who has not truly looked to God and sought him. There must be a genuine desire to seek God and his ways in the deepest recesses of our being and, conversely, a real desire to turn away from evil.

Recognizing the presence of all kinds of supernatural evil influences, the psalmist calls on the people of God to make the Most High their dwelling place and shelter (Ps. 91:1, 9). God then extends supernatural protection and help. He even commands "his angels concerning you to guard you in all your ways" (Ps. 91:11). His power enables his people to "tread upon the lion and the cobra" and to "trample the great lion and the serpent" (Ps. 91:13), images of the demonic in the Old Testament and Jewish context (cf. Luke 10:17).

Turning to God is something that occurs deep in a person's soul. James reiterates the importance of this in the subsequent verse: "come near to God and he will come near to you" (James 4:8). This is a decisive act of the will that results in the softening of the heart to the impulses of the Spirit of God. It involves prayer, worship, and exposing oneself to God's will through the Scriptures.

B. Resist the Devil and His Foul Spirits (James 4:7; 1 Peter 5:9; Eph. 6:11–13)

The second part of the instruction from James is to "resist the devil." The command is so important, it is reiterated by both Paul and Peter. This phrase is exceedingly well known among Christians, but what does it mean? What does it look like for a person to resist the devil? Successful resistance entails a set of nine convictions and actions.

1. GIVE ATTENTION TO THE AREA THAT HAS MADE YOU SUSCEPTIBLE TO DEMONIC ATTACK

In order for a person to turn away from a sin or make a break with an impure allegiance, he or she must first recognize and acknowledge that there is evil that needs to be dealt with. As we think of various forms and degrees of demonic influence, it is helpful to consider the ways evil spirits seek to assert their dominance.

Avenues of Demonic Influence

Intentionally inviting their presence	False religions Witchcraft, sorcery Channeling
Residual influence from the past	False religions Witchcraft, sorcery Channeling Intergenerational ("familial") spirits
Unintentionally inviting their presence	Habitual practice of sin (Eph. 4:27)
Special attacks against Christians	Deception Temptation Physical attack

Special attacks against Christians (cont.)

Special period of
attack (Eph. 6:13)
Demonic opposition
to carrying out the
mission of the
church, especially in
sharing the gospel

Intentionally inviting their presence. As we discussed earlier, there were many people who became Christians in the New Testament world who explicitly invited spirits to come and reside with them. I suggested that it may very well have been these people out of whom Paul cast spirits during his ministry in Ephesus. We also noted that for the next few centuries, the church continued to minister in this way to new Christians converted from pagan cults and with a background in magic, witchcraft, and sorcery.

In the past few years, we have witnessed a dramatic rise of interest in various spiritualities in the West. Americans seem to have developed a voracious appetite for experiencing the supernatural. A few years ago, a concerned member of Biola University's board of trustees showed me an article in a trendy magazine advocating "Tarot Therapy." The article stresses the limitations of traditional psychology and encourages the use of tarot cards so that a person can encounter helpful spiritual guides and mentors. The author notes, "It is beautiful to witness the bonding between these eternal transpersonal powers and an individual in need. During this process many people learn how to allow this new spirit guide into their daily life."[58] The obvious question for us to ask is what spiritual powers these people are getting.

Duane Garrett, a professor at Canadian Southern Baptist Theological Seminary, has recently written a very informative analysis of the recent angel craze in a book he has titled *Angels and the New Spirituality*.[59] He takes a careful look at a number of books that are typically sold in the New Age section of the local bookstore. They include titles such as *The Angels within Us, Ask Your Angels, A Book of Angels, Guardians of Hope,* and *Angels of Mercy.* Garrett concludes that the so-called new spirituality is not new at all, but a reversion to the ancient traditions of polytheism and household gods. The angels people are calling on are not the angels of the biblical and Christian tradition, but spirits from a different source altogether. He warns that "despite the appearance of a soft, personal form of Christianity, these books offer an altogether different gospel. The flutter you hear is of the wings of bats, not angels."[60]

One of the characteristics of many forms of the new angel spirituality is invoking the presence of an angel. This spirit-being can provide protection, comfort, guidance, and even empowerment. During the course of his analysis, Garrett poses the question of whether people who get into this form of spirituality are simply imagining things when they speak of experiencing and conversing with angels, or whether there truly is some kind of transaction and intercourse taking place with the spirit realm. Garrett sees at least some of what is going on as the outcome of incredible imaginations. Nevertheless, he is convinced that many angel-lovers have actually made friends with spirits from the retinue of Satan.

With the launching of cyberspace and the ability to surf innumerable sites on the World Wide Web has come a new medium of access for information on how to call on angels and channel supernatural beings. There are pages and pages of material available providing instructions on how to communicate with angels as well as records of what angels have said to people. In one brief session on the Web, I found this set of instructions allegedly from the archangel Raphael instructing people on how to get in touch with angels:

> To start working with your higher self and guides, Sananda, an Archangel, or an Ascended Master, all you need to do is invite them in. You do not need to know how to formally meditate or channel to do this. Just relax in a sitting or laying [sic] position and state your intention to work with them. As you become sensitive to your higher self's energy you can set up a communication system with them. . . . When you can feel their energy strongly you can ask questions of them and get responses through the energy.

Another page, purportedly giving information from St. Germain, attempts to dispel the concern Christians may have about becoming involved in these mediumistic experiences by assuring that "the Bible is full of channeled material and channeling experiences." Many of these practitioners actually conceive of Jesus as on the same level as the angels and make him an object of channeling. Of course, the ostensible appeal for calling on these angels is to benefit from their kindness and their powerful aid. "They will always do their best to help you meet your goals for spiritual advancement and to help you with any problems that you have in your life in any way that they can."

All of this illustrates a growing tendency for people to explicitly open their lives up to the inhabitation and control of spirit-beings. When Christians involve themselves in such practices, they willingly yield their minds and the members of their bodies to the dominating influence of evil spirits. It is crucial that they recognize this as an avenue of demonic influence and begin to deal with it.

Residual influence from the past. People who have become Christians and have had a background in channeling, witchcraft, sorcery, or other religious practices, and have not yet renounced these beliefs and practices, may have left themselves open to continued and direct demonic influence. The hall closet needs to be unlocked, these things need to be repudiated, and a fresh confession of allegiance to Christ needs to be made.

Virtually every practitioner of contemporary deliverance ministry speaks of the reality of intergenerational (or "familial") spirits. This concept finds no direct biblical support, in spite of the appeals to the Old Testament texts that speak of the sins of the fathers being visited on the descendants up to the third and fourth generations (Exod. 20:5; Deut. 5:9). These verses speak of guilt and consequential punishment, not about familial spirits passed on to the third and fourth generations. Nevertheless, the concept of intergenerational spirits may receive indirect biblical support in a couple of other ways. First, in his ministry to the severely demonized boy, Jesus finds out from the father that his son had been in that awful condition "from childhood" (Mark 9:21). The demonization was therefore not the result of the boy's own sin or his choice to give his allegiance to false gods. The spirits were passed on to him from some other source, the most likely of which would be his family. Second, children tend to act out many of the same sinful patterns of behavior that their parents engaged in. Thus, when we read Old Testament historical books such as 1 and 2 Kings and 1 and 2 Chronicles, we find the kings of Israel typically following in the evil steps of their ancestors. The biblical writer often asserts in the narrative a line such as "he committed all the sins his father had done before him" (1 Kings 15:3). These tendencies may not only be genetic and environmental, but may also have a spiritual root. This is particularly apparent when we investigate the allegiances to other gods that the kings of Israel repeatedly gave themselves to.

Unintentionally inviting their presence. When Paul speaks of giving ground to the devil in Ephesians 4:27, he is teaching that the habitual practice of sin can lead to an increased involvement of Satan in the life of a believer. As we discussed earlier, Paul speaks of this as yielding habitable space to an evil spirit, which is tantamount to surrendering control over an area of one's life. Although in the context of Ephesians 4 Paul explicitly mentions excessive anger, living and speaking falsehood, and stealing, the concept appears to be that the ongoing practice of any sinful behavior yields control to the devil. Satan reasserts his reign in an area where Christ should reign.

Some recent interpreters fail to take this text into consideration when they criticize those involved in deliverance ministry for assuming that there may be a sin problem in a person's life that has attracted a demonic spirit.[61] Demonic affliction may come as a result of sin. This important text—Ephesians 4:27—stands behind the title and presentation of Jim Logan's helpful recent book on spiritual warfare entitled *Reclaiming Surrendered Ground.* Logan rightly observes, "If I cherish sin in my life, Satan will seek to exploit it."[62] As my colleague, Dr. Doug Hayward, often observes when counseling an individual, demons like to pour gasoline on a fire that is already burning. A moral issue that begins with succumbing to the evil influence of the flesh may escalate into a greater spiritual problem. Just as flies and rats are attracted to garbage, unclean spirits are drawn to unclean thoughts and behaviors. This does not mean that everyone who falls into a period of sinful behavior will end up becoming demonized. It does, however, underline the seriousness of sin and the need to get rid of the garbage and extinguish the fires.

Special attacks against Christians. There will be times that Satan attempts to assert his insidious influence on believers in the absence of past allegiances or sin. In the classic passage on spiritual warfare, Paul envisioned periods when the powers of darkness would strike with exceptional power and ferocity. It is for these times that he urges Christians to be prepared with the armor of God. He encourages them to "put on the full armor of God, *so that when the day of evil comes,* you may be able to stand your ground" (Eph. 6:13). This was surely the experience of Peter when he succumbed three times to the temptation to deny Christ. Just prior to his fall, Jesus warned him, "Simon, Simon, Satan has asked to sift you as wheat" (Luke 22:31).

Temptation, attempts at deceiving Christians, and even physical affliction (2 Cor. 12:7) are just some of the ways Satan may attempt to reassert his control. We can also expect Satan to do all that he can to prevent the church from fulfilling its mission.

2. Determine to Resist

After spending time discerning specifically how an evil spirit may be attempting to gain dominance, it is crucial to make a decision to oppose him. This is the natural complement to seeking God and taking steps to draw close to him.

This act of faith entails that we believe that God is capable of enabling us to conquer a seemingly impossible situation. There appears to be a climate of despair among people who perpetually view themselves as victims. Part of determining to resist is beginning to believe that we are not stuck in a predetermined rut; that there is a way out to a better place.

God himself can stimulate this sort of faith. The beginning of our response in drawing close to him is asking for the ability to believe that he is able "to do immeasurably more than all we ask or imagine, according to his power that is at work within us" (Eph. 3:20). The prophet Isaiah eloquently expresses the kind of determination the Lord seeks: "Because the Sovereign Lord helps me, I will not be disgraced. Therefore, *I have set my face like flint,* and I know I will not be put to shame" (Isa. 50:7, italics mine).

3. KNOW WHO YOU ARE IN CHRIST

Part of resistance involves knowing the truth so that the devil cannot convince us of the lie. It is especially important to know and believe the truth about our new identity in Christ. We are no longer to see ourselves as corrupt at the core of our beings, but as pure and holy before God.

This has been the emphasis and the strength of Neil Anderson's approach to deliverance ministry as expressed in his two influential books, *The Bondage Breaker* and *Victory over the Darkness.*[63] Neil stresses the importance of leading people into grasping that they truly are forgiven for each and every sin, justified as the gift of God, and sealed as belonging to God for eternity. He points to the efficacy of Jesus' promise, "you will know the truth, and the truth will set you free" (John 8:32). He correctly observes that many people in our churches are living defeated lives because they have not properly understood the work of Christ on their behalf. The "accuser" has convinced these dear believers that they are still worms, filthy sinners, and undeserving of God's grace. As the apostle Paul repeatedly emphasized, believers are to consider themselves as righteous and members of the family of God. Because we are clothed with Christ, God now highly values us as his own precious inheritance (Eph. 1:17).

4. KNOW YOUR RESOURCES IN CHRIST

Closely related to apprehending this new identity is becoming aware of the basis for one's authority to resist Satan and his forces of evil. This is rooted in Christ's work on the cross and our identification with him in that work. The Bible reveals that Christ not only made satisfaction for sin by his blood, but that through this sacrifice and his resurrection and exaltation, he defeated the principalities and powers (Col. 2:15).

When people become Christians, they enter into a relationship with Jesus Christ. Many people think only of the communing with and fellowship with Christ that flow out of this new relationship. There is another, practical dimension to this relationship that is often overlooked. Being "in Christ" means that we have become united with him in his death, resurrection, exaltation, and new life (see esp. Rom. 6; Eph. 2:1–10; Col. 2:9–15). The apostle Paul explicitly associates Christ's resurrection and exaltation with his present authority over the demonic realm. In Ephesians 1, Paul prays that believers would gain a full and complete appreciation for God's "incomparably great power for us who believe. That power is like the working of his mighty strength, which he exerted in Christ when he raised him from the dead and seated him at his right hand in the heavenly realms, *far above all rule and authority, power and dominion, and every title that can be given*" (vv. 19–21, italics mine). In the very next chapter, Paul underlines that believers are in Christ and that they participate with Christ in his resurrection and exaltation: "And God raised us up with Christ and seated us with him in the heavenly realms in Christ Jesus" (Eph. 2:6). The implication of all of this is that just as Christ wields authority now over the realm of the demonic, so do his people. Paul makes this even more explicit in Colossians 2:9–10, where he declares, "For in Christ all the fullness of the Deity lives in bodily form, and you have been given fullness in Christ, who is the head over every power and authority." Once again, Paul wants believers to know that by virtue of their relationship with Christ, they share in his headship over the realm of the demonic. This means that we have the authority to counter and overcome evil spirits in whatever ways they attempt to divert us from the path that God has laid out for us to follow.

Our relationship to Christ also involves the reception of his very own Spirit. The presence of the Spirit is not only an empowering resource, but is the basis for our new identity as believers. The Spirit incorporates us into the body of Christ and is a present experience of the blessings of the age to come and the kingdom of God. The Spirit empowers us in our ongoing struggle with evil inclinations (Rom. 8:13) and with the influence of the hostile powers of darkness (Eph. 5:18; 6:18).[64]

Who we are in Christ and our new resources in Christ are realities that are not immediately grasped by believers. This prompted Paul not only to explain doctrinal truth to the new believers in Ephesus and Asia Minor, but also to engage in intercessory prayer for them to gain an awareness of these important concepts. He knows that these truths needed to be revealed to them by the Holy Spirit and that they needed to be grasped emotionally as well as intellectually. He therefore relates that he asked the Father to give them a "Spirit of wisdom and revelation" and "that the eyes of your heart may be enlightened in order that you may know . . ." (Eph. 1:17–18).

5. DEAL WITH THEIR GROUND FOR ATTACK

Part of resisting Satan involves renouncing and severing any associations with evil. In order to draw close to our holy and pure God, we must necessarily make a break with what our Lord detests. Conversely, to repel Satan, we must repudiate all that attracts him. What follows represents the response to the avenues of demonic influence we discussed earlier.

Renounce and decisively turn away from ungodly involvements. The apostle Paul commended a group of new Christians because they had "turned to God *from idols* to serve the living and true God" (1 Thess. 1:9). These recent believers in Thessalonica had severed their connections to Dionysus, Isis, Sarapis, the cult of the Cabirus, and many other religious groups. Renunciation of previous ties to other religions became an integral and critical part of the discipleship of new Christians in the early church. New believers were instructed to disavow their connections to the cults, magic, divination, and astrology and leave these practices altogether.

Charles Kraft, a professor at Fuller Theological Seminary's School of World Missions, refers to this as an "allegiance encounter." This involves "a change in one's ultimate allegiance from the world and its values to God and his kingdom."[65] In speaking of his experience as a missionary in Nigeria, he describes how some Christians there maintained an unhealthy dual allegiance—they had prayed to receive Christ, but simultaneously remained loyal to their traditional religious beliefs and practices.[66] When they were sick or troubled by a spirit, rather than turning to Christ, they would turn to the local shaman. These dear believers needed to give their full devotion to Christ, who was sufficient and powerful to meet their needs.

This principle applies not only to people in animistic cultures, but also to people in the West. Christ calls us to turn aside from every idol (which includes money or sex; see Eph. 5:5; Col. 3:5), every unholy relationship, and every object of devotion that diverts our devotion from him. This renunciation involves confessing it to God as sin and trusting in his faithfulness to forgive (1 John 1:9).

Renounce your connection to ungodly lifestyles, deeds, and affiliations in your extended family. The succession of kings in Israel and Judah after Solomon were evaluated in 1 and 2 Kings by whether they turned away from the sins of their fathers and grandfathers. Notice what is said of just a few of the kings:

Abijah: "He committed all the sins his father had done before him" (1 Kings 15:3).

Nadab: "He did evil in the eyes of the LORD, walking in the ways of his father and in his sin" (1 Kings 15:26)

Baasha: "He did evil in the eyes of the LORD, walking in the ways of Jeroboam and in his sin" (1 Kings 15:34)

Ahaziah: "He did evil in the eyes of the LORD, because he walked in the ways of his father and mother and in the ways of Jeroboam son of Nebat" (1 Kings 22:52).

It is important to recognize that it is typical for sinful patterns in a family to repeat themselves in succeeding generations. The kings of Israel often made commitments to other gods and goddesses (in reality, demonic spirits; see Deut. 32:17) that continued generation after generation until someone sought the Lord, renounced these false gods, and tore down or removed all of their trappings. Because of the vows and pledges made to these deceitful spirits by the kings of Israel, it is likely that the demons laid claim to their sons and daughters, thereby continuing the cycle of bondage.

This principle is still valid today. Spiritual dedications and commitments made by our parents and ancestors have a direct impact on us. Demonic spirits associated with these past vows will claim their rights on the next generation. Similarly, evil spirits will seek to exploit the familial patterns of sinful behavior in the succeeding generations. If there is, for example, a pattern of sexual sin or marital unfaithfulness in the family of a new Christian, this will likely be an issue he or she will struggle with. This may, in part, be explained by genetic predisposition as well as by a set of poor examples, but there is probably also a spiritual, supernatural aspect to it. This is an area where Satan will strike by powerfully tempting the individual working in concert with the sinful inclination already there.

The solution is to recognize the sinful tendencies and the past ungodly commitments, ties, and allegiances of one's family and to disavow them. It is especially important to note that this is not a repudiation of one's family, only a renunciation of the sinful patterns and connections. The early church of the first three centuries placed a strong priority on leading new Christians to make these renunciations at the time of conversion.

The disavowal should be followed by a proclamation of loyalty to the new family—the family of God. We can then call on God to help us cultivate the character traits of this new family.

Turn from sin. Believers may unwittingly invite increased demonic involvement in their lives by nourishing a sinful practice in their lives. It is essential, therefore, to turn away from sin, to confess it (1 John 1:9), and to ask the Spirit of God to strengthen them to resist. Turning from sin and appropriating righteousness is the breastplate in the armor of God for successful spiritual warfare (see Eph. 6:14).

Ask God to grant strength for endurance and perseverance. Not all demonic affliction comes as a result of sinful behavior or through past unholy allegiances. God may permit Satan to attack for his own purposes or simply because we still live in the present evil age. When Paul experienced his "thorn in the flesh," inflicted by an angel of Satan, he left us an important model (2 Cor. 12:7–10). Since he discerned demonic involvement, he initially dealt with it accordingly: "three times I pleaded with the Lord to take it away from me" (2 Cor. 12:8). But after discerning the Lord's purpose in allowing this physical affliction, he then began to rely on the power of God to endure the daily difficulties of his situation. God assured Paul and also us: "My grace is sufficient for you, for my power is made perfect in weakness." Paul experienced the power of God in the midst of suffering.

Intercessory prayer is another way of surmounting this sort of diabolical obstacle. After Jesus warned Simon that Satan asked to sift him like wheat, Jesus consoled him by affirming, "But I have prayed for you, Simon, that your faith may not fail" (Luke 22:32). Jesus had already prayed for Peter—asking God to strengthen him so he could stand. Paul modeled this kind of intercessory prayer for the Christian communities he ministered to. He told the Colossians that he was praying that they would be "strengthened with all power according to his glorious might so that you may have endurance and patience" (Col. 1:11).

6. IF NECESSARY, DEAL DIRECTLY AND FIRMLY WITH THE DEMONIC SPIRIT

The strategy we have outlined for dealing with demonic spirits thus far has said nothing about "casting out" spirits. This is not always necessary. As a person draws near to Christ, renouncing sin and appropriating the resources in Christ, demonic spirits will often flee. James says, "Resist the devil, and *he will flee from you*" (James 4:7). As we have been attempting to show, resistance involves a set of actions that may or may not include a firm command to a spirit to depart.

There may be times, however, when it is entirely appropriate and necessary to exercise one's authority in Christ to command a spirit to leave. This involves first of all knowing that the basis for one's authority to issue such a command is derived from union with Christ. In such instances, we act in his authority, not in our own. We are united to him and have been filled by him and thus share in his authority over the realm of the demonic (see Col. 2:9–10). Such a situation requires a firm verbal command addressed to a demonic spirit; this is not a prayer to God (although the whole confrontation is prepared for and supported in prayer).

There has been some controversy among people who have written about deliverance ministry on whether it is appropriate to take authority in Christ and command a spirit in another person to leave. In other words, as we minister to an individual who is clearly troubled by a demonic spirit, should our goal be strictly to enable him or her to exercise authority in Christ to command any residing spirits to depart? Or, upon discerning their presence, should we intervene and demand that the spirits leave?

This issue is sometimes described as the difference between a "truth encounter" or a "power encounter" approach. Such labels oversimplify the issue, however, since both approaches rely on the power of God and encourage people to know and appropriate the truths of the Christian faith. The real distinction is over what we might call "self-deliverance" or an intervention-based approach. Even this distinction is somewhat artificial since those who practice a "truth encounter" approach do intervene to a certain extent by discerning the presence of spirits and even directly commanding them to silence and not to manifest their presence in any way.

While I applaud the emphases of the truth encounter approach, which seeks to help people apprehend and apply the basic truths of the faith (e.g., forgiveness of sin, freedom from guilt, unity with Christ), I don't find substantiation for what it denies—that is, the advisability of a mature believer to act on behalf of another person to command a spirit to leave. The example of Jesus, the Twelve, the Seventy, and Paul as well as numerous examples from the early church point to the propriety of an interventionist approach.

It may help clarify the issue to use a brief analogy. If I come upon the scene of a serious automobile accident and find a victim lying in the middle of the street with severe lacerations, it is essential that I apply pressure to stop the bleeding. It would not be appropriate to encourage and instruct the person on how to bandage himself or herself. There will come a time, of course, when the person is well enough to change his or her own bandages. But at this time the person requires loving and skillful help.

The early church recognized the need for Christian leaders to intervene in cases where people had recently professed faith in Christ and were just beginning their growth. There are far fewer examples in the early history of the church of an intervention approach for people who had been Christians for an extended period of time. Yet in comparing the early church to the church today, we need to keep in mind that rarely are demonic issues dealt with in the assimilation process of new Christians in contemporary churches. In fact, the quality of training and discipleship of new believers often looks woefully inadequate when we compare it to the three-year catechumenate of the pre-Nicene churches. This may mean that there are more unresolved issues of sin and demonic influence among Christians today who have professed Christ for five years or more than among Christians in the early church.

Of course, one of the key issues is *when* is it appropriate to take authority in the name of Christ and demand a spirit to depart. And, closely related to this is the issue of *how one discerns* the presence of a demonic spirit and distinguishes it, for example, from simply the "lust of the flesh." I do not presume to have a well-established set of criteria that will enable a person to discern the presence of a demonic spirit with the kind of certainty we can have in diagnosing a bacterial infection, for example. There are many who have attempted to create a list of symptoms that point to the kind of demonic activity that would require direct confrontation.[67] Unless the person manifests some sort of supernatural power or abilities, such as levitation or superhuman strength, it is difficult to diagnose the presence of a spirit merely by a set of symptoms. There are often legitimate psychological explanations for many symptoms that were previously understood to be clear signs of a demonic spirit. Voices in the head, the presence of different personalities, bizarre behavior, hallucinatory experiences, seizures, all may have a medical or psychological explanation. On the other hand, however, they may point to demonic affliction. Various kinds of channeling experiences and mediumistic activity could also suggest the potential for demonization.

Spiritual issues require spiritual discernment. We need to develop our sensitivity to the leading and impressions from the Holy Spirit as we minister to people. Empirical verification will often be difficult to come by as we seek to discern what is really going on. Any of us, for example, would be quite pressed to give empirical evidence demonstrating or proving the presence of the Holy Spirit in our lives. We could point to our changed behavior, or to the sense of joy, purpose, and satisfaction in our lives, but these would not be regarded as scientific evidence. But the Holy Spirit is God's guiding and empowering presence in our lives who can lead us into ministering in the most appropriate way to people.

When there is evidence pointing to the presence of a spirit and the Holy Spirit confirms this conclusion to us, we can then exercise our authority in Christ to order the spirit(s) to depart. There may be occasions when it is appropriate simply to say, "If there is a demonic spirit causing this problem, I now command you in the name of the Lord Jesus Christ to depart!"

Much more can and needs to be said about the process of discernment and then directly confronting demonic spirits. Our purpose here is merely to assert the fact that we have the authority in Christ to take such direct action and that there may be occasions when it is appropriate.

7. BE MEANINGFULLY ATTACHED TO THE BODY OF CHRIST

Much spiritual vulnerability comes from being detached from the body of Christ. The Book of Acts is not only the story of the spread of the gospel, but a story about the development of Christian communities. It was not enough for the apostle Paul simply to proclaim the gospel in a new area. He worked diligently to bring the new believers together into communities that met regularly for worship, teaching, fellowship, and prayer. In each of his letters, he evaluates how these communities are doing on the basis of the way they are tangibly expressing love for one another.

The message and the community go hand in hand. When a person becomes a Christian, the Holy Spirit not only unites the person to Christ, but also to other Christians. Believers need each other as they grow to maturity.

There are not many themes in the New Testament about which more is said than community. Yet it appears that there is less community now in the church than at any other time in its history.

Being meaningfully attached to the body of Christ involves much more than attending a big celebration each Sunday morning or Saturday evening. It means meeting weekly (or more often) with a small group of believers or a spiritual mentor, studying the Scriptures, relating the Word to daily struggles, sharing intimately with one another, and praying earnestly for one another. It means having a "family" that cares for you and is always there for you.

One Christian counseling center that understands the role of the demonic and will not hesitate to cast out demons if they are discerned also understands the vital role of the Christian community in the deliverance/healing process. They make it a requirement for every counselee not only to attach himself or herself to a local church, but to have a spiritual mentor and a group of four to five people that will serve as prayer partners. The professional counselor then is only one member of a larger team that is working together to help a person come to whole-ness in Christ.

8. Pray and Solicit Prayer Support

Prayer is the heart and essence of spiritual warfare. In the delineation of the armor of God, Paul mentions prayer most prominently. But how do we pray?

We start by praying for ourselves. Prayer represents intimate com-munication with God and by it we are soliciting our omnipotent Father to fight for us. But it does not end there. We need other believers to pray for us. The apostle Paul recognized his own need for prayer and urged the Ephesians to pray for him. On the other hand, he recognized how much they needed prayer and reports how he engaged in intercessory prayer for them. As I discussed in chapter 1, I am convinced that we need to view our times of small group prayer as a chance to arm each other for spiritual warfare.

9. Expect Christ to Give Victory! (James 4:7)

Those who are struggling with demonic influence and attack need to think optimistically. They are not trapped in a situation from which there is no escape. There is hope in Christ. Following his exhortation, James gives a promise: "Resist the devil, and *he will flee!*" (James 4:7, italics mine).

Excesses to Avoid

A cloud of controversy surrounds the whole topic of spiritual war-fare. Some of this has to do with our culture—many people do not believe in the reality of evil spirits. But some of it has to do with a lot of erratic, unbalanced, and unsound ideas and practices. Many of the crit-icisms raised against contemporary deliverance ministry are justified. Here are a number of excesses we all need to avoid as we attempt to honor Christ, engage in effective ministry, and maintain a balanced bib-lical perspective.

"When in Doubt, Cast It Out"

Some people are quick to see a demon as the primary instigating force behind almost every problem a person may have. They are quick to rush in, with little or no awareness of a person's psychological or medical background, and engage in aggressive denunciation of various spirits, ordering them to leave the person. This approach is both scary and dangerous. It could leave the person more full of fear and generally worse off than before the encounter.[68]

Uncritical Acceptance of the Testimony of Demons

There is significant controversy over the advisability of instructing a demon to manifest its presence and speak, forcing it to answer questions. Whatever position one takes on this issue, considerable discernment needs to be used in evaluating whatever is said. It goes without saying that demons are inveterate liars and commonly referred to in early Christianity as "deceitful spirits."

I remember talking to one person involved in deliverance ministry who used to write down everything that was ever said by a demon talking to or through a person. He would then use this information to inform his strategy, learn about demonic hierarchies and methods, and find out about the local plans and workings of demons. As he grew in wisdom and discovered that little of what was said appeared to correspond to reality, he quickly gave up this practice.

A "Lone Ranger" Approach to Counseling

With the advent of modern deliverance ministries has come a collection of individuals who view themselves as independent deliverance experts. Often deprecating the help churches have traditionally given through pastoral counseling and frequently maligning psychotherapeutical assistance, these people style themselves as knowing how to deal with spiritual problems quickly and effectively through deliverance ministry techniques.

The church has no place, however, for spiritual shamans. While gifted people should be recognized and a context provided for the exercise of their gifts, the manifestation of individual giftedness is carried out within the body. That is, deliverance ministry is only one link in a chain of ministries to help people grow in Christ.

Expecting Too Much Too Soon: Circumventing the Discipleship Process

People not only have a natural tendency to overrely on techniques, programs, and formulas, but they want an immediate outcome. This is particularly true in American culture. There is a significant danger in deliverance ministry of short-circuiting the discipleship process, which Jesus himself instituted for the believer's growth and development. This is not only a problem in the way that it is carried out by certain practitioners, but it is even more of a problem of perception by those who are being counseled.

My former colleague at Talbot School of Theology, Neil Anderson, has tried to help believers struggling with demonic issues by putting together what he has called "Steps to Freedom in Christ."[69] Many people have received significant help from working through these steps, which leads them into a better understanding of their identity in Christ and how this knowledge helps them gain victory over sin and demonic influence. Unfortunately, some people have looked at these seven steps more as a magical formula that will insure them success. They complete each of the steps and then complain that nothing has really changed for them and begin to wonder if there is something very seriously wrong with them.

This is a problem of perception. The "Steps to Freedom in Christ" are to be used within the larger context of meaningful discipleship relationships, worship, prayer support, fellowship, teaching, and growth. They are not a technique for obliterating temptation or lifting the ongoing struggle out of the believers' warfare.

As I explained in the first chapter, spiritual warfare is a wholistic way of looking at life. Healing and growth take time and patience. While I believe that God can and does deliver his people from various forms of bondage, I also know that he has created the body of Christ to provide the wounded with a caring environment for continued recovery and growth.

Winning a Battle, but Losing a War

We also need to be alert to avoid the pitfall of becoming so focused on a particular demonic issue that we neglect the care of the whole person. What good is it if we help a person deal with demonic influence in the area of night terrors if we do not provide counsel for poor marital communication patterns and the couple ends up getting divorced?

Forms of "Christian Magic"

For the entirety of my academic career, I have not only written about the Bible, but also about Greco-Roman era magic, witchcraft, astrology, and mystery cults. As a result of that research and writing, I have seen the remarkable way that the apostle Paul continually stressed the primacy of a *relationship to Christ* and tried to move young believers away from a magical worldview and approach to God. This research has also made me quite sensitive to forms of developing "Christian magic" that

seem to be surfacing today, especially in much of the contemporary discussions about spiritual warfare.

This was also a struggle for the Christians in the early history of the
church. As believers dealt with the influence of the demonic in the first
few centuries of the church, they often relied more on their former
practices and techniques than on their relationship to the exalted Christ.
Not following the example of the Ephesian believers in Acts 19 who
renounced and burned their magic books, some continued to mix Christianity with magical practices and beliefs. They emphasized technique
over relationship to Christ; they stressed the use of angels rather than
reliance on the power of the indwelling Christ and his Spirit; they
invested Christian symbols, names, phrases, and verses with magical
power, just to name a few examples of their syncretistic approach. Their
practices are known to us through a number of sources: Christian magical papyri written in Greek or Coptic, Christian magical amulets, and
Jewish magical documents edited and preserved by Christians. In fact,
Harper San Francisco recently published a whole collection of Christian magic texts, most dating from the third to the tenth centuries. The
book is entitled *Ancient Christian Magic.*[70] There are four areas where I
see a similarity between ancient magical practices and contemporary
deliverance ministries.

1. *An emphasis on formulaic prayers:* Some modern books on spiritual
   warfare give model or pattern prayers that, at times, border on
   the formulaic. None are of the variety that we find in the news-
   paper suggesting that if we pray a certain prayer to St. Jude seven
   times we will get what we ask for. But some include comments
   like, "this is an effective prayer," thus giving the impression that
   the power resides in the prayer rather than in the one the person is praying to. But part of the problem, again, is in the way
   people respond to pattern prayers. Rather than properly seeing
   these prayers as models, some people erroneously take them as
   powerful formulas. The same principle holds true for the Lord's
   Prayer, which is to serve as a model rather than as a formula for
   recitation.
2. *An overemphasis on "what works":* Just as Hellenistic magicians sought
   techniques and rituals that guaranteed success, some in deliverance ministry are making a pseudoscience out of spiritual warfare
   by cataloging every strategy that appears to work effectively in the
   deliverance process. In doing so, there is often a devaluation of the
   person of Christ with the corresponding elevation of technique.

3. *An emphasis on immediate cures:* As we discussed earlier, expectations are sometimes subtly communicated or mistakenly held that one or two sessions will totally alleviate a particular issue or struggle in a person's life. Even if demons are driven away, there are a set of ungodly influences, bad habits, and the presence of sin that will need to be dealt with over the long haul.

4. *An emphasis on angels and invoking angels:* Early Christian magic was enamored with angels, whom they called on regularly for deliverance from demons. One document preserved and used by early Christians (Testament of Solomon 18) even identifies which angel to invoke to thwart a demon responsible for provoking a certain symptom. Some people involved in deliverance ministry are attempting to learn more about and develop lines of communication with angels who will work with them in deliverance ministry. Paul's letter to the Colossians gives an unequivocal response to this practice, which apparently was being advocated by a group in the Colossian church. Paul urges them not to invoke angels (2:18) but to rely solely on Christ, who leads and empowers his people (2:19), who defeated the powers at the cross (2:15), who is the creator (1:16) and ruling head over every power (2:10), and who unites us to himself and grants to us a share in his authority over the realm of darkness.

Belief in an Internationally Networked Satanic Cult Conspiracy

Over the past twenty years, especially in the past decade, there has been an unprecedented surge of speculation and debate about the existence of multigenerational satanic cults perpetrating vile forms of ritual abuse. Much of the sensationalism in Christian circles was initially fueled by Michael Warnke's extraordinarily popular book, *The Satan Seller* (1972).[71] Reportedly totaling sales of three million copies, the book recounts Warnke's alleged preconversion experience as a satanic high priest. He reveals details of a worldwide networked satanic cult that perpetrated all sorts of awful crimes in the name of Satan. The cult engaged in various forms of ritual worship of Satan, including gang rape, animal sacrifice, and the consumption of blood. Warnke claimed to be the leader of a coven in San Bernardino, California, that grew to a membership of 1,500. Together with his second best-seller, *Schemes of Satan,*[72] his many high-profile public appearances (including "The Oprah Winfrey Show," "Larry King Live," and ABC's "20/20"), and his ambitious national speaking schedule as a Christian comedian, many Americans were alerted to the horrors of what purported to be the world's best-kept secret—an underground satanic cult perpetrating all kinds of heinous crimes.

Twenty years later and after two years of intense investigation, journalists John Trott and Mike Hertenstein wrote an article for *Cornerstone* magazine exposing many of the details of Warnke's story as implausible, grossly exaggerated, and patently false.[73] They subsequently penned a nearly 500-page book telling the entire story of their investigation into the background and claims of Michael Warnke.[74] Warnke initially responded not only by denying what was written against him, but by accusing the journalists of being members of an extremely powerful satanic cult that was out to destroy his ministry.[75] He later admitted that he was "guilty of embellishment and exaggeration . . . not in an attempt to deceive but to entertain." He also confessed to ungodliness in his personal life and asked forgiveness for being a failure as a husband (he was married four times) and a father.[76] In a subsequent editorial in *Christianity Today,* Tim Stafford chided evangelical believers for blithely swallowing Warnke's improbable and chilling tales.[77] As Trott and Hertenstein had done in their exposé, Stafford properly called his readers to be discerning in what they read or hear and to place a higher priority on searching for the truth.

The notion of an internationally networked multigenerational satanic cult has received much more attention in recent years from numerous people claiming to be surviving victims of the cult. The majority of these individuals have been treated by mental health professionals who have uncovered "repressed memories" of ritual abuse carried out against their patients by people from the cult. The recovery of these memories is often tied to a diagnosis of Multiple Personality Disorder (now officially called Dissociative Identity Disorder).[78] Therapists discover that in addition to the primary personality (the host), the victim may have many different alter personalities that emerge in the process of counseling. As the therapist makes contact with these alters and dialogues with them, scenes of "Satanic Ritual Abuse" (SRA) may be described.[79] Counselees mention recollections of ritual activities involving child and animal sacrifices on satanic altars, group sex, the engraving of pentagrams, consumption of chalices of blood, and elaborate baby-breeding schemes to provide child sacrifices. As these vivid episodes are recounted, mental health professionals as well as pastoral counselors are faced with the dilemma of how to respond to the information that is conveyed. Many have assumed the historical reliability of the accounts and have taken steps to do something about the alleged abuse by contacting the police, finding a safe place for the patient to live, separating the patient from his or her family, or writing and speaking out about the SRA phenomenon. Other therapists have continued to work with their patients and have suspended judgment about the "recovered memories." Still others have doubted the veracity of any of these ritual abuse stories retrieved through memory work.[80]

The difficulty we face in accepting the incredible testimony of many of these patients is that seldom can any of the pertinent details of their story be corroborated with physical evidence. No body parts can be found, no traces of blood are discovered at the alleged scene of the crimes, no witnesses come forth, no satanic cult paraphernalia is uncovered, nor can any other physical evidence of the crimes be found. This leads us to ask about the reliability of the "recovered memories"—about which I say more below. It also leads us to ask if there is any evidence pointing toward the existence of a large internationally networked satanic cult conspiracy that is responsible for thousands of human sacrifices each year.

At this point there is very little hard evidence pointing to such a cult conspiracy. Kenneth Lanning, an FBI agent in charge of investigating SRA crime for the past fifteen years, has concluded that "law enforcement has been aggressively investigating the allegations of victims of ritualistic abuse. There is little or no evidence for the portion of their allegations that deals with large-scale baby breeding, human sacrifice, and organized satanic conspiracies."[81] In the past few years, many well-researched books have been written confirming Lanning's conclusions and calling into question the idea of a multigenerational satanic cult conspiracy, such as the collection of essays in *The Satanism Scare* (1991), Robert Hicks's *In Pursuit of Satan* (1991), Jeffrey Victor's *Satanic Panic* (1993), and now, most recently, the outstanding work of Debbie Nathan in *Satan's Silence* (1995).[82]

In his excellent recent book on the SRA phenomena, psychiatrist Colin Ross—who previously was more sympathetic to the credibility of SRA victim testimony—has aptly summed up the evidence by asserting that "there is no objective public proof of the existence of such cults" and "no authoritative body, agency, or professional society has endorsed the reality of orthodox multigenerational satanic cults."[83] This is a significant statement from a therapist who has had clinical contact with about three hundred cases of MPD/DID, in which the individuals had memories of involvement in a destructive satanic cult. Of the eighty cases in which Ross had considerable involvement, he writes, "In none of these cases has the reality of the memories been objectively verified, and in several of them collateral history has proven that patient claims of Satanic ritual abuse were false."[84]

On the other hand, there is ample evidence of crimes (even murders) carried out in the name of Satan and various other forms of ritual and abuse. Ross points to four other levels of satanic crime that are indeed well documented:[85]

1. *Isolated Criminal Deviants:* Richard Ramirez, the "Night Stalker," claimed devotion to Satan, but public records say that he was never involved in an organized satanic cult and that his crimes were carried out alone.
2. *Teenage Dabblers:* In many cities, teenagers are becoming interested in satanic worship and committing capital crimes. For various reasons—curiosity, gaining spiritual power, sex, and drugs—teenagers band together in groups and try out various rituals and deviant practices, including animal sacrifice and murder.
3. *Noncriminal Public Satanic Churches:* Although Anton LaVey's "Church of Satan" is a blasphemous and disgusting affront to Christ and the church, his satanic rituals involve no criminal activities.
4. *Narcosatanistos:* Ross points to the Matamoros, Mexico, drug-smuggling group as an example of the most well-organized satanic group. These drug-smuggling satanists captured worldwide attention in 1989 for their ritual murder of a Texan pre-med student. The body had been ritually dismembered, boiled in a pot, mixed with animal blood, and cannibalized. They believed that the ritual would give them magical power that would protect them from the police.

The current available evidence points conclusively to various sorts of crimes, even murders, carried out in the name of Satan. In spite of aggressive investigation by various levels of law enforcement and private groups and individuals, there is as yet no evidence establishing the veracity of the worldwide-networked conspiracy theory.

Uncritical Acceptance of "Recovered Memories"

Pastors and Christian counselors, unfortunately, have been among those who have uncritically accepted "recovered memories" that are demonstrably untrue or that are not supported by corroborating evidence. This is tragic when it involves civil litigation, public attention and shame, and the separation of family members.

It is important for any Christian worker to realize that there are at least four possible explanations for memories recovered during the counseling process:

1. *Authentic:* they are genuine recollections of actual historical events.
2. *Confabulation:* they are actual images in the mind of the patient, but they do not correspond to historical events. We cannot underestimate the power of the mind to create images and to associate images from another context (like a horror movie) with one's own prior experience. Nor should we underestimate the ability of the Evil One to present a series of images to one's mind that could mistakenly be taken as a memory.
3. *Malingering:* the patient is intentionally making up the events and feigning illness to avoid responsibilities or for some kind of personal gain (e.g., winning a civil suit and a large sum of money).
4. *Iatrogenesis:* the therapist or counselor has unwittingly or inadvertently suggested images that the patient makes his or her own.
5. *Combination:* the "memory" could have a grain of truth or even an authentic framework, but many of the details could have come from other sources.

Ross comments: "It is my opinion that many of the Satanic ritual abuse memories described by the patients I treat are confabulated and comprise things that never actually happened."[86] Nevertheless, he exercises an appropriate caution by not moving to the other extreme and doubting that it never happens. He notes, "I am cautious in this opinion because I cannot know for sure that it is correct. I assume, for the sake of discussion, that 10 per cent of the content of such memories could be historically accurate and based on distorted recall of childhood participation in small Christian cults; small, isolated groups of Satanists; deviant elements of the Ku Klux Klan; pornography; or other forms of abuse that a child could misinterpret."[87]

Once again I reiterate that there is ample evidence pointing to numerous awful crimes committed in the name of Satan. Thus, when someone in your church comes and says that he or she was ritually abused as a child in a satanic cult, there is a possibility that it actually happened. To immediately respond with disbelief would be inappropriate and not conducive to ministering to that person. Nevertheless, there may be other explanations for the images recovered in the counseling process (as we noted above). The point is that we need to exercise critical and spiritual discernment as we minister to people who claim they have had ritual abuse experiences, especially when they indict family members and others in the church or in the city.[88]

Violence

As far as I am aware, no evangelical Christians are advocating any form of harsh treatment or violence toward people who are diagnosed as having a demon or have some affiliation with witchcraft. Deliverance ministry is commonly understood to be a calm, controlled time of counseling, prayer, and verbal renunciation of evil spirits done with the consent and involvement of the counselee. There is no hint of a return to the atrocities like those surrounding the inquisitions under Pope Innocent VIII or the Salem witchcraft trials when Scripture (Exod. 22:18: "do not allow a sorceress to live") was twisted and misapplied in support of a violent effort to extirpate witches.

There are extremists on the fringes, however, who resort to violence against people, assuming that they are attacking a spiritual entity. This was certainly the case with two of the situations I mentioned in chapter 1: the five women in Emeryville, California, who beat a woman to death in an exorcism ritual and the tragic situation in New Mexico, where a father beheaded his son in an effort to beat back the demons. And just recently, a South Korean woman died after a six-hour exorcism ritual in Los Angeles, which involved a great deal of physical force in an attempt to expel the evil spirits from her body.[89] A Korean pastor denounced the event as "an extreme case, involving a fringe group of the Korean Christian community."

Events of this nature should be denounced by all. Physical violence toward a person is never justified in counseling or dealing with demonic issues. We have the authority in Christ to command spirits not to manifest their presence. This enables us to maintain control over a counseling situation and point the person to the Lord Jesus Christ, the only deliverer.

Summary

1. Christians cannot be demon-possessed if one means by that expression ownership of a believer by Satan or demons. Believers are the property of God and belong exclusively to him.
2. Christians can be inhabited by demons, but only if they provide the spirits with the space to occupy through protracted sin or by inviting their presence. One needs to recognize that this sort of spatial language is a metaphorical way of speaking of spiritual presence and control.

3. The behavior of Christians can be controlled by demons, but only if they have yielded that control to the spirits. Just as sin can "reign" over one's body, so a demon can assert a high level of control.

4. Christians can yield so much control to a demon that they may even display an altered state of consciousness and manifest the presence of an intruding demon (with the demon speaking through the person, etc.).

5. Christians can be delivered from evil spirits and that is what God wants for them. God does not want his people to live defeated lives, in bondage to sin and impurity or to unclean spirits. The power of God is infinitely greater than the power of the enemy and his realm. Believers can experience freedom and victory from the compelling influence of Satan and his forces.

6. Resisting Satan and finding deliverance from the influence of evil spirits is an entire way of life in the context of Christian community. It involves drawing near to God in faith and prayer, becoming immersed in the Scriptures, attaching oneself to other believers in meaningful relationships, and understanding and appropriating the work of Christ.

7. Resisting a demonic spirit on some occasions may involve exercising authority on the basis of one's relationship to Christ as his disciple and firmly commanding an evil spirit to depart.

8. It is important to recognize the wide variety of ways that demons seek to exert their unhealthy influence on the church. To become overly fixated on the dramatic symptoms of what has classically been called "possession behavior" could cause one to lose sight of the ways he works to harm relationships, thwart the evangelistic mission of the church, or distort what one thinks of Christ and his work.

Recommended Reading

Books Affirming That Christians Can Be Demonized

Anderson, Neil T. *The Bondage Breaker: Overcoming Darkness and Resolving Spiritual Conflicts*. Eugene, Ore.: Harvest House, 1990; *Victory over the Darkness: Realizing the Power of Your Identity in Christ*. Ventura, Calif.: Regal, 1990. Anderson advocates what he calls a "truth encounter" approach and advises Christian counselors not to intervene by commanding an evil spirit to depart from the person they are working with. His "Steps to Freedom in Christ" have proved to be a practical set of guidelines in helping people deal with sin and spiritual issues in their lives.

Dickason, C. Fred. *Demon Possession and the Christian*. Chicago: Moody, 1987; reprint, Westchester, Ill.: Crossway, 1989. Dickason, chairman of the theology department at Moody Bible Institute, attempts to make a biblical and theological case for the possibility that Christians can be demonized. His book also includes case studies and practical insights based on his experience in counseling demonized people.

Kraft, Charles H. *Defeating Dark Angels: Breaking Demonic Oppression in the Believer's Life*. Ann Arbor: Servant, Vine Books, 1992; *Deep Wounds, Deep Healing: Discovering the Vital Link between Spiritual Warfare and Inner Healing*. Ann Arbor: Servant, Vine Books, 1993. In his first volume, Kraft attempts to provide support for the notion that Christians can be demonized and then gives perspective on how to minister to believers in this condition. In the second volume, he advocates a controversial "inner healing" approach and makes a case for its relevance in ministering to people who are struggling with powerful demonic influence.

Logan, Jim. *Reclaiming Surrendered Ground: Protecting Your Family from Spiritual Attacks*. Chicago: Moody, 1995. Logan, counselor at the International Center for Biblical Counseling (ICBC) in Sioux City, Iowa, uses Ephesians 4:27 as a starting point for his book. He attempts to provide practical counsel to Christians who have allowed evil spirits to gain control over aspects of their lives.

Murphy, Ed. *The Handbook for Spiritual Warfare*. Nashville: Thomas Nelson, 1992. Formerly a career missionary with OC (Overseas Crusades) International, Murphy has put together the most detailed book about spiritual warfare currently available. This 600-page volume treats many topics, but especially the issue of the demonization of Christians.

White, Thomas B. *The Believer's Guide to Spiritual Warfare: Wising Up to Satan's Influence in Your World*. Ann Arbor: Servant, Vine Books, 1990. White, director of Frontline Ministries in Corvallis, Oregon, has put together a concise and practical guide on the topic of spiritual struggle and dealing with the demonic.

Books Denying That Christians Can Be Demonized

Ice, Thomas, and Robert Dean Jr. *Overrun by Demons: The Church's Preoccupation with the Demonic*. Eugene, Ore.: Harvest House, 1990. This book is a highly polemical critique of contemporary deliverance ministry, going so far as to compare it to the final apostasy during the end-times of the church age.

Powlison, David. *Power Encounters: Reclaiming Spiritual Warfare*. Grand Rapids: Baker, 1995. Powlison, lecturer in practical theology at Westminster

Theological Seminary and editor of the Journal of Biblical Counseling, provides a strong critique of modern deliverance ministry. He argues strenuously against the need for or advisability of a "casting out" form of ministry.

Rommen, Edward, ed. *Spiritual Power and Missions: Raising the Issues.* Evangelical Missiological Society Series 3. Pasadena, Calif.: William Carey Library, 1995. This volume contains an important essay by Robert J. Priest and two of his colleagues at Columbia International University, suggesting that much of the modern deliverance ministry reflects more of an animistic worldview than a biblical view of reality.

Historical Perspective on the Early Church

Kelly, Henry A. *The Devil at Baptism: Ritual, Theology, and Drama.* Ithaca, N.Y.: Cornell University Press, 1985. This is an outstanding historical study illustrating how the early church dealt with the issue of the demonization of those who were becoming Christians.

Are We Called to Engage Territorial Spirits?

Maximón is defeated!"[1] News of this victory for Christians in Guatemala brought great rejoicing to believers in Latin America and the United States who were familiar with this territorial stronghold. Maximón is a Mayan deity who has been worshiped in Guatemala for centuries. Many Christians in the city of Quezaltenango and the surrounding regions have seen Maximón, however, as a powerful territorial spirit over a large section of Guatemala who revels in blood sacrifice and death and works to keep people from turning to Christ when the gospel is proclaimed.

The June 24, 1994, edition of *Crónica Semanal,* a Guatemalan news magazine, ran a cover story on this once-popular idol titled "The Defeat of Maximón: Protestant Fundamentalism Alters the Culture of the Altiplano and Turns the Native Religions into Tourist Attractions."[2] For many years, groups of Christians in the area had engaged in spiritual mapping and aggressive warfare prayer against the territorial spirits, including Maximón. In addition, four teams of intercessors from Guatemala City had gone to four points of the nation on June 25, 1994, to pray for the country on a specially designated day of prayer. On that day, seventy thousand people participated in the March for Jesus in Guatemala City, announcing to the principalities and powers (Eph. 3:10) that Jesus, not the Mayan spirits, is Lord over Guatemala. The magazine appeared on the newsstands the following week reporting that "the fraternity of Maximón and its followers has been reduced to a mere handful of individuals . . . but the central meeting places of the day are the huge quantity of evangelical churches."

This is truly news worth getting excited about. It reminds us of some of the amazing events in the first century, when the people "turned from idols to serve the living and true God" (1 Thess. 1:9). Where it varies slightly is in method. Although the preaching of the gospel is still central, an incredible emphasis is now being placed on preparing the ground by dealing with the high-ranking evil angels—territorial spirits—over the region.

This unique emphasis on battling territorial spirits has also become a key element in a variety of ministries in the United States. One example is the ministry of a church called The Dwelling Place in Hemet, California. Over a decade ago, Pastor Bob Beckett began to have recurring visions of a bearhide stretched out over this large southland community as he sought the Lord during times of personal prayer. Each of the four corners of the bearhide had claws firmly anchoring the hide into the area. Down the middle of the hide was a strong backbone.[3]

What did this image represent? The pastor was convinced that this was the ruling demonic spirit over the area. He later discovered that the name of the spirit was Taquitz. He believed that God was giving him specific information so he could lead his people in warfare prayers to bring down this territorial spirit and, ultimately, increase the effectiveness of the church in its outreach and ministry in the community. The pastor then led a group of people from the church in praying against this evil principality. As they prayed, they gained the strong impression that the backbone of the beast was breaking apart and that it was losing its spiritual grip on the area.

Further research by the pastor into the history of the area helped him identify the four strongholds of the bear's claws—a Transcendental Meditation center, an Indian reservation (which actively engaged in traditional shamanism), a retreat facility for followers of the Maharishi Yogi, and a Church of Scientology resort. As the pastor sought the Lord's direction, he sensed that the Lord was telling him to drive stakes into the ground at four points and raise up a "prayer canopy" over the area, thus claiming the territory for Christ that once belonged to this evil spirit. After the church took this prophetic action and continued in intercessory prayer for the area, they began to have tremendous success in ministry: the congregation doubled in size in less than a year, a spirit of love and unity pervaded the church, and there was a new expression of unity among pastors in the community.

Numerous stories of Christians effectively battling principalities and powers are surfacing from all over the world, including Korea, Argentina, Canada, and elsewhere. A few Christian leaders are now culling insights from these accounts and advocating new and specific strategies for battling higher-ranking spirits that wield influence over neighborhoods, cities, geographical territories, and even whole countries. Using the references in Daniel 10 to the evil angelic princes over Persia and Greece as a starting point, these leaders are contending that Christians need to begin doing battle against the territorial spirits in order for successful and effective Christian ministry to occur.

Have these leaders rediscovered a vital aspect of our warfare long neglected by our churches? Even if aspects of the strategy sound strange, different, or even absurd, can we question it in light of its apparent successes?

Argentina has been a focal point for the implementation of this strategy. One of the most notable examples has been Argentine evangelist Carlos Annacondia. Observers of his ministry claim that nearly two million people throughout Latin America have registered decisions for Christ in his crusades since 1982. Annacondia has strongly emphasized spiritual warfare and practices "binding the strong man" over the areas where he holds his crusades.[4] Omar Cabrera, pastor of the 90,000-member Vision of the Future Church in Argentina, also practices this method. In preparing for an evangelistic thrust into a new area, he spends five to seven days in solitude, aggressively praying for the binding of the strong man, or prince, who controls the darkness of that particular area.[5]

In the United States, this mode of spiritual warfare has been popularized by missiologist C. Peter Wagner. He has coined the phrase "Strategic-Level Spiritual Warfare" (SLSW) to describe the strategy and to distinguish it from exorcism or "deliverance ministry." Wagner presents the strategy in detail in his book, *Warfare Prayer* (Regal, 1991). He has also edited two other books that advocate the strategy: *Engaging the Enemy: How to Fight and Defeat Territorial Spirits* (Regal, 1991) and *Breaking Strongholds in Your City: How to Use Spiritual Mapping to Make Your Prayers More Strategic, Effective, and Targeted* (Regal, 1993). These books contain essays by pastors, evangelists, and missionaries, including John Dawson, Tom White, David Yonggi Cho, Larry Lea, Cindy Jacobs, George Otis Jr., Bob Beckett, Harold Caballeros, and Victor Lorenzo. Most recently, he has attempted to provide a biblical and theological basis for the practice in a book titled *Confronting the Powers: How the New Testament Church Experienced the Power of Strategic-Level Spiritual Warfare* (Regal, 1996).

All of these people are involved in an international group of Christian leaders called the "Spiritual Warfare Network" (SWN). The group was formed after the 1989 Lausanne II Conference held in Manila in response to the tremendous interest generated by five workshops relating to territorial spirits in the context of the task of world evangelization. The first meeting of the SWN took place at Lake Avenue Congregational Church in Pasadena, California, on February 12, 1990, led by Wagner, Charles Kraft, Cindy Jacobs, and Gary Clark. SWN was founded for the purpose of seeking God's wisdom and direction as to the ways in which Christians could pray to measurably advance the cause of world evangelization.

I became involved in the SWN in 1991 at the invitation of Peter Wagner and Charles Kraft to serve as a biblical-theological resource person, sharing with them a commitment to world evangelization and a desire to think about strategy in light of the opposition of the Evil One to the spread of the gospel. I have continued in dialogue with various SWN members over the past few years and recently participated with Wagner, David Bryant, and Tom White as a consultant for the development of "The Philosophy of Prayer for World Evangelization Adopted by the AD 2000 United Prayer Track."[6]

Description of the Strategy

In describing the distinctive traits of SLSW, I focus primarily on Wagner's articulation of the strategy because he has become the principal and most influential spokesperson for the approach. Without the publication of his many books on the topic, there would be little awareness of "Strategic-Level Spiritual Warfare." I have come to realize, however, that there really are a variety of *strategies* even within the SWN and that it is not correct to speak of one uniform strategic-level spiritual warfare method. Although it may not be readily apparent in the literature, some would disagree with Wagner on certain aspects of the strategy, emphasizing certain parts to the minimization or exclusion of other parts.

At the heart of SLSW is a threefold approach: (1) discern the territorial spirits assigned to the city, (2) deal with the corporate sin of a city or area, and (3) engage in aggressive "warfare prayer" against the territorial spirits. I describe each of these facets of the strategy in turn.

1. Discern the Territorial Spirits Assigned to a City

This aspect of the method, of course, assumes not only the reality of hostile supernatural beings intent on hindering the progress of the gospel, but it also assumes a demonic hierarchy with powers of greater and lesser rank having specific geographical assignments.

Most Christians would have no problem affirming the reality of Satan and demons. Not to do so entails a conscious or unconscious acceptance of a hermeneutic influenced by an a priori scientific naturalism. The concept of hostile angels associated with territories also has biblical support in Daniel 10:13, 20, 21, which speaks of a "prince of Persia" and a "prince of Greece" struggling in heaven with the angel Michael, one of the "chief princes" of the heavenly host.

Wagner contends that it is crucial to learn the names and nature of the assignments of the demonic princes over a given area as a first step in this kind of spiritual warfare. He cites the example of Resistencia, Argentina. He claims that "one of the keys to the substantial evangelistic results in the city of Resistencia was naming the spirits over that city: Pombero, Curupí, San La Muerte, Reina del Cielo, witchcraft, and Freemasonry."[7] In a more recent discussion of SLSW, he reaffirmed how important it had been to discern the names of these six spirits as part of the strategy.[8] Other Christian workers have emphasized the naming of the powers as well. Pastor and evangelist Larry Lea describes how he asks God to show him the enemy forces at work in the particular town or church in which he is ministering.[9] Similarly, John Dawson, international director of urban missions for Youth With A Mission, relates how he asked the Lord for discernment regarding the "strong man" or territorial spirit over Amazonas and Manaus in Brazil prior to a time of ministry there.[10] In contrast to Wagner, Dawson contends that "getting the exact name of demons at any level is not necessary, but it is important to be aware of the specific nature or type of oppression."[11] In the prescriptive section of *Warfare Prayer,* Wagner instructs his readers as follows: "To the degree possible, the intercessors should seek to know the names, either functional or proper, of the principalities assigned to the city as a whole and to various geographical, social or cultural segments of the city."[12] In his most recent book, Wagner reiterates the importance: "Effective spiritual warfare does not *require* knowing the names of the spirits, but experience has shown that when we are able to identify them specifically by name, we seem to have more authority over them, and therefore we can be more effective."[13]

This is where the concept of spiritual mapping comes in. This expression was coined by George Otis Jr., president of the Sentinel Group and coordinator with Wagner of the AD 2000 & Beyond Movement's United Prayer Track, where he heads the spiritual mapping division. He defines spiritual mapping as "superimposing our understanding of forces and events in the spiritual domain onto places and circumstances in the material world."[14] By this he means discerning what is happening in the spiritual realm that keeps people from responding to the light of the gospel. His concept of spiritual mapping amounts to engaging in detailed research on the religious history of a city or country. He seeks to uncover not only the official religious background, but also the folk beliefs and practices. His research is based on the assumption that malevolent spirits are behind these other religious beliefs and practices and are using them to blind people to the gospel. The first fruits of this kind of research have recently been published in a volume titled *Strongholds of the 10/40 Window*.[15] Unlike Wagner, Otis does not suggest that intercessors need to discern the names of the spirits. He is more concerned to uncover the nature of their deception in its varied manifestations from place to place.

It is also important to observe that Otis does not advocate "mapping" in the sense of drawing lines on a map from one religious or occultic center to another as a means of detecting demonic corridors of power. This is a principle that some in the SWN give credence to (including Wagner), but it does not represent what most in the SWN are doing.

2. Deal with the Corporate Sin of a City or Area

Many in the Spiritual Warfare Network are now emphasizing the importance of dealing with the corporate sin of a city or area as an integral part of the overall strategy of fighting territorial spirits. The assumption here is that "the sinful behavior has provided openings for high-ranking principalities and powers to establish spiritual strongholds that will not be loosened other than through corporate humility and repentance."[16]

The strongest advocate of this has been John Dawson. He has coined the expression "identificational repentance" to encapsulate the essence of what is needed. In his best-selling book, *Taking Our Cities for God,* Dawson stressed the importance of identifying with the sins of the city and then confessing and repenting of these sins as a means of effecting reconciliation and thereby breaking Satan's grip on a city.[17]

He has developed this approach in a more recent book titled *Healing America's Wounds.* He focuses in particular on our country's sins against Native Americans, African Americans, women, and the poor. He explains to the contemporary generation that it has inherited the legacy of its ancestors and is therefore partly responsible before God for their past transgressions. He urges Americans to identify with these sins, publicly confess them, and allow the offended parties to release forgiveness. In the spiritual domain, he contends, "Satan is terrified by reconciliation."[18]

Wagner has made this aspect of the SLSW strategy central to the United Prayer Track of the AD 2000 & Beyond Movement. He says, "no aspect of warfare prayer is more important than identificational repentance."[19] In his view, casting down the ruling spirits over an area is insufficient; they may return if their legal jurisdiction is not annulled. He says, "One of the reasons evil spirits succeed in returning is that the strongholds on which they had based their legal rights to control that area and its people have not been thoroughly removed. . . . Through accurate and sensitive spiritual mapping we can identify strongholds rooted in unremitted sins of past generations."[20] These need to be dealt with by identificational repentance and Wagner points to Dawson's book as the most important guide.

Problematic

3. Engage in Aggressive Warfare Prayer against the Territorial Spirits

The final step in SLSW is to engage in aggressive warfare prayer against the territorial spirits identified. After naming the six ruling spirits over Resistencia, Argentina, Wagner says that "under the coaching of Cindy Jacobs, the Argentine Pastors prayed strongly and specifically against these principalities."[21] This sort of praying is "designed to bind the strongman and weaken his powers over the souls" of people in a city who have not yet received Jesus Christ.[22]

Cindy Jacobs is president of Generals of Intercession, based in Colorado Springs, Colorado. She has had a significant and formative influence on Wagner's thinking and on the direction of the prayer movement. She is a strong advocate of praying against the territorial spirits after adequate spiritual preparation for the confrontation. She describes her method:

> Once sin has been repented of, I usually ask the local pastors who have strong anointings and authority to lead in the actual prayer against the territorial spirits and command their power to be broken. This must not be done until the sins have been remitted or the power of the strongholds will not be broken. This is an area where one must rely carefully on the leading of the Holy Spirit. The leadership has a great responsibility for those they have taken into battle with them. To attempt to rail against the territorial spirits when it is not the time can be disastrous. God puts tremendous peace and faith into the hearts of the pastors and leaders when it is time to pray against the spirits.[23]

Jacobs appears to find warrant for this method in the example of Jesus in his temptation. She says, "We sometimes overlook the few, but powerful, words that Christ used in the wilderness. Ending the battle, He said with great authority, 'Away with you, Satan!' (Matt. 4:10). The Bible says that he left Jesus and the angels came and ministered to Him."[24]

Victor Lorenzo describes the aggressive warfare prayer against the six ruling powers they discerned in Resistencia, Argentina. He says that with Cindy Jacobs and a group of trained intercessors

> we battled fiercely against the invisible powers over the city for four hours. We attacked them in what we sensed was their hierarchical order, from bottom to top. First came *Pombero,* then *Curupí,* then *San La Muerte,* then spirit of Freemasonry, then Queen of Heaven, then the Python spirit whom we suspected functioned as the coordinator of all the forces of evil in the city. When we finished, an almost tangible sense of peace and freedom came over all who had participated. We were confident that this first battle had been won and that the city could be claimed for the Lord.[25]

Wagner points to other people who have prayed effectively against territorial spirits. Among these is Larry Lea, who prays against the powers located in every direction surrounding his church. For instance, Lea issues an explicit command to the personified direction "North": "North, you have people God wills to become a part of my church. I command you in the name of Jesus to release every person who is supposed to become a part of this body."[26]

Biblical and Church Historical Foundations

When we turn to the Scriptures for insight about the so-called territorial spirits, we do not find much, but there are a handful of important passages that clearly affirm the reality of demonic spirits associated with territories, especially nations.

Angels over Nations (Deut. 32:8; Psalm 82)

The first passage that refers to territorial spirits is Deuteronomy 32:8. This verse strongly affirms God's sovereignty over all people and nations, but also informs us that he has given angels a measure of responsibility over the nations of the earth:

> When the Most High gave the nations their inheritance,
>   when he divided all mankind,
> he set up boundaries for the peoples
>   according to the number of the sons of Israel.

This division of humanity by *'Elyon* ("Most High") took place in a heavenly council, where all the angels, or "holy ones," were present.[27] The Lord apportioned humanity into groupings "according to the number of the sons of Israel" or, as the Septuagint and a scroll of Deuteronomy from Qumran put it, "according to the number of the sons of God"—a reference to angels. The passage thus appears to be teaching that the number of the nations of the earth is directly proportional to the number of angels. Certain groupings of angels are associated with particular countries and peoples.

Some of these angelic rulers evidently have rebelled against the Lord. Rather than direct the people's worship to the one true God, they have sought veneration for themselves and have falsely presented themselves to the people as "gods" (Ps. 82:1–8).[28] Instead of inspiring the human leaders of these nations to reign in justice, righteousness, and goodness, they have stimulated idolatry, wars, hatred, injustice, and every kind of wickedness and perversity. For these misdeeds they will face the strict judgment of God in the heavenly assembly (Ps. 82:1–8). The masquerade of these "sons of the Most High" will be brought to an end. People will then know that the one God is truly the "Most High" *('Elyon)*. He alone is sovereign and worthy of worship. All the nations are his inheritance (Ps. 82:8).

The prophet Isaiah also speaks of the impending judgment of these patron angels of the nations:

> In that day the LORD will punish
>   the powers in the heavens above
>   and the kings on the earth below (Isa. 24:21).

These heavenly powers wielding territorial influence through the kings of the earth may truly be powerful, but they have underestimated the infinite wisdom and almighty power of their Creator. They will most assuredly meet their doom.

All three texts give clear testimony to the reality of fallen angels that wield significant influence over nations. Rather than their reign over a particular geographical territory, the emphasis seems to lie more on ethnic people groupings. These passages reveal a very close connection between the affairs of humanity and the activity of the angels.

The Gods of the Nations Are Really Demons (Deut. 32:17; Ps. 96:5; 106:37–38)

Two Old Testament passages in particular highlight the depraved nature of some of these angels over the nations. The same chapter that reveals the allotments of humanity to angelic guardianship (Deut. 32:8) speaks of Israel provoking God to jealousy by embracing foreign gods (Deut. 32:16). In reality, however, "they sacrificed to demons" (Heb. = shēdim; Gk. = daimonia; Deut. 32:17). They forsook the one true almighty God and gave their devotion to fallen angels, to demonic spirits. Of course they did not realize that they were worshiping evil spirits. These principalities and powers pulled off an effective hoax by deceiving people into thinking that they were the omnipotent rulers of heaven and earth.

The Psalms poetically remind the people of God that the one they worship is the Sovereign of the universe: "For you, O LORD, are the Most High over all the earth; you are exalted far above all gods" (Ps. 97:9). This is by no means to be misconstrued as an endorsement that other gods truly exist. The Septuagint version of Psalm 96:5 unmasks the true identity of the various gods of the nations: "For all the gods of the nations are demons, but the Lord made the heavens."[29]

All the rituals, prayers, sacrifices, and worship offered to the gods of other nations were not really offered to "gods" at all. They were accorded to angelic imposters usurping the rightful place of the one true God. What is especially appalling about this grand demonic deception is the horrific sacrifices these rebellious angels demanded of the people as their "gods." They went so far as to elicit human sacrifice. The psalmist laments one of these sad chapters in the history of Israel:

They worshiped their idols,
    which became a snare to them.
They sacrificed their sons
    and their daughters to demons.
They shed innocent blood,
    the blood of their sons and daughters,
whom they sacrificed to the idols of Canaan,
    and the land was desecrated by their blood (Ps. 106:36–38).

The gods and goddesses of the Canaanites were, in reality, demonic spirits. They tempted the people of Israel and solicited their worship under the guise of local deities. They were what many today are calling "territorial spirits."

After the conquest of Canaan, the people of Israel often succumbed to the temptation to worship these local deities. The Old Testament historical books, the prophets, and the Psalms are replete with stories of the people of God compromising their fidelity to Yahweh by embracing idols. There were numerous gods in the Canaanite religion, but "El" was extolled as supreme. The people also worshiped the goddess Ashtoreth, a deity closely related to the Babylonian and Assyrian goddess Ishtar. In the Old Testament and other religious texts from this time, we also find numerous references to the god Baal, the supreme fertility god of the Canaanites. Every locality venerated its own Baal and often named him after the city or territory where he was worshiped, such as Baal-hermon, Baal-hazor, Baal-gad, and Baal-peor. There were many other regional deities in Canaanite religion. Chemosh of Moab, Milkom of Ammon, Mclqart of Tyre, and Eshmun of Sidon are just a few of the assorted territorial deities.[30]

A variety of other Canaanite deities had no regional association, but were revered because of some special function they performed. Ilib, for instance, was the patron of ancestor veneration, Hadd (or, Hadad) was responsible for storms, Yam was the god of the sea, Mot reigned over death, and Rephesh was connected to pestilence. Therefore, it was common for people to worship more than one deity. Old Testament scholar Peter Craigie has suggested that a Canaanite dwelling in a particular city might worship (1) the principal deity of that city, (2) a fertility deity, (3) a deity associated with the dead, or (4) a personal or familial deity.[31]

The Old Testament makes it clear that all of these idols—whether associated with a country, city, territory, the sea, or even if they claim to wield power over a function such as death, fertility, or storms—are in reality rebellious angels, or demons, masquerading as "gods." They are pridefully diverting to themselves the worship that properly belongs only to the one true God. The apostle Paul taught the same truth to the Corinthians when he said, "the sacrifices of pagans are offered to demons, not to God" (1 Cor. 10:20).

The idols fashioned from stone, wood, or precious metals are still mere images (the meaning of the term "idol"). There is nothing to the actual statues. But there is a spiritual reality associated with them that is exceedingly dangerous. Demons stand behind the idol worship and animate it as part of their attempt to subvert the plan of God and seek worship for themselves.

Angels over Nations at War with Good Angels (Dan. 10:13, 20, 21)

The notion of territorial spirits receives unequivocal support from the Book of Daniel. The term "territorial," however, actually understates the nature and function of these angelic powers. Perhaps a better expression would be "empire spirits."[32]

The text describes angelic powers that have specific connections to the successive empires of Persia and Greece. These evil angels are mentioned to Daniel by an interpreting angel, perhaps Gabriel (see Dan. 9:21), who came to explain a vision God had given to him. Gabriel reveals that there was a heavenly struggle that hindered his coming to Daniel for three weeks:

> The prince of the Persian kingdom resisted me twenty-one days. Then Michael, one of the chief princes, came to help me, because I was detained there with the king of Persia (Dan. 10:13).

Later, Gabriel informs Daniel that the heavenly warfare would continue, but would now include a struggle with another angelic prince:

> Soon I will return to fight against *the prince of Persia,* and when I go, *the prince of Greece* will come. . . . (No one supports me against them except Michael, your prince) (Dan. 10:20–21, italics mine).

Both the prince of Persia and the prince of Greece in these passages are not references to human rulers, but to angelic forces. There is a clear consensus among Bible scholars on this foundational point.[33] This interpretation is strongly suggested by the fact that the archangel Michael is also referred to as a "prince." The Septuagint (Theodotion) translation of the Hebrew term *sar* is *archōn,* a word that was used by Paul (see 1 Cor. 2:6, 8; Eph. 2:2), John (John 12:31), and other first-century and early Christian writers for angelic powers.

Daniel received his vision during the third year of the reign of Cyrus, king of Persia, in 535 B.C. He had been praying and fasting for the people of Israel. Many of them were still in the Mesopotamian cities of Babylon, Persepolis, Susa, and Ecbatana, many miles from Palestine, their homeland. Cyrus, however, had just allowed some of the Jewish exiles to return to Palestine. This first wave of returnees unfortunately encountered hostility from the local inhabitants (colonists originally settled there by the Assyrian kings) and incredible opposition to their efforts to rebuild the temple and the city of Jerusalem (see Ezra 1–6). We can only imagine Satan's displeasure over the favorable turn of events for Israel with the possibility that they would return to their land and once again worship Yahweh from a reconstructed temple.

Daniel, now an old man, engaged in a period of focused intercessory prayer for the people of Israel. This was a critical time. He withdrew from the city of Babylon to somewhere along the banks of the Tigris River, the closest point of which would have been twenty miles from the city. The text says that he "mourned for three weeks" and committed himself to at least a partial fast, eating "no choice food," meat, or wine.

While he earnestly prayed for his people, he received a heavenly visitation that some Bible scholars have understood to be an appearance of the preincarnate Christ himself.[34] His vision was of a man dressed in linen, "his face like lightning, his eyes like flaming torches, his arms and legs like the gleam of burnished bronze, and his voice like the sound of a multitude" (Dan. 10:6; cf. Rev. 1:12–16). Immediately after this (Dan. 10:4–9) he is visited by an angel (Dan. 10:10ff.) sent by God to reveal what would happen to the people of Israel in the future (Dan. 10:14).

The interpreting angel then provides not only prophetic knowledge about the future, but insight into the nature of the spiritual struggle in the supernatural realm. Daniel finds out that there was and will continue to be war in heaven. Gabriel has already faced twenty-one days of struggle with the angelic prince over the Persian kingdom, but the archangel Michael came and helped provide a temporary victory. Gabriel explains that after he leaves, angelic warfare will continue not only with this Persian prince, but with the angel given responsibility over the ascending empire of Greece.

The events of Daniel 10 took place in 535 B.C. On the human plane, the Greek Empire did not surface to prominence until the rise of Alexander the Great, almost exactly two hundred years later. For the next two centuries, the Persian Empire remained the dominant power in the Ancient Near East. It is important, then, to observe that the text does not teach that Daniel, by his prayer, was able to bind, cast down, or evict the Persian prince—he remains powerfully influential for two hundred years. Of course, casting down a territorial ruler was not the objective of Daniel's prayer anyway.

What the angel reveals to Daniel only whets our appetites for more insight into the nature of the heavenly warfare. More is not given. What the Book of Daniel does impress on our hearts and our minds so clearly is the absolute sovereignty of God. He is in control of world history. God knows and has predetermined the succession of empires. He is infinitely superior to the heavenly powers; "he does as he pleases with the powers of heaven" (Dan. 4:35). Nothing will catch him by surprise. But, more important, he is building an eternal kingdom. "It will crush all those kingdoms and bring them to an end, but it will itself endure for ever" (Dan. 2:44).

We also learn from this revelation that the angelic powers are intimately involved with the earthly kingdoms. Daniel models for us earnest intercessory prayer to our Almighty Father on behalf of the people of God. This made a dramatic difference.

A Key Old Testament Assumption: Demons Are behind the Idols of the Nations

I have often heard people say that the Old Testament simply does not say much about demons. When compared to Jesus' numerous encounters with demons in the Gospels, Paul's many references to "principalities and powers," and the angelic warfare in the Book of Revelation, there are not as many explicit references to demons.

But there is much more just beneath the surface. The inspired writers of the Old Testament assumed the presence of the demonic in many places where demons and angels are not directly mentioned. We have already discussed some key verses that point to a foundational Old Testament worldview understanding that demons are behind the national and local idols and that they are closely intertwined with the affairs of an empire. This suggests that the role of the demonic is far more pronounced in the Old Testament narratives than we might initially realize on a surface level. It suggests that when the kings of Israel compromised their relationship to Yahweh and served the gods of the nations, they were actually worshiping, serving, and trafficking with demons. When Ahab went and consulted Baal-Zebub, the god of Ekron (2 Kings 1:2), who was he actually consulting? When the people of Judah "set up for themselves high places, sacred stones and Asherah poles on every high hill and under every spreading tree" (1 Kings 14:23), who was really receiving their worship? When Ahaz, king of Judah, sacrificed his son in the fire to one of the local gods, who inspired this tragic behavior and who reveled in this kind of devotion? According to the Old Testament worldview, demons were behind all of this.

New Testament Teaching about Territorial Spirits

The New Testament gives us little direct teaching about angelic patrons over cities, territories, regions, or nations. Jesus says nothing about these higher-level spirits. Neither does the Book of Acts contain explicit teaching about them.

Paul's references to the "principalities and powers" say nothing about regional or city spirits. His teaching is focused on the variety of ways evil spirits directly oppose believers. There are a few passages, however, where we might infer references to powerful spirits. One such text would be 1 Corinthians 2:6, 8, where Paul speaks of "the rulers of this age" who incited the crucifixion of Christ.[35] Another might be Paul's reference to "world rulers" *(kosmokratores)* in Ephesians 6:12, but the whole context of this passage has to do with the believers' daily direct struggle with the demonic.

There is no other explicit teaching about these territorial rulers until we come to the Book of Revelation. In Revelation 12, as in Daniel 10, there is insight given about war in heaven. Here the warfare includes Satan himself and his entire retinue of evil angels (Rev. 12:7–9). All the powers of darkness are decisively defeated by Michael and his angels. No specific mention is made, however, of territorial responsibilities of any of these angels. The epic drama carried out on this celestial stage has overtones of an endtime battle that results in the satanic forces losing their place in heaven.

The letters to the seven churches in Revelation 2 speak of angels associated with the churches in the seven cities (e.g., "To the angel of the church in Pergamum write. . . ," Rev. 2:12). Nearly all recent commentators assume that the "angels" addressed are actual angels, and thus would be a type of territorial angel. This would be particularly true in a large metropolitan city like Ephesus, where there would probably have been a network of house churches, but only one "church" and "angel" addressed. This, of course, says nothing explicit about the opposing realm of darkness and whether there is an evil angel over the city.

There is one passage that specifically connects demons to a city. Babylon, a symbolic way of referring to the city of Rome, will be a magnet for evil spirits in the last days prior to her doom and judgment:

Fallen! Fallen is Babylon the Great!
   She has become a home for demons
and a haunt for every evil spirit (Rev. 18:2).

This passage does not explicitly speak of territorial rulers, but could include them. More important, Babylon is personified as a woman in Revelation 17 and is depicted as riding on a beast. This animal represents a demonic power since it came up out of the Abyss (Rev. 17:8). The passage thus affirms and illustrates the close nexus between a city and a demonic power that influences the human rulers of the city.

Some of the Church Fathers Speak of Territorial Spirits

Explicit references to demons over territories—villages, cities, provinces, regions, or countries—are quite rare in the church fathers. No mention of territorial spirits is made in the Apostolic Fathers. Justin Martyr (2nd century A.D.) makes reference to "the power of the evil demon that dwelt in Damascus" (*Dialogue with Trypho* 78). He blames this territorial ruler for holding the Magi in bondage and inspiring them to commit all kinds of evil deeds. Justin believed that the coming of Christ somehow broke the sway of this spirit over the region, enabling three of the Magi to revolt from that dominion and come and worship Christ. In the very next chapter, Justin speaks of evil angels that dwell in the city of Tanis (or Zoan) in Egypt. He asserts, "for the princes in Tanis are evil angels" (*Dialogue with Trypho* 79).

Many of the early Christian writers, however, reflect the Old Testament teaching that the idols and so-called gods of the nations are demons. In the third chapter of his *Exhortation to the Greeks,* Clement of Alexandria bluntly speaks of "these gods of yours, who are but demons." He bemoans the bloodthirstiness of the demons animating these cults:

> Well, now, let us say in addition, what inhuman demons, and hostile to the human race, your gods were, not only delighting in the insanity of men, but gloating over human slaughter . . . that they might be able abundantly to satiate themselves with the murder of human beings (*Exhortation to the Greeks* 3.1).

He goes on to speak of human sacrifices made in honor of the Ithometan Zeus, Tauric Artemis, Dionysus, and a variety of other deities.

Minucius Felix (2nd or 3rd century) also unmasked the gods, including Saturn, Sarapis, and Jupiter, as demons. He attributed many of the supernatural aspects of their cults to the work of demons. They inspired the cultic prophecies, they lurked under the statues and images, they dwelt in the shrines, they animated the fibers of the animal entrails in divination practices, and they appeared to heal by releasing what they had bound (*Octavius* 27). The evil spirits associated with these cults would also often "creep secretly into human bodies" and cause sickness, madness, and various other maladies. He also points out how Christians have effectively ministered to these people by driving the demons out of their bodies and bringing healing.

The Christian apologist Lactantius (A.D. 240–320) elaborated on the demise of the patron angels of the nations. He relates that God had sent them to be guardians of the human race, but having fallen into corruption and now wanting to destroy humanity by keeping people away from God, they have posed as gods so "that they themselves may be worshipped, and God may not be worshipped" (*Divine Institutes* 2.15). He continues by explaining:

> But they who have revolted from the service of God, because they are enemies of the truth, and betrayers of God attempt to claim for them-

selves the name and worship of gods; not that they desire any honor. . . , nor that they may injure God, who cannot be injured, but that they may injure men, whom they strive to turn away from the worship and knowledge of the true Majesty, that they may not be able to obtain immortality (*Divine Institutes* 2.17).

Feigning to be gods, the demons are present in the temples and "are close at hand at all sacrifices." They also deceive through prodigies and enter secretly into the bodies of the worshipers. They can cause diseases, but when appeased with sacrifices and vows can then remove them. They can also send dreams full of terror (*Epitome of the Divine Institutes* 28). Christians, however, "excel in power" and can minister effectively to those who have been afflicted by these deceitful spirits (*Divine Institutes* 2.18).

The church of the first four centuries did not display much concern about the hierarchies of demonic authority that extended to spirits over territories. So many of the writers, however, share the assumption that demons were integrally involved in the various religions of the time as a means of blinding people to the revelation of the one true God in the Lord Jesus Christ. There are frequent reports of dealing with demonized people who were affiliated with these cults, but no accounts of Christian leaders attempting to cast out a high-ranking spirit over an area or a temple.

Summary

The biblical and historical evidence supports the idea that there are "territorial spirits." These are fallen angels that wield some kind of dominion over people groups, empires, countries, or cities. They exercise their supernatural power not only to bring harm and misery, but most important, to keep people from coming to a knowledge of the one true God. Historically, this has happened most commonly when these spirits create, animate, and maintain deviant religions and cults to which people give their devotion and worship.

At no time is there any intimation that these powers in any way rival God or present a serious threat to the fulfillment of his plan and purposes. God is sovereign and is infinitely more powerful than any of the spirits or angels. The Father earnestly seeks the full devotion of his people. He wants believers to call directly on him for wisdom, strength, and help.

The evidence does not appear to suggest a strategy for dealing with territorial spirits similar to what some are proposing today. In spite of the widespread consciousness of the people of God throughout history of the existence of high-ranking hostile angels, we do not find them naming the powers, rebuking them, binding them, or trying to cast them out of a region.

Responding to Strategic-Level Spiritual Warfare

Given the reality of territorial spirits and their hostility to the gospel and the people of God, how do we respond to the new strategy for dealing with them? Strategic-Level Spiritual Warfare (SLSW) is making a profound impact on international missions, the prayer movement across our land, and urban ministries. Nevertheless, many people have concerns about the strategy. In July 1993, for example, the Intercession Working Group of the Lausanne Committee on World Evangelization met in North Carolina to discuss the issue of spiritual warfare. The committee issued a statement cautioning Christian leaders about SLSW. The statement read: "We are cautious about the way in which the concept of territorial spirits is being used and look to our biblical scholars to shed more light on this recent development."[36]

From my perspective, it has been a healthy move for the Western church to think more deeply about the pervasiveness of Satan's influence at many different levels. Proponents of SLSW certainly have and will continue to stimulate the church to consider the nature of Satan's work at a macrolevel. This is assuredly a positive result especially insofar as believers are roused to a greater dependence on God and more fervent prayer.

I am also deeply encouraged by the spirit of cooperation toward reaching the lost exhibited within the prayer track of the AD 2000 & Beyond Movement. As the Day of the Lord draws near, as demonic hostility intensifies, as the vast majority of people in many countries (especially in the 10/40 Window) still do not know Christ, we desperately need to lock our arms and hearts together in fulfilling the commission the Lord has given to us. There are so many issues we can agree to disagree on while we work side by side laboring for the sake of the gospel.

It is clear to me that what motivates the various advocates of SLSW is a passion for the lost. There is an overwhelming desire to see cities and countries that have long been resistant to the gospel finally crack and a flood of people come to know the Lord Jesus Christ. The 10/40 Window appears to be a special concern to many proponents of SLSW. I am deeply inspired by what Peter Wagner says in his recent book, *Warfare Prayer:*

God's highest priority is evangelism, calling out a people who will honor and glorify His name. This is my highest priority as well. I have given over 35 years of active ministry to missions, evangelism and church growth. If I have 10 more years to serve God, I want them to make a difference in the number of souls that are saved around the world. My interest in warfare prayer is directly proportional to its effectiveness in enhancing evangelism.[37]

What about "Discerning," "Naming," and "Praying Down" Territorial Spirits?

Although territorial spirits are not prominently featured in Scripture, there is enough evidence to say that the Bible clearly teaches the reality of evil spirit entities assigned to geopolitical units. The Bible also seems to suggest that these high-ranking angels are behind the national idols. We gain little insight from Scripture, however, into how these ruling angels organize other spirits under themselves, how they relate to one another (especially when one nation goes to war with another), and a host of other questions.

Of even greater significance for the issue confronting us is the fact that the Bible nowhere narrates, describes, or instructs us on how, or even whether, we are to engage these high-ranking territorial spirits. This has led some to say that we have no authority or responsibility to take on these forces; God will sovereignly deal with them (perhaps with his angels) as he deems fit. Others in the spiritual warfare movement, such as advocates of SLSW, find inspiration in Jesus' words to the Seventy: "I have given you authority . . . to overcome *all* the power of the enemy" (Luke 10:19). They would contend that Scripture's silence on the issue of engagement and strategy by no means implies that we should not take on these territorial rulers as we undertake the mission Jesus gave to us.

Still, the silence of Scripture on the issue of strategy is quite evident. When we consider that the New Testament records the spread of the gospel into pagan lands (Syria, Asia Minor, Greece, and Italy) where idols and occultism held sway, it is very surprising to find no mention of a strategy that stresses discerning, naming, and praying down territorial spirits. This observation is made all the more conspicuous by the fact that none of the early church fathers mention anything at all about discerning, naming, or praying against territorial spirits. They believe in the reality of territorial spirits; they frequently talk about the significant role of exorcism in the early church; but, a strategy for taking on territorial spirits is absent. *These observations do not instantly make this facet of the strategic-level spiritual warfare strategy wrong or unbiblical, but it should cause us to pause and reflect on just how important or key this new strategy is.*

God Directs His Angels for Us

Almost all advocates of SLSW cite Daniel 10 in support of the strategy. As I have already shown, the passage does support the notion of angelic beings over nations, but actually models something quite different from what many proponents of SLSW would say. I think it is very instructive to observe that Daniel had no idea of what was happening in the spiritual realm as he prayed. *There is no indication that Daniel was attempting to discern territorial spirits, pray against them, or cast them down.* In fact, Daniel only learned about what had happened in the angelic realm *after* the warring in heaven. Furthermore, God grants the vision to Daniel only in response to his piety and faith, not because he was seeking this information. The angelic messenger told Daniel: "Since the first day that you set your mind to gain understanding and to humble yourself before your God, your words were heard, and I have come in response to them" (Dan. 10:12).[38] It seems to me that it is God himself who sovereignly directs his angels to war against the territorial rulers. Our role is to walk humbly and obediently before our God, bringing our needs and the needs of the people of God before him in prayer. We can take great comfort in the fact that as we pray and intercede for people, God can direct his angels to fight key battles in the heavenly places on our behalf. Perhaps this is just one of the ways his promise in Psalm 91:11 is fulfilled: "For he will command his angels concerning you."

Focusing on People: Minister to the Demonized

Exorcism appears to be one of the ways that the early Christians helped people who came to Christ from a background in the pagan cults. This was done in a context of care within the Christian community where these new believers were receiving instruction in the Scriptures and mentoring from mature Christians who would help them develop a Christian lifestyle. There are many sources from the mid-second century on that mention the exorcism of new believers prior to or in conjunction with their baptism.[39]

I have recently become fascinated by the early 300s conversion of Firmicus Maternus, a Roman who had been involved in astrology and mystery religions and came to know Jesus Christ around the age of forty. He subsequently wrote a book titled *The Error of Pagan Religions*. He sets out to demonstrate that the pagan cults are demonic counterfeits. In describing the cult of Sarapis, he says, "At this statue, just as at those of others, the foul spirits of demons gather." Maternus thinks that the demons are particularly attracted to the blood of the sacrificed victims. He never speculates, however, that Sarapis is the name of a powerful territorial ruling spirit. He merely emphasizes how the cult attracts a horde of demons. He then mentions that the former devotees of the cult had been freed from bondage to demonic spirits through the ministry of exorcism.[40] To put it in contemporary terms, it seems that Firmicus was into deliverance ministry but was not into strategic-level spiritual warfare. Of all Christian leaders in his age, he would seem to be one of the most likely candidates for advocating such a method, given his pre-Christian background. Yet he never speaks of praying down Sarapis or Mithras in Rome.

Avoiding a Compromise with the Spirit Realm

The emphasis on attempting to discern and name territorial spirits reflects the assumption that if you can somehow get the name of the demonic ruler, then you have more power over it. Wagner explicitly states that it will "make them more vulnerable to attack."[41] This was the common assumption of people involved in the occultic arts in antiquity. They believed that if you could identify the name of a spirit-being, then you had a means of control over that entity.[42] It seems to me that Paul wrote precisely against this kind of mind-set when he reaffirmed to the Ephesians that Christ had been raised, "far above all rule and authority and power and dominion, *and every name that is named*" (Eph. 1:21 NASB, italics mine). Why do we need to find the name of a territorial ruler if we are in union with a Lord who has been exalted high above every conceivable power, regardless of its name or title?

Praying versus Commanding or Rebuking

The very idea of "warfare prayer" is misleading. As the prayer statement for the AD 2000 & Beyond Movement affirms, "the essence of all prayer is a personal relationship with God made possible through the redemption purchased by the blood of Jesus Christ on the cross."[43] We engage in prayer with humility and respect for our awesome God. Because of the nature of the battle we face, however, we may ask God to fight for us, defeat our enemies, and advance his kingdom purpose.

To challenge principalities and powers, however, is not prayer. This is exercising authority in the name of Jesus Christ to directly address and rebuke them. This is an aggressive confrontation of the evil spirits that is not properly called prayer. The real issue continues to be whether we have the authority to take territorial spirits on at all in some kind of direct fashion.

This distinction is often confused in the SLSW literature. Writers often speak of praying over a city in the same breath that they tell of confronting the territorial demons, but these are two different activities. It is the latter that is in question. This is why I think it is inappropriate to speak of "praying down" or "praying against" a demonic ruler when we really mean exercising authority in Christ to directly command the spirit to leave.

The Issue of Authority

I can find no scriptural evidence suggesting that we have the right or authority to "serve notice," "evict," or "bind" spirits over cities, regions, or nations. This is perhaps the central issue to the debate about SLSW.[44] Wagner would say that the authority of the believer extends to the territorial rulers whereas I, and other Christian leaders such as John Wimber, limit the authority of the believer to dealing with demons afflicting individuals.[45]

When Jesus spoke of giving the Seventy authority "to overcome all the power of the enemy" (Luke 10:19), this did not extend to angelic rulers over cities and nations. This is made clear when the Seventy exclaim to the Lord with excitement, "even the demons submit to us in your name" (Luke 10:17). They were ministering to people afflicted in various ways by demons. And this is what they continued to do after the day of Pentecost. There is no hint in the text that the Seventy were casting demons out of villages, cities, or temples. The authority of the believer with regard to demonic spirits is depicted in figure 3.1.

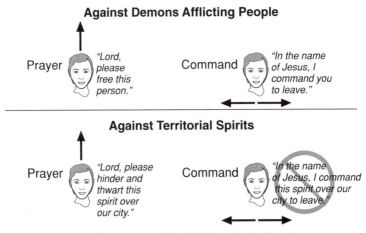

Against Demons Afflicting People

Prayer — *"Lord, please free this person."*

Command — *"In the name of Jesus, I command you to leave."*

Against Territorial Spirits

Prayer — *"Lord, please hinder and thwart this spirit over our city."*

Command — *"In the name of Jesus, I command this spirit over our city to leave."*

Fig. 3.1 Extent of the Believer's Authority

Figure 3.1 illustrates that prayer and appeal to God are always appropriate. Peter urges us to cast all our anxiety upon our Lord because he cares so deeply about us (1 Peter 5:7). In the very next verse, he speaks of the devil as our enemy, who prowls around like a roaring lion seeking someone to devour (1 Peter 5:8). If we are concerned about the influence of territorial spirits in our neighborhood, city, or region, we have every right to pray to our God about this. We can appeal to him to hinder and thwart their activities. The diagram also shows that believers do have the authority to utter a word of command to a demonic spirit that is afflicting the life of an individual. This may include a demonic spirit attacking me individually, or it may refer to me helping and ministering to another person. The fourth panel, however, reveals the limitation. We do not have the right to directly command a demon to leave a city, territory, or country. Where sin is present, Satan and his spirits have a claim. This is why Jesus did not cast out the devil from Jerusalem, Judea, or from the entire Roman Empire and send him packing to Neptune or Pluto during his earthly ministry. Jesus defeated Satan by making atonement for sin by his blood shed on the cross. We defeat the devil through the application of the blood of Jesus.

Some Points of Hesitation

1. *Some biblical passages sound a note of caution.* Passages such as Jude 8 and 2 Peter 2:10–11, in spite of the fact that they are notoriously difficult to interpret, would seem to caution the believer against ever directly rebuking a high-ranking angelic power. Second Peter 2:10–11 is probably the clearer of the two texts. In this passage, Peter is criticizing a group of people in the churches of Asia Minor who were "not afraid to slander celestial beings." It is clear that Peter is not criticizing a core of earnest Christians who are trying to take authority over evil principalities and powers in their efforts to advance the gospel in their regions of the country. Peter is denouncing "false prophets" (2:1) who introduced destructive teachings and advocated a form of Christian freedom that evidently justified their indulgence in sexual immorality, drunkenness, and other compromises of Christian virtue. No one really knows for sure how they were railing on spirit powers,[46] but the point is that Peter cautions them that "even [good] angels, although they are stronger and more powerful, do not bring slanderous accusations against such beings in the presence of the Lord" (2:11). This should make us think twice about *directly rebuking* a territorial spirit.

2. *We do not find Jesus, John, Peter, James, or Paul ever attempting to take on a territorial spirit.* Why don't we find Jesus railing against the territorial

prince over Jerusalem who blinded the eyes of the Pharisees, scribes, and religious leaders—so much so that they successfully conspired to put to death the Son of God? Why don't we see Peter, after he was filled with the Holy Spirit at Pentecost, evict the territorial ruler over Jerusalem? The Spirit empowered Peter to preach the kingdom of God and the gospel of the Lord Jesus Christ. Many responded, but a short time later Peter was in jail. In fact, this first center for Christianity experienced increasing persecution, causing many believers to flee from the city. The situation grew so bad by the time of the outbreak of the Jewish war that the entire Christian population fled from the city to Pella in A.D. 66. If Jesus and the apostles did not evict Satan from a city, are we not somewhat presumptuous to think we can by properly implementing a new method? Given the characteristics of the city of Rome in the first century, it seems to me that Paul would have had ample reason to cast out a spirit of *porneia,* or greed, or pride, or destruction from the city. He did, however, send a request back to his intercessors while he was imprisoned in the city. He asks the readers of Ephesians to pray *for boldness,* that he would make known the mystery of the gospel boldly as he ought (Eph. 6:19–20).

3. *We do not have the right to tell a spirit to leave if it has an open invitation to stay.* In other words, if the people of the city have not put away their sinful thoughts and practices, the minions of the enemy would have a legal right to remain. Some in the movement recognize the difficulty of this point and have quit using the language of "casting the spirit out" or "bringing it down" in favor of "weakening its grip." Still, it does not follow that, if Christians rail on an evil principality or a power, that its grip is any less strong if the people it holds in bondage defiantly continue their evil ways in rejection of God. When a Christian leader commanded the spirits over San Francisco to leave a few years ago, there was no sign that they left. The people of God need to do hand-to-hand combat on the streets by proclaiming the message of deliverance and ministering to those victimized by sin and the demonic.

4. *Paul's power encounters do not illustrate taking authority over territorial spirits.* Accounts of Paul's ministry in Acts such as his confrontation with Elymas (Acts 13:6–12) and his exorcism of the young girl with a spirit of divination (Acts 16:16–18) do not illustrate SLSW. In neither of these instances does Paul try to identify a ruling spirit nor does Luke give any indication that a territorial spirit had possessed Elymas or the slave girl. Of course we have no way of knowing the "rank" of the spirit behind Elymas or the slave girl. Because Elymas had such influence over the proconsul of the entire island, it might be possible to assume that it was a

high-ranking spirit. The point, however, is that Paul did not come to Cyprus with a strategy of trying to discern the territorial spirit and bring it down as a prelude to his work of evangelism. He encountered demonic opposition along the way as he focused on bringing the gospel to the island. Based on his authority in Christ, he dealt with it.

5. *Paul's ministry in Ephesus does not illustrate the binding of a territorial spirit.* Many advocates of SLSW point to Artemis/Diana as the territorial spirit over Ephesus that Paul effectively cast down, resulting in his fruitful ministry in that key city of Asia Minor (Acts 19). This celebrated case of tearing down a territorial stronghold, again, does not seem to me to illustrate or validate this aspect of the methodology of SLSW. For one thing, Luke never identifies this goddess as a manifestation of the major territorial spirit over the area. Neither is there any indication that Paul himself regarded "Artemis" as the high-ranking spirit over Ephesus and the west coast of Asia Minor, nor do we see Paul confronting or instructing his converts to engage the territorial spirit behind the Artemis worship. *I am sure, however, that Paul was convinced that there was all kinds of demonic activity associated with the Artemis cult.* Accordingly, he seems to have been busily engaged in "ground-level spiritual warfare" (Acts 19:11–12). We must remember too that there were up to fifty other deities worshiped in Ephesus during Paul's time, not to mention all of the occultic activity (i.e., the magical practices). What Luke stresses in his account of Paul's ministry in Ephesus is Paul's "evangelistic teaching" (in the synagogue and then in a lecture hall) and his "deliverance" work.

6. *Ephesians 3:10 is not a mandate to "serve notice" to the territorial spirits.* Some have erroneously reached the conclusion that we have the responsibility of serving notice to the powers based on this verse, which reads: "His intent was that now, through the church, the manifold wisdom of God should be made known to the rulers and authorities in the heavenly realms." This verse, however, does not teach that God has commissioned us to proclaim a message to the principalities and powers.[47] The main verb is the *passive* voice of "to make known" *(gnōrizō):* "the manifold wisdom of God is made known to the principalities and authorities in the heavenly places through the church." This refers to the fact that *the very existence* of the church reveals God's wisdom to the powers. Those who use this text to support taking authority against the high-ranking powers also lose sight of the subject of the verb in the sentence: the manifold wisdom of God. It is not a message of eviction that we are responsible to proclaim, nor is it a biblical warrant to tell them to leave. The high-ranking angelic powers are made aware of God's incredible wisdom.

There was a common Jewish understanding that the angelic realm is carefully watching the unfolding of events on earth and God's dealings with people. This is why angels were often called "watchers" in the first century. Paul spoke of this in 1 Corinthians 4:9 when he described himself as a "spectacle" to the angels as he suffered as an apostle.

This verse really points to the amazing drama of how God brought salvation to his people in spite of intense demonic hostility. It is the story of how God foiled the wisdom of the demonic powers who thought they could end God's redemptive plans by inciting the political and religious leaders to put Jesus to death (1 Cor. 2:6–8). Jesus' death on the cross, however, turned out to be God's very means of dealing with the most important problem of all—how to deal with the issue of sin. God did not leave Jesus in the tomb, but raised him and exalted him high above every rule and authority. Jesus has assumed the position of "head" of "his body," the church, which the principalities and powers now see actively redeeming the lost world. *What remarkable wisdom!* No demonic plan can foil what God has purposed to do. The very existence of the church makes that abundantly clear to the powers.

7. *Matthew 16:19 is not a mandate for believers to bind territorial spirits.* A common assumption among people practicing SLSW is that Jesus' words, "whatever you bind on earth will be bound in heaven," are an authorization to believers to bind down the spirits over an area. Thus, an evangelist coming into a city might declare, "By the authority of Christ, I bind you spirit of idolatry; I bind you, you spirits of greed, hatred, and witchcraft!" But this is not what Jesus is teaching his disciples in this passage.

Jesus is granting "the keys of the kingdom" to Peter as a representative of the apostles and of all authentic believers. A "key" is used to unlock or lock a door. In this case the doorway is entry into the kingdom of God. The apostles and the believers throughout the centuries have possessed the "keys" that would open the doorway of salvation and thereby grant admission into a relationship with the living God. What is this "key" that has such extraordinary power—the power of life and death? That key is nothing other than the message of the forgiveness of sin available through Christ, the Messiah, who gave his life so that we may have eternal life. In an excellent article entitled "The Power of the Keys," Fuller Theological Seminary emeritus professor Geoffrey Bromiley writes,

> All confessing believers may thus exercise the "power" of the keys as they offer forgiveness to others through faith in the crucified and risen Jesus. . . . On the basis of Christ's saving work and the divine commission, min-

isters of God's Word can boldly state that those who respond in faith to the gospel will have forgiveness, whereas those who do not will still be under the divine judgment unless and until they convert and believe.[48]

Using the keys, therefore, has nothing to do with confronting high-ranking demonic powers. It has to do with offering people entry into the kingdom of God (unlocking) or with the issue of church discipline (locking), which Jesus elaborates in Matthew 18:18 (see also John 20:23).

Conclusion: It appears, then, that we bear no responsibility for discerning, naming, or tearing down territorial strongholds. We can trust our powerful and providential Father to deal with these wicked beings as he wills.

Are There Examples of SLSW in Church History?

As I have thought of this strategy in light of the testimony of many church fathers who have used a lot of ink writing about the workings of demons, I have found no mention of or even allusion to anything close to praying against territorial spirits. When one reads, for instance, the *Shepherd of Hermas,* Ignatius, *Epistle of Barnabas,* Justin Martyr, Tertullian, Hippolytus, Cyprian, Origen, Irenaeus, and many others, one finds numerous references to dealing with demonized people, exorcisms, and the fact that demons are closely associated with idolatry, magic, and the pagan religions. But nothing is found illustrating the practice of individuals in the church praying against demons over territories.

In his most recent book on SLSW, Wagner claims to have found a few examples. He points to a legend regarding the apostle John confronting the goddess Artemis of Ephesus (4th century A.D.) and accounts from the ministries of Gregory Thaumaturgus (A.D. 213–270), Martin of Tours (A.D. 316–397), Benedict of Nursia (A.D. 480–550), and Boniface, "the Apostle of Germany" (A.D. 680–754).[49]

Wagner points to a fascinating story in an apocryphal book titled *The Acts of John.*[50] There is one passage in the book that purports to describe a major confrontation between the apostle John and the cult of Artemis. During a dedication festival for the temple, John put on black clothing and went into the temple, where he chastised the worshipers for their unswerving commitment to Artemis and failure to devote themselves to the one true God. He then directly confronts the demonic spirit that he perceives to be behind the cult, saying, "now let the demon that is here take flight" (*Acts of John* 41). At this, the altar split into many pieces and half the temple was destroyed. The priest of the cult was killed when the roof collapsed on him. John then implored the people to flee the cult and acknowledge the living and true God. The people immediately went and destroyed what was left of the temple and turned their hearts to God, confessing their error in following Artemis (*Acts of John* 42–45).

If true, the story represents a remarkable illustration of successful strategic-level spiritual warfare. As wonderful as the story is, however, it does not represent what really happened. First, as one of the seven wonders of the ancient world, the temple of the Ephesian Artemis was an immense and impressive marble edifice. There are a number of independent historical sources that attest to it standing long after the apostle John's death. These texts date the destruction of the temple around A.D. 268 during a Gothic incursion.[51] Second, the *Acts of John* contains many other legends that have little claim to historical accuracy. For instance, the book relates a tale about a time when John and his traveling companions spent the night at an inn, where they were terribly bothered by bed bugs (*Acts of John* 61). None of the party could sleep and when John could stand it no longer, he gave firm orders to the bed bugs to leave their home for the night and to keep their distance from the servants of God. No longer troubled by the bugs, the group slept soundly the rest of the night. When they arose in the morning, one of John's companions found the bugs all huddled by the door of the room. John then told them that since they had behaved themselves for the night and obeyed his command, that they could now return to the bed. Immediately the bugs scurried back to the bed.

The New Testament Apocrypha has been widely recognized by Christian leaders throughout the centuries as full of legendary and unhistorical tales. This is why the leaders of the churches did not allow them to be read. In fact, the fifth session of the Nicene Council of 787 went so far as to make the following pronouncement on the *Acts of John:* "No one is to copy (this book): not only so, but we consider that it deserves to be consigned to the fire."[52] This does not mean that there is absolutely nothing in the book that is of historical value. Obviously there was an Artemis cult in Ephesus and there is corroborating tradition that the apostle John lived in the city. It is impossible, however, that this account of the temple's destruction corresponds with historical reality. For this reason, I believe it is very important for advocates of SLSW to discontinue relating this story as what really took place.

After nearly three centuries of persecution, it was a time for rejoicing when a Christian actually became the emperor of the Roman Empire. With Constantine the Great (A.D. 306–337) a whole new era had begun. Christians became the dominating political force. But this raised some significant new questions. If the ancient enemy and his demonic hordes were really the animating force behind the pagan cults, how should Christians respond to the cults, especially now that they had the political power to effect change? Many believers advocated tolerance and suggested winning them to Christ through the demonstration and proclamation of the gospel. Others, however, drawing inspiration from the biblical kings, pushed for the destruction of the idol temples and even the persecution of pagan priests and worshipers.

Constantine himself practiced tolerance to the pagan cults and did not advocate persecuting the adherents or forbidding these ancient religions. Many of his successors did not share this opinion. Theodosius I (A.D. 379–395) was one of the worst. He gained the reputation of being the final suppressor of paganism. Under his reign, more pagan temples were destroyed in Egypt, Greece, Italy, and Asia Minor than during the reign of any other emperor. A number of Christians exercised violent force against the temples, confiscating the property and razing the buildings to the ground. In Gaul (France), Martin of Tours led the forceful destruction of many temples and cultic images. This was regularly done in the face of stringent opposition from the pagan population of a village or city. The victims often became so enraged that they struck back in fury at the Christians and murdered them. This was not evangelism by persuasive proclamation of the gospel in the power of the Spirit, but evangelism by sledgehammer and force.

Many Christian leaders spoke out against such destructive and violent strategies. John Chrysostom pleaded, "Christians are not to destroy error by force and violence, but should work the salvation of men by persuasion, instruction, and love." This was sound counsel and remains so today. Augustine also appealed to Christians not to forcefully destroy the idols of their pagan neighbors. He said, "Let us first obliterate the idols in the hearts of the heathen, and once they become Christians they will either themselves invite us to the execution of so good a work (the destruction of the idols), or anticipate us in it. Now we must pray for them and not exasperate them."[53]

Not only did Martin of Tours engage in destructive and unwelcome attacks on pagan cultic images and temples in the name of Christ; so did Benedict of Nursia and Boniface. All three adamantly believed that they were tearing down powerful demonic strongholds, but they did so without the consent of the people they were trying to reach with the gospel. No doubt many of the pagans were surprised when these Christian leaders were not struck dead by the gods and were thereby stimulated to consider the claims of the gospel. But the end does not justify the means. Would it not have been more appropriate to first lead these people to

Christ, then encourage them to destroy their own cultic paraphernalia (as Paul did in Acts 19), and, ultimately, to tear down their temples? This kind of violence was an ugly stain on Christian history and one that we need to remember as we consider the future.

By recalling this era, I am not at all suggesting that any proponent of SLSW favors any form of physical violence against temples, cultic images, or any occultic center. I have never heard even a whisper that is reminiscent of the strategy of the post-Constantinian church. I raise this because a recent book espousing SLSW lifts up Martin of Tours, Benedict of Nursia, and Boniface as examples of Christian leaders who effectively practiced warfare against territorial spirits. These Christians certainly perceived themselves as doing battle with demons, but not in a way that we could conscientiously endorse today.

The one example that Wagner cites that merits attention is the ministry of a third-century Christian leader in Asia Minor, Gregory Thaumaturgus ("Gregory the Wonderworker"). The biography of Gregory was written about a century after his death by one of his admirers, Gregory of Nyssa (*Patrologia Graecae* 46.893–958). In the biography, Gregory of Nyssa tells a dramatic story of Gregory's battle with demons (913D–924C). In fact, he gives it the heading: "Gregory the Great begins his heroic combat against the demons." The story is set at the time when Gregory Thaumaturgus approached his hometown of Neocaesarea and, because he needed to find immediate shelter from a torrential rainstorm, spent the night in a pagan temple. Because Gregory made the sign of the cross upon entering and spent the night praying and singing hymns, the demons who usually revealed oracles to the priests of the cult fled and were too terrified to return. Eventually the local priest and many of the citizens of this city conceded that the power of God manifested in Gregory was greater than the power of the demons. Many people soon became Christians—so many, in fact, that one ancient writer says that only seventeen remained who were not Christians by the time Gregory died.

Wagner contends that this is an illustrious example of successful strategic-level spiritual warfare. He suggests that the principality who was over the temple "was presumably a well-known territorial spirit."[54] Gregory directly engaged him in spiritual warfare and the principality was defeated, resulting in a wonderful increase of conversions in the city.

There are at least four difficulties, however, with Wagner's analysis of this episode as an example of SLSW: (1) The text itself does not identify one ruling spirit, but simply and consistently speaks in the plural of demons who were involved in the cult. In fact, at the outset of the account, the author states, "the whole region was under the grip of demons." He bases this conclusion on the fact that Christianity had not yet penetrated the area and "the entire city and surrounding area was filled with pagan altars, sacred places, and all the people were devoted to images." (2) The text gives no indication that Gregory engaged in spiritual mapping, discerning the name of the territorial ruler, or taking authority in the name of Jesus and commanding it to leave. It appears that simply the presence of Gregory in the temple area frightened the demons and they left. Furthermore, there is no indication that this was the main pagan temple of the region. As we have already pointed out, this was merely one among many. (3) The initial results were actually quite negative. When the priest of the cult could no longer get prophetic inspiration from the demons, he threatened to use force against Gregory or to bring him before the local magistrates. The magistrates subsequently acquired the support of an imperial edict from the Roman emperor Decius and a proclamation from the provincial governor that forced Gregory to leave the city and hide in the mountains.[55] (4) It is difficult to separate fact from fiction in Gregory of Nyssa's account. As with many of the tales in the New Testament Apocrypha, there is legendary material in this biography (all of which came to Gregory of Nyssa in oral form).[56] One of the more dubious accounts in the biography is a story of Gregory handling a dispute between two brothers who were arguing over who had the legal right to a particular lake (924C–929A). Gregory responded by miraculously drying up the lake and, thus, effectively ending any debate.

The episode does, however, illustrate the widely held early Christian belief that demonic spirits were profoundly involved in the pagan cults and opposed the spread of the gospel through them. The story also shows that prayer, hymn-singing, and confidence in God cause demons to shudder (see 916A and B).

There are still no examples in church history that I have seen illustrating a Christian leader taking authority in the name of Christ, directly addressing a ruling spirit over a "territory" (an empire, province, region, city, or village), and commanding it to leave.

If It Works, It Can't Be Wrong! Or Can It?

How can you argue with results? If thousands of people are coming to Christ in Argentina and Guatemala where evangelists and Christian leaders have taken authority in Jesus' name over the ruling principalities, how could their approach be wrong or misguided?

We must remember that railing against territorial spirits is not the only thing that Christians have done in Guatemala, Argentina, or numerous other places where the church is growing. As we reflect on the success of the gospel in penetrating an area, we need to be sure that we take into account all the factors. If a group of praying Christians has reached a point where they are attempting to discern and pray down hostile powers in their effort to reach a city for Christ, many other crucial ingredients are already in place. They have organized into prayer meeting groups, they have prayed for the lost and for each other, they have sought and worked for unity among themselves, they have dealt with issues of personal sin, they have begun sharing the gospel, they have planned outreach events, and perhaps taken many other important steps. There are also other sociological factors that make people ripe for the gospel. Prior to the explosive growth of the church in Argentina, for example, the country had faced a series of major catastrophes, including losing the Falklands War, oppressive military rule, economic stagnation, and runaway inflation.[57] It is also important to note that churches and evangelists in Argentina that are not practicing SLSW are also experiencing extraordinary growth and responsiveness to the gospel.[58] As we consider what factors led to the explosive growth of churches in particular areas, we need to have a wholistic perspective.

What about a City with a Covenant Relationship with a God or Goddess?

There are many accounts in the missiological and spiritual warfare literature of cities in the non-Western world where the citizens have taken some kind of vow to a local deity. These vows and dedications are often renewed each year in ritual celebrations. Would it not be appropriate on these occasions to exercise spiritual authority in Christ and command this territorial ruler to be gone or at least loosen its grip?

The apostle Paul found himself in this kind of situation repeatedly as he took the gospel to the Gentiles throughout the Mediterranean world. The city of Ephesus, for instance, did indeed have an official covenant bond with the goddess Artemis.[59] As I have already observed, however, we have no indication that Paul attempted to "pray down" or cast out the high-ranking demons associated with this cult. But he sure got his fill of dealing with demonized persons in the city and he aggressively proclaimed the gospel in every conceivable venue.

In his recent book about angels (both good and evil), Old Testament scholar Duane Garrett confidently affirms the reality of the demonic connection to pagan religions. He observes: "Missionaries must recognize that real demons are behind the religion of the tribes to whom they preach. They must expect to face genuine conflict with the spirits, pray intelligently and seriously for the breaking of the demonic power, and be prepared to face hostile reactions from the devotees of the spirits."[60] There is no question that Christians should pray. This involves asking the Holy Spirit how we should pray and appealing to God to break the compelling power of the demonic deception among the people whose lives are touched by the false religion. In some places of ministry, it will be abundantly obvious where the devotion of the people lies. Just as Artemis/Diana enjoyed a covenant bond with the citizens of Ephesus, Maximón appears to have had a similar relationship to the people of Altiplano, Guatemala. We can and should pray fervently for God to fight the heavenly battles for us and at the same time ask him to lift the veil of blindness from the eyes of people in the village or city. Yet, for the reasons I have already discussed, I do not think that God has authorized us to stand on a hilltop or near a temple and directly address a territorial ruler, commanding it to leave.

What about Spiritual Mapping?

If there appears to be no warrant for discerning, naming, and casting out territorial spirits, what role is there for spiritual mapping? For some, spiritual mapping is the process of identifying the precise boundaries of the jurisdiction of a territorial spirit. This district is then marked out on a map, along with the zones of authority for every other demonic ruler that has been identified.

I have seen a number of these mapping projects in which a city or regional map is covered with triangles, diamonds, and squares that are thought to represent the assignments of various high-ranking demonic powers. Sometimes these are discerned by drawing lines between key points on the map—points that indicate the location of a cult center, the site of a violent crime, a pornography shop, a Masonic lodge, a totem pole, or even a rock outcropping on a hill that was once thought to have spiritual significance. The lines themselves are often thought to represent corridors of demonic traffic and are, thus, dangerous places to be. One SLSW advocate has actually been drawing extensively on the occultic concept of "ley lines" as a means of discerning the networks of spiritual power in a territory.[61] This expression is commonly used in modern occultism and psychic research to refer to "alignments of ancient megaliths, dolmens, and stone circles, whose patterns are said to constitute grids of 'power,' or ley-lines."[62] For the spiritual warriors, however, the "ley lines" represent demonic highways that intersect to form elaborate grids of power. Within each triangular, square, or rectangular cell on the grid is a territorial ruler who is the strategic opponent to do battle with. When this principality is brought down, the lesser demons go with it. These maps then serve as key intelligence information for intercessors who feel called to this kind of high-level warfare. They believe that they have the responsibility to move out and evict or bind these territorial spirits.

This kind of mapping explicitly draws on non-Christian understandings of occultic power. The concept of "ley lines," in particular, depends on tribal and occultic religious beliefs about the movements of spirit powers. At the minimum, this is an exercise of imagination and incredible speculation. At the worst, it is a dangerous syncretistic adaptation of occultic beliefs that only plays into the hands of the Evil One. I find no warrant for this kind of mapping and the consequent reviling of the high-ranking spirits.[63]

I am convinced, however, that there is a significant role for "spiritual mapping" in the way that it is described and carried out by George Otis Jr. As we pointed out earlier, Otis defines mapping as the creation of a spiritual profile of a city or area based on careful research.[64] The purpose of this profile is to guide intercessors as they pray for the people in this location—people whose eyes have been satanically blinded to the truth of Christ when the gospel is proclaimed. Otis wants Christians to be able to pray intelligently and specifically, yet he does not explicitly advocate the practice of attempting to cast demons out of a city or even learn their names.[65]

It is biblically sound to encourage people to pray with specificity and this is the common practice of the church. Who doesn't give time in small group prayer for sharing specific requests? What church doesn't ask its missionaries to send prayer letters so its members can pray intelligently? In my estimation, the October 1995 campaign to pray for the "100 Gateway Cities" of the 10/40 Window is the kind of strategy we need to encourage. It greatly heightened the awareness and participation of many Christians in the mission of the church to the places of greatest spiritual darkness. I know of a number of churches who have adopted cities in the 10/40 Window and are now focusing their efforts and prayer on the spread of the gospel in those cities. Spiritual mapping information facilitates this greatly.[66] Awareness of the means by which the enemy has kept these peoples from a knowledge of the truth helps the church pray more specifically. As the Lord instructed us to pray, "deliver us from evil/the evil one" (Matt. 6:13), out of love we can pray for those in bondage to evil, "Lord, deliver them from the evil one."

The kind of in-depth research that Otis calls for in spiritual mapping can be helpful in at least two other ways that do not seem to be emphasized in the writings of SLSW advocates or in his own books: most important, this information needs to be used in developing contextually relevant training programs for new believers. Closely related to this is the later stage of developing a contextualized theology for the nation.

In the apostle Paul's day, new Christians had major worldview shifts to make in light of their newfound faith in Jesus Christ. For example, their discipleship in the faith led them to the realization that

- there are not many gods, but only one true God
- our faith is not wrapped up in the alignment and movements of the stars, but God has chosen us before the foundation of the world
- we no longer have to worry about a god that acts capriciously; the one true God acts out of love, righteousness, and mercy
- Jesus is not a lesser god or an exalted mediator figure (like Hermes, Hekate, or one of the *paredroi* [helper spirits]); he is the Son of God and the one true Lord
- we no longer approach deity with incantations, sacrifices, and rituals but view him as a caring Father through the Lord Jesus Christ

The apostle demonstrates a keen awareness of the areas of the new Christians' belief structure and behavior patterns that need to change and communicates theology in a relevant manner. Extensive teaching was of paramount importance to Paul's missionary strategy. He evidently spent many hours every day teaching his new converts about Jesus and the kingdom of God. How else can we explain, for example, the high level of knowledge on the part of the Thessalonians he assumes when he wrote his first letter to them (less than a year after he had planted the church there)? Given that he was there only a couple of months, he must have held many intense teaching sessions.

The results of the research carried out under what is called "spiritual mapping" will have a vital role to play for knowing what kinds of things to teach new believers. This would seem incredibly important for people who come to know Christ in the 10/40 Window. They have much to rethink in light of their newfound faith in Jesus Christ.

What about "Identificational Repentance"?

The raw nerve of racism in its abundant forms will cause many people to listen carefully to what John Dawson has to say in his new book, *Healing America's Wounds.* His previous book, *Taking Our Cities for God,* sold over a quarter million copies. Joe C. Aldrich, president of Multnomah School of the Bible, has said, "*Healing America's Wounds* ought to be required reading. John Dawson's call to repentance and reconciliation is a message that needs to be implemented."[67]

In his first line of the foreword to Wagner's collection of essays on fighting territorial spirits, Dawson comments, "I'm not really interested in territorial spirits. What is God up to, that is the question."[68] This does not mean that Dawson does not take seriously the reality and presence of territorial spirits; rather, he deemphasizes the need to identify who they are and cast them down in the terms described by Wagner and Jacobs. Dawson's greatest concern is in treating the corporate issues of sin that, in his words, attract demons like flies to a gaping wound.

In a social climate of Western individualism, Dawson's attempt to make us aware of corporate responsibility is a welcome biblical emphasis. While it is correct to say that we are individually responsible and accountable for our own iniquity, sinful traits and tendencies are passed on from one generation to the next. To deny that we resemble our parents—for good or for ill—is to deceive ourselves. Similarly, to deny that we are infected by ungodly attitudes in our social and cultural context can be equally deluding. I believe that it is important for Christians to carefully search their hearts and deal with sinful tendencies that they have in common with their families and with the larger social group from which they have come. Confession and repentance through the empowering work of the Holy Spirit are certainly God's prescribed remedy. It also seems appropriate, when an entire community of Christians recognizes their collective transgression and experiences sorrow for sin, for a leader to function as a representative of that community, confessing and repenting on behalf of his people to the offended parties or someone representing the offended parties.

Many advocates of "identificational repentance" see more to it than this. They contend that a profound spiritual transaction takes place when we identify with the corporate sins of a group and confess them. This is brought out clearly in the position statement on the philosophy of prayer for world evangelization for the AD 2000 & Beyond Movement's United Prayer Track:

> Responsible spiritual mapping will frequently uncover sins of a nation or city which have been committed in the past, sometimes generations ago, and which have become strongholds of the forces of darkness, allowing them to keep multitudes in physical misery and spiritual captivity. When we corporately confess those sins of our nation through what many

are calling "identificational repentance," *they can be remitted through Jesus' blood shed on the cross, and the strongholds can be removed.* [69]

What is striking about this statement is the assumption that there is an efficacy of proxy confession in the application of Jesus' blood for forgiving sin. A surface reading of this statement would lead one to believe that Christians can apply the atoning sacrifice of Christ not only to their own lives, but to the lives of other people. Others in the Spiritual Warfare Network have likewise stressed the efficacy of identificational repentance. Kjell Sjöberg, national coordinator for Sweden of the Spiritual Warfare Network of the AD 2000 & Beyond Movement's United Prayer Track, clarifies his understanding of the difference between personal confession and confessing the sin of other people:

> It is important to understand the difference here between individual sin and collective sin. When unbelievers repent and confess their personal sins and believe in Jesus, they are saved. No one else can take their place and confess their sins for them. This, however, is not true for collective sin. Intercessors can confess collective sin even though they did not personally participate in the sin, and something that has displeased God can be removed. When that happens, God can pour out his Holy Spirit. It then becomes easier for unbelievers to hear the gospel of Christ, repent of their personal sins and be saved. This is how strategic-level intercession paves the way for effective evangelism. [70]

Sjöberg also speaks of this confession of collective sin as "remitting" it. He does so in the context of describing a prayer journey to West Africa, where he and a group of people "confessed and remitted" some of the corporate sin rooted in the slave trade. [71]

When I first heard this notion of remitting the sins of others, I reacted strongly, describing this teaching as "dangerous" and "unbiblical." It seemed to me to be something similar to the Mormon doctrine of performing baptisms for the dead to remit their sins. I later came to find out through prolonged discussion with Spiritual Warfare Network members that this is not what they mean when they speak of "remitting" the sins of others. Peter Wagner has clarified for me that they are thinking solely of removing the curse and penalty for the sins of others that is visited upon the subsequent generations and upon the land. [72] I do not think that there is anyone in the AD 2000 & Beyond Movement that thinks he or she can confess the sins of other people and thereby apply the justifying work of Christ and bring these people into a relationship with the Lord. Victor Lorenzo better explains the idea in his description of what the Christian leaders prayed for La Plata, Argentina: "The leaders humbly begged God to erase the consequences of the sin and to remove the curse from the city."[73]

Of course, this is not the way that "remission" is used in Scripture or in the history of Christian thought. The term does not even appear in some of the modern translations, but was rather common in the King James Version for a word that is now translated "forgiveness" *(aphesis).* For instance, on the day of Pentecost when Peter preached to the multitude at the temple, he urged them, "Repent, and be baptized every one of you in the name of Jesus Christ for the remission of sins" (Acts 2:38 KJV). The term *remission* has a long history of usage in the English language to denote the *forgiveness* and *pardon of sins.*[74] I believe that it is unwise for leaders in the spiritual warfare movement to use the word *remit* in a sense different than the way it is used in the Bible and in Christian theology. At the minimum, it is quite confusing and could also lead to dangerous theology and practice.

The problems with "identificational repentance" in the way that it is being advocated and practiced by many run still deeper. I point to two fundamental flaws.

BELIEVERS CANNOT REMOVE THE CURSE ON UNBELIEVERS

There does not appear to be scriptural evidence supporting the notion that believers can vicariously confess the sins of other people and remove God's temporal penalty, or curse, on the corporate sin. It is true that Daniel and Nehemiah identified themselves with the sins of their people and confessed those to God. But the situations were different in that they were fellow members of God's covenant community (an issue we discuss below).

What we do not have in the Old Testament is any example of a leader, judge, or king of Israel confessing the sins of any of the neighboring pagan cities or countries. We do not find, for instance, Daniel identifying with the sins of Nebuchadnezzar and confessing these to God in the hopes that the Persians would soften their hearts to the living God. Nor do we see the prophet Isaiah identifying with the sins of the Babylonians, Egyptians, or Moabites and confessing them to God, assuming that the curse on these nations would be broken. Similar observations could be made about the leaders in the early church. The apostle Paul never identifies with the sins of Roman imperialism, sexual immorality, and idolatry as a means of severing the ground held by ruling principalities.

How can anyone confess the sins of other people and expect to accomplish anything in the spiritual realm? If a Christian leader today publicly confesses his or her city's sins of drug abuse and prostitution, what good does this do if those involved with these evils have not made a confession of faith in Christ—who alone can change their hearts and behavior? If the same number of pimps and drug dealers are still walking the streets, no amount of vicarious confession will change anything. The demonic spirits will continue their insidious work in the lives of the people of the city because the welcome mat is still out on the porch, the light is on, and the door is wide open for them.

COVENANT PROMISES TO ISRAEL CANNOT BE DIRECTLY APPLIED TO CONTEMPORARY NATIONS AND CITIES

As much as we may like to think that our nation is specially chosen, the fact is that the United States is not the covenant people of God. A covenant relationship with God is no longer established on the basis of nationality. One does not need to be an Israelite to be in the covenant. Entry into the covenant is based on accepting the reconciling work of Jesus Christ, accomplished through his shedding his blood for us on the cross. The Holy Spirit joins us to the universal body of Christ. This new covenant people of God transcends all national, ethnic, racial, cultural, social, and every other boundary that we can think of.

Many advocates of "identificational repentance" incorrectly assume that Christians function in a priestly role in the covenant God has with their nation. John Dawson, for instance, points to Jonathan Edwards's assertion that America has a covenant relationship with God and enjoys the consequent protections and blessings of the covenant as long as it is honored.[75] The problem is that America has not maintained fidelity to the covenant because of its idolatry and injustice and is thereby subject to the covenant curses as stipulated in Deuteronomy 27–28. The only solution is for the church to take the priestly action of confessing the sins of the nation before God—as Nehemiah did for Israel (Neh. 1:6)—to lift the curses that the nation is ready to reap.

The problem with this scenario is that America is not Israel nor is America the covenant people of God. The New Covenant consists of people "from every tribe and language and people and nation" who have become the people of God because of Jesus Christ—"because you were slain, and with your blood you purchased men for God" (Rev. 5:9).

My former colleague, Pastor Joe Hellerman, brings further clarification to this issue in a position paper he wrote for the Promise Keepers organization on the topic of racial reconciliation.[76] Hellerman notes that when the Roman Empire became tolerant of Christianity under Constantine (A.D. 312) and openly Christian under Theodosius the Great (A.D. 379–395), Christians now began to think of their state as a divinely sanctioned institution. Tragedy struck, however, in A.D. 410, when Alaric the Goth and his armies sacked the city of Rome. There were profoundly different responses from the two greatest Christian leaders of the time. Hellerman observes that Jerome reacted in horror, exclaiming, "Jerusalem has fallen!" Jerome had taken the covenant promises of Israel and aligned them with the Roman Empire. Augustine, by contrast, had concluded that no earthly empire or nation now could ever be understood to be God's covenant nation. He penned his classic *The City of God* to proclaim that God's true covenant people are authentic believers of the past (in heaven) and the present (on earth) from every nation.

Hellerman concludes that history has vindicated the Augustinian perspective. No country throughout modern history can lay claim to having enjoyed a covenant relationship with God. It is important to realize that God himself is the one who takes the initiative to establish a covenant with a corporate entity. He has done that only once—with the people of Israel. Therefore it is inappropriate to conceive of any nation today—the United States, Great Britain, or any country—as enjoying a covenant relationship with God as Israel once did prior to the coming of the Messiah.

IDENTIFICATIONAL REPENTANCE AMONG THE PEOPLE OF GOD

Because the believing church represents the covenant people of God today, the appropriate application for identificational repentance would be within the body of Christ. Second Corinthians 3 is the key passage that points to the establishment of the New Covenant. God has not chosen any particular nation or ethnic group to bear his glory. By his Spirit, his glory lives in the church—people from every nation who have experienced the regenerating work of Christ and who now live in him. Although we are vessels of the Lord's glory, we are in need of moral transformation by the power of his indwelling Spirit (2 Cor. 3:18). This is where the concept of identificational repentance comes in.

In the first New Testament letter written, James (the brother of the Lord and leader of the church at Jerusalem) calls believers in Palestine and Syria to repentance. He implores them: "Wash your hands, you sinners, and purify your hearts, you double-minded. Grieve, mourn and wail. Change your laughter to mourning and your joy to gloom. Humble yourselves before the Lord, and he will lift you up" (James 4:8–10). Too many of the Christians were chasing the idol of wealth, some were showing favoritism to the wealthy in public gatherings, some were taking advantage of day laborers, and others were incredibly sharp-tongued and were inflicting wounds on their brothers and sisters. James sees the hand of Satan at work among these believers (James 4:7). He calls them to corporate repentance and to dependence on the power of God for transformation. The stains of sin on these dear believers were not unique to them. They simply continued to reflect attitudes and behaviors prevalent in contemporary Palestinian society. But this is not acceptable for Christians. We are called to a higher level of ethics.

It is in this context where the intercessory prayers and identificational repentance modeled by Nehemiah and Daniel are very appropriate and have incredible potential. Both leaders humbled themselves before God and prayed earnestly for their people, identifying themselves with their sin *in spite of the fact that they did not personally participate in the sinful behaviors.* While the people of God still suffered the plight of Babylonian captivity, Daniel "turned to the Lord God and pleaded with him in prayer and petition, in fasting, and in sackcloth and ashes" (Dan. 9:3). He prayed

> *We* have sinned and done wrong. *We* have been wicked and have rebelled; *we* have turned away from your commands and laws. *We* have not listened to your servants the prophets. . . .
> Therefore the curses and sworn judgments written in the Law of Moses, the servant of God, have been poured out on us, because *we* have sinned against you (Dan. 9:5–6, 11, italics mine).

Daniel has been very highly esteemed because of his obedience and sensitivity to God. Nevertheless, he identifies with his people's sinfulness and confesses it to the Lord as a corporate representative.

About a hundred years later, Nehemiah "mourned and fasted and prayed before the God of heaven" (Neh. 1:5) on behalf of the people of God:

> I confess the sins we Israelites, including myself and my father's house, have committed against you. We have acted very wickedly toward you. We have not obeyed the commands, decrees and laws you gave your servant Moses (Neh. 1:6–7).

In his prayer, Nehemiah specifically confesses not only his own culpability, but also the sins of his family. As a representative of Israel, he also confesses the sin of his people.

Neither of these leaders of the people of God identifies with or confesses the sins of the Assyrians, the Babylonians, the Medes, or the Persians. They repent only on behalf of the covenant people of God.

In a similar way, our priestly role to the nations does not amount to confessing their sins. We recognize our own sin and confess it before

God. These passages support the appropriateness of representative corporate confession. The apostle Paul clarifies our priestly response to the sin of the nations in his continued discussion about the covenant. We have a ministry of reconciliation and function as ambassadors to the world. Paul says that "we try to persuade men" (2 Cor. 5:11) that Christ died for them, becoming sin on their behalf, so that they might become righteous before God and thus be reconciled to him (2 Cor. 5:13, 20, 21). We cannot "remit" the sins of the nations by confessing them. We can, however, present Christ to the nations (as ambassadors of God) and give them the opportunity to enter a relationship with Christ so that their sins are not counted against them (2 Cor. 5:19).

The current practice of identificational repentance, in fact, does appear to be having its most significant impact within the church. There are many inspiring stories of reconciliation among estranged groups of Christians. In large public gatherings, whites have repented of the sin of slavery and the associated racist attitudes, and blacks have repented of bitterness and hatred toward whites; Japanese have repented of atrocities carried out by their ancestors toward Koreans, and Koreans have repented of their anger toward the Japanese; police officers have confessed acts of brutality, and others have confessed their lack of respect and foul attitudes toward the police. These kinds of public meetings have gone a long way toward healing some of America's wounds—within the Christian community.

Biola University and Talbot School of Theology recently had to face the issue of dealing appropriately with the sin of one of its forebears. In the summer of 1994, a Talbot School of Theology student brought certain written statements by Dr. Louis T. Talbot to the attention of Dr. Dennis Dirks, dean of the School of Theology. Among the statements were some biblically inaccurate and highly offensive comments regarding African Americans which had been made by Talbot on a radio broadcast and published in a book in 1938. Because some current students were concerned that the faculty condoned Louis Talbot's teaching on this issue, the dean brought the matter to the attention of the faculty. The faculty was shocked by the discovery; only one or two were even aware that Talbot had made such comments. The members of the faculty then went on record as unanimously disavowing Talbot's views regarding blacks as wholly inaccurate and apologizing to the African and African American constituency who had been offended by these particular views of the founder and namesake of the seminary. In September 1995, the dean then read the statements at a chapel service and at a special conference on racial reconciliation involving students and members of the local evangelical community. The statement and apology have gone a long way in clearing up much misunderstanding and suspicion.

IDENTIFICATIONAL REPENTANCE AND TERRITORIAL SPIRITS

What happens in the supernatural realm when Christian leaders lead their groups in identificational repentance? As Dawson says, "such action often releases healing grace in the hearts of bitter people"[77] and, as Hellerman adds, "it helps us to come to terms with our own hidden prejudices."[78] By dealing with these hidden prejudices, we unmask the work of the Evil One in our own lives and begin to deal with the foothold he may have where he fans the flames of bitterness, anger, and hard feelings.

Dawson is also probably correct in saying that Satan is terrified by corporate confession of sin. Do the high-ranking spirits over a city leave as a result? I don't think so. It seems to me that they will work just as hard to sow seeds of discord, mistrust, and suspicion to destroy the unity achieved. Spiritual warfare and struggle continue. But, as John pointed out to believers in the city of Ephesus years ago, "greater is he that is in you than he that is in the world" (1 John 4:4). Christians have the resources in Christ to set the standard for racial unity through the church.

What, Then, Is the Level of Our Engagement of Territorial Spirits?

God has not given us the responsibility of directly engaging territorial spirits. It is therefore not necessary for us to discern them, name them, and try to cast them out. We are called to continue proclaiming the Word in the power of the Spirit and ministering the kingdom of God. We can have confidence that God will deal with these high-ranking spirits as he sees fit, just as he did for Daniel.

Nevertheless, God has revealed to us through his Word that there are powerful malevolent spirits assigned to territories. Once again, Daniel's example is instructive. He prayed. We, too, should pray with a renewed vision of our need to depend on God. Recognizing the supernatural potency of our opposition should jar us into the realization that we need our God to fight for us.

We should also pray according to the guiding and prompting of the Spirit (as Paul instructs in Eph. 6:18, where he says, "pray in the Spirit on all occasions"). If the Spirit clearly impresses someone or a prayer group to pray for a particular matter in a certain way, they should by all means follow his guidance.

As we endeavor to follow Christ and engage in the mission he has called us to, fully recognizing that there is powerful demonic opposition at all levels, what should we do?

Strive for Personal and Corporate Purity

First and foremost, God has called his people to integrity, purity, and holiness. Righteousness is the breastplate of the Christian's armor. This involves a recognition that we have had the righteousness of Christ bestowed on us, but it also involves making progress down the road of transformation. The Father wants his children to resemble him.

In the Old Testament, the kings who were counted as great in the eyes of the Lord were those who devoted their hearts to the Lord and then removed all of the idols from the temple, the cities, and the land. Likewise, we need to be in the process of removing all the idols and high places that provide the demonic with an opportunity for control. Such idols are not always cultic gods or goddesses. They may be greed or sexual impurity (Col. 3:5). All of these strongholds need to be recognized, confessed, and rooted out. This is true on the corporate level as well. Sin in the community needs to be dealt with in a community way. This is where corporate confession and identificational repentance come in.

A renewal of our commitment to God and his purposes combined with the renunciation of everything that stands between us and the Father is foundational. David Bryant has been calling the church to purity and revival for over fifteen years as he leads "Concerts of Prayer." He recently declared,

> I believe revival is the greatest *offensive* that the Church has in world evangelization—*it is the highest form of spiritual warfare.* For example, if Satan's tactic is to divide the Church and conquer, it is through revival that God reverses these tactics and brings about a new level of unity and oneness of vision and labor. Again, if Satan's tactic is deception and lies, it is by revival that God brings about a revelation of the glory of His Son and of the truth that is in Jesus, that sets the Church free from the spirit of "anti-Christ."[79]

Recognize That Demons Exploit Culture to Hold People in Bondage

It is important for all believers to recognize that demons not only afflict individuals, but they attempt to exert their influence on the societal and cultural levels. The value of acknowledging this is that it helps us realize that we can only effectively engage in our mission through spiritual means and not merely with new strategies, technologies, and programs. Above all, it prompts us to depend on our God in faith and prayer.

As we have already observed, demons exert powerful influence over whole people groups through inspiring the worship of other gods and thereby receiving for themselves the veneration that is due to the one true God. They are also active in various kinds of occultic beliefs and practices as well as in popular folk beliefs. Just as Elymas the magician tried to keep Sergius Paulus, the governor of the island of Cyprus, from hearing the gospel (Acts 13:4–12), demonic spirits work through a variety of means to influence civic and national leaders.

Another area exploited by the demonic is culture and social systems. In an important volume entitled *Transforming Culture,* Sherwood Lingenfelter has challenged the long-held view that culture is basically a neutral vehicle.[80] He contends that every culture is inextricably infected by sin. He points to the apostle Paul's remarks in Romans 11:32, where he describes all of humanity as in a prison, a cell of disobedience: "For in shutting all mankind in the prison of their disobedience, God's purpose was to show mercy to all mankind" (NEB). Every culture and social system have been perverted by the Evil One into a prison of disobedience, entangling people into a life of conformity to shared values, beliefs, and lifestyles that are fundamentally at variance with God's purpose for humanity as expressed in Jesus Christ. Although Lingenfelter's book is not explicitly about spiritual warfare, it provides significant help to the church by assisting Christians in recognizing the multitude of ways Satan has worked on a corporate level to blind people to the gospel and keep them in bondage through perpetuating beliefs and practices that are contradictory to the gospel. In the third volume of his trilogy on the powers of darkness, Walter Wink is quite correct in asserting that people need to be "reborn" from their primary socialization in a culture by taking on the radical values of God's kingdom. He chides conservatives for being "generally too acculturated themselves to go that far."[81]

Part of "spiritual mapping" (or, "spiritual diagnosis") then should include not only the overt and explicit ways the demonic has operated in a city or culture (e.g., idols, occultic practices, etc.), but also the more implicit ways it has held people in bondage (e.g., economic issues, social power relationships, etc.). We can never underestimate the manifold ways our enemy seeks to keep people in bondage.

Pray

The heart and essence of spiritual warfare at any level is prayer. As the covenant people of God, Christians can appeal to God as their divine warrior. Here are a few foundational aspects of prayer in light of the recognition of powerful demonic hostility.

1. *Ask God for guidance on how to pray.* Jesus promised that he would send the Holy Spirit to serve as a counselor and guide for us (John 14:16, 26; 15:26). Part of the ministry of the Holy Spirit is in providing direction and guidance in how we pray (Eph. 6:18). As we seek to reach our community with the gospel or intercede for another country, we should begin by asking the Spirit how we should pray. This is at the basis of what some are calling "prophetic intercession." We listen to the Spirit and exercise sensitivity to what he impresses on us to pray for.

2. *Ask God to provide inroads into the community or area.* Knowing with full confidence that God wants to use us as his ambassadors to reach the lost, we can pray for God to work in such a way that the gospel would have an opening into the community. Paul prayed this way. He asked the Thessalonians to join him in praying "that the message of the Lord may spread rapidly and be honored, just as it was with you" (2 Thess. 3:1).

3. *Ask God to hinder the hostile working of known spirits.* As we become increasingly familiar with the community or country we are interceding for through information that we receive, we can begin to pray more specifically about the obstacles to the gospel. It is entirely appropriate to ask God to hinder the influence of the Evil One, and, more specifically, to thwart the influence of demonic spirits associated with particular cults and false religions.[82] As we pray for countries and cities where few people know the Lord Jesus Christ, the kind of information that has been made available in books like *WindoWatchman, Strongholds of the 10/40 Window,* and Patrick Johnstone's classic *Operation World* will help us pray with greater specificity.[83] A more intimate awareness also enables us to pray with more passion.

Zealously Do the Work of the Kingdom

As ambassadors of Christ, we need to focus less on territorial spirits and more on the task of being ambassadors. We are representatives of the King sent out to do kingdom business. As his envoys, we pursue the following objectives with zeal.

1. *Proclaim the gospel.* The gospel is "the power of God for the salvation of everyone who believes" (Rom. 1:16). It is also "the sword of the Spirit," which the believer uses as part of the offensive aspect of spiritual warfare. The apostle Paul recognized well the spiritual dimension of the battle in taking the gospel to people. He told the Corinthians, people who just a decade earlier had still been worshiping idols, that "the god of this age has blinded the minds of unbelievers, so that they cannot see the light of the

gospel of the glory of Christ" (2 Cor. 4:4). Yet he also recognized the power of God at work in the presentation of the gospel. In the same context, he emphasized proclamation and presentation, speaking about preaching the Lord Jesus Christ and declaring the truth plainly. This was how the Holy Spirit worked to bring the Corinthians into a relationship with Christ. The Holy Spirit continues to work powerfully through the presentation of the gospel message. This has been and continues to be the foundational part of our ministry.

2. *Reach out in acts of kindness, love, compassion, and service.* As representatives of the kingdom of God, we are also called to minister in tangible ways in our communities. Jesus has sent us to be lights in the midst of darkness. He wants us to reflect his selfless love and his commitment to justice in the world. Any act of kindness to our neighbor expresses to this person the tender care of Jesus Christ and may lead to opportunities to present the good news of Christ at a later point.

Unite with Other Believers in Prayer and in Carrying Out the Mission

The goal of carrying out the Great Commission will not be accomplished by one individual, church, or denomination. The people of God will need to work together in unity to effectively carry out this task. It begins with prayer.

The past five to ten years have been a very exciting time for this. Observers have begun to speak of a "prayer movement" that is touching Christians not only across our land, but across the world. David Bryant has documented this well in his book *The Hope at Hand.*[84] Literally hundreds of prayer networks have been created to stimulate corporate prayer for those who do not know Christ all over the world. The catalyst to pray has brought together people across denominational lines in a spiritual unity with a passionate desire to set people free from the bonds of Satan so they can enter into a relationship with the living Christ. Campus Crusade, World Prayer Crusade, Christian Information Network, Concerts of Prayer, Esther Network International, Every Home for Christ Jericho Chapters, Generals of Intercession, and Southern Baptist Bold Mission Prayer Thrust are just a few of the many groups that are gathering people together to pray.

There also seems to be a new vision for mobilizing people to pray for the cities. In November 1995, four different prayer conferences were held in Los Angeles to intercede for the city. Similar events are being held in other cities. Perhaps even more important, informal networks of people from various churches meet in some cities to pray together for their cities on a weekly basis.

It pleases the Lord for his people to work together in unity. The apostle Paul urged the network of churches in the metropolis of Ephesus to "make every effort to keep the unity of the Spirit through the bond of peace" (Eph. 4:3).

Models for Doing Spiritual Warfare at the Church and City Levels

The vast majority of books and articles on spiritual warfare deal with the subjects of exorcism and deliverance ministry; few make an attempt at suggesting how to deal with the adversary at the corporate level of church or city. There are a handful of possible models that could be mentioned here, but I focus on two that I believe to be biblically rooted and practically helpful.

At the Church Level (Neil Anderson and Charles Mylander)

All churches struggle with various issues that surface, but some churches seem to have had all of their vitality sapped right out of them. Members are discouraged because a damp blanket seems to cover their feeble attempts at worship, which have become more perfunctory than full of life. The pastor is discouraged because over 90 percent of his time is spent trying to put out fires; the other 10 percent is used for quickly piecing together his Sunday messages and a few Bible studies.

Rightly recognizing that Satan strategizes to nullify the vibrancy of the love and ministry of each local church, Neil Anderson and Charles Mylander have put together some thoughts and a plan for helping the church deal effectively with issues of corporate sin.[85] Anderson, my former colleague at Talbot School of Theology and now president of Freedom in Christ ministries, and Mylander, general superintendent of the Friends Church Southwest, contend that there are often issues that need to be dealt with on a corporate level if a church is to experience freedom in Christ to fulfill its calling.

They have put together a strategy that involves gathering all the leaders of the church and taking a Friday night and Saturday retreat to work corporately through this seven-step plan. In preparation for the retreat, Anderson and Mylander encourage the participants to work through the personal "Steps to Freedom in Christ." The essence of their model is outlined in the following list:

Setting Your Church Free

1. *Our Church's Strengths:* Discern and list all of the strengths of your church and then summarize the greatest strengths.
2. *Our Weaknesses:* Discern and list all of the weaknesses of your church.
3. *Memories:* Ask the Lord to remind you of the best memories as well as the most traumatic events in the church's past. Thank the Lord for the good memories. Ask the Lord for courage to face the pain of the bad memories and for the grace to forgive the offenders. Declare to Satan that you now retake any ground given to him through your response to these painful memories.
4. *Corporate Sins:* List and ask forgiveness for any corporate sins that have been committed by the church.
5. *Attacks of Spiritual Enemies:* Discern and list the ways Satan has attacked your church, its leaders, and its people because of what it is doing right. Renounce all satanic assignments.
6. *Prayer Action Plan:* Place four sheets of paper on the wall in front of the group with the headings: we renounce. . . , we announce. . . , we affirm. . . , and we will. . . . Based on all that has been done so far, discuss, synthesize, and pray.
7. *Leadership Strategy:* Devise a leadership strategy for implementing and holding people accountable to the prayer action plan.

The plan is predicated on a huge assumption: that all of the members of the leadership team of a church have worked through Anderson's "Steps to Freedom in Christ" and are thus spiritually healthy people. For Anderson, this does not mean that they are living sinless lives, but that they have a good understanding of their identity in Christ and that they are actively appropriating Christ's power in overcoming temptation. It seems to me that if the leaders of the church have reached this stage in their Christian experience, they are already far down the road of leading the church in a healthy direction.

Nevertheless, Anderson and Mylander assert that there are often issues of *corporate* sin that need to be confronted. The heart of the strategy is leading the church to face these issues, to confess any corporate sins, and to seek the forgiveness of God and those offended by the actions (or possibly inactions). The plan also involves grappling with issues that have resulted from painful memories, direct satanic attacks, or simply the weaknesses of the church.

As part of the agenda for a specially focused retreat for the leadership of a church, they advise the group to ask the Lord to help them discern all of the corporate sins of the church under past as well as present leadership and to list these (this would include such things as power struggles, apathy and complacency, a critical spirit toward other churches, etc.). The group leader would then give opportunity for a time of group prayer:

> At this point, the facilitator will invite everyone to search their own hearts. Ask for the Holy Spirit to reveal each one's participation in the church's corporate sins. Each person, as directed by the Holy Spirit, should then pray out loud, confessing personal involvement in these corporate sins. Alert everyone that it is off-limits to confess someone else's sins. (The participants will usually laugh when the facilitator says this, but it prevents a big mistake from happening.)[86]

In the context of the leaders of the church meeting together to deal with such sin issues, Anderson and Mylander would find "identificational repentance" inappropriate. Although they do not specifically address the concept, I wonder if the next natural step would be for these leaders, upon returning home, to lead the entire church in a time of prayer, confession, and repentance. For the church to witness and participate with their leaders in such a time could be extraordinarily significant in bringing healing and restoration of God's blessing on the body.

The strategy is therefore not really a method for casting a territorial demon out of the church; a central part of the plan deals with sin and, thereby, robbing the devil of the ground that has been handed over to him as a base for his operations. Because of the strong concept of individual responsibility in our culture, little thought is often given to the notion of corporate sins or corporate responsibilities. This is precisely what Anderson and Mylander hope to see the church deal with more effectively.

The kinds of corporate sins they have in mind are the kinds that many churches have struggled with. To name just a few examples,

- mean-spirited public criticism of the pastor or another leader in the church
- lack of commitment to each other
- self-focus that produces apathy toward the lost
- lack of commitment to and practice of spiritual disciplines
- intolerance of other races
- highly critical attitude toward charismatics or non-charismatics, toward different denominations, or toward other churches in the community
- insensitivity to the poor or the marginalized in the community

Anderson and Mylander argue that such corporate sins need to be unmasked and dealt with corporately.

The authors also suggest a more direct engagement with the enemy involving public renunciation of Satan and all his ways in tandem with a fresh public announcement of allegiance to Christ and all his ways: "We renounce you, Satan, in all your works and in all your ways," followed by "We announce that Christ is Lord of our lives and choose to follow only his ways."[87] There are also times when they advise making a pointed declaration to Satan, such as, "In Jesus' all powerful name we retake any ground that Satan may have gained in our lives and in our church through these painful memories. Because we are seated with Christ in the heavenly realms we command Satan to leave our presence, our ministries and our church."[88]

Perhaps the most direct engagement with the Evil One takes place in step 5, where they suggest asking the Father to reveal "the attacks of Satan against us, our pastors, our people and our ministries." They understand these to be curses and various "satanic assignments." Once these are discerned, they teach that each form of attack should be renounced one by one with a declaration like the following: "In the name and authority of our Lord Jesus Christ, we renounce Satan's attacks of ————. We resist them and come against them in Jesus' all-powerful name. Together we declare, 'The Lord rebuke you, the Lord bind you' from any present or any future influence upon us."[89]

At the City Level (Edgardo Silvoso)

How do we reach an entire city for Christ? This is the question that Argentinian evangelist Edgardo Silvoso deals with in his recent book, *That None Should Perish*.[90] He seeks to answer this question by taking into account the fact that evangelism represents a frontal assault on the kingdom of Satan. Silvoso's work is particularly significant because many leaders in the Spiritual Warfare Network have looked to his strategy for reaching La Plata and Resistencia, Argentina, as models of what is possible.[91] In both cities, thousands of people turned to Christ and became viable members of churches as a result of the networked outreach of Christians.

What is significant for our inquiry is that Silvoso recognizes the reality of demonic opposition at all levels, but he does not stress identifying and directly confronting the demonic powers over the city.

Central to Silvoso's plan is prayer. He urges the creation of numerous prayer groups scattered throughout the city; they should be composed of people from different churches who share a common passion for seeing people come to know Christ. These prayer cells would then pray not only for the city in general but also for people in the immediate neighborhood. He suggests that pairs of people go through the neighborhood, engage people in conversation, and ask them if they have some issues they would like prayer for. He observes, "the openness of the lost to intercessory prayer on their behalf has been the greatest surprise I have encountered in our city-reaching ministry."[92] In Resistencia, over six hundred prayer cells were formed; "not a single neighborhood was left without a prayer house."[93] It seems to me that the effectiveness of this part of the strategy will be directly proportional to the quality of relationships that are built with these non-Christian neighbors in the community. As friendship and trust develop, there will be a greater inclination to ask for prayer. Silvoso's strategy is outlined in the following list:

Six Steps for Reaching a City for Christ

1. *Establish God's perimeter in the city:* Look for people who make up the "faithful remnant," those who are waiting for the kingdom of God to come to their city. Such a group forms a microcosm of God's kingdom in the midst of Satan's dominion.

2. *Secure God's perimeter in the city:* Recognize that the enemy has infiltrated not only the city but also the church through sin, anxiety, and strongholds. Counter Satan's schemes and tear down the strongholds. Practice "keeping the unity of the Spirit in the bond of peace."

3. *Expand God's perimeter in the city:* God uses the faithful remnant to establish a model. With that model now in place, others whose hearts God has been preparing must gradually be brought inside the perimeter to build up the army of saints who will eventually launch the attack on the forces holding the city in spiritual darkness.

4. *Infiltrate Satan's perimeter:* From a secure base of operations, make the enemy's base insecure by parachuting behind enemy lines through a massive "air assault" of specific and strategic intercessory prayer. This is done by establishing hundreds of prayer cells throughout the city to weaken Satan's control over the unsaved and produce a favorable disposition to the gospel by finding favor with the people.

5. *Attack and destroy Satan's perimeter:* Begin the "frontal assault." Launch the spiritual "takeover" of the city, confronting, binding, and casting down the spiritual powers ruling over the region. Proclaim the message of the gospel to every creature in the city. Disciple the new believers through the established "Lighthouses."

6. *Establish God's new perimeter where Satan's once existed:* Loot the enemy's camp. Entirely dispossess him of his most prized possession—human souls. Unless spiritual warfare results in solid, tangible conversions that are incorporated into a growing number of churches, nothing of consequence has happened.

Silvoso bases this prayer strategy in part on Paul's injunctions to the church in 1 Timothy 2:1–8, which encourages that "requests, prayers, intercession and thanksgiving be made for everyone" with the ultimate goal of seeing people come to know Christ. The passage also stresses lifting up *holy* hands in prayer (2:8), which Silvoso takes seriously. Those who commit themselves to a prayer cell must be dealing with personal sin in their lives through repentance and appropriating the power of God to live with purity.

Some people will undoubtedly take exception to Silvoso's (over)use of battle imagery throughout his presentation. The whole ethos of his approach stands in strong contrast to the many books of the past generation that describe evangelism as a kind of technology, a sort of skill that people polish and use. Silvoso's emphasis reminds us of an important biblical concept that we have already discussed in the first chapter, a conception that understands evangelism to be spiritual battle. We must also be careful not to read too much into the triumphalistic-sounding notion of engaging in a "spiritual takeover" of a city. Here Silvoso is merely extending the metaphor used by our Lord of plundering the strong man's house. This is not to be misunderstood along political lines or as leading to a proscription of other religions in a city. For Silvoso, this is a metaphorical way of speaking of a huge outpouring of people turning their hearts to Christ in response to the proclamation of the gospel.

Although a "six-step" approach has the ring of American pragmatism and program orientation, Silvoso's method is probably more culturally Latino-Christian. It is less a program than a call to prayer and to mobilization to get serious about what Christ has commissioned his church to do.

Many churches rally around programs involving literature distribution, big events, doing surveys, or telephone calling campaigns. What strikes me about Silvoso's model is that he is calling the church first and foremost to assemble for prayer. The intercession, however, is not to be focused on ourselves, but on others—on finding the one lost sheep that the good shepherd left the ninety-nine to find.

One of Satan's strategies among the churches in a given city has been to create dissension and spiritual arrogance. Silvoso, in fact, considers disunity among churches as one of Satan's deadliest strongholds. To help restructure our thinking about the church, Silvoso tries to emphasize that there is only one church in a city that meets in many congregations. He cites the example of a group of pastors leading "Pray Stockton" in Stockton, California, who introduce themselves to non-Christians as pastors of the church in Stockton, purposely avoiding any reference to their denominational affiliation. He thus calls for the walls of disunity to come down in a display of unity around the Great Commission. For him, this starts in groups of prayer, where the focus is on Jesus (not a program). In many instances, it will be essential for genuine repentance and forgiveness to take place within these groups. Where attitudes such as superiority, apathy, and racism have been present, these will need to be confessed in order for true brotherly love to exist and authentic unity to take place.

These initial groups, which Silvoso refers to as "the remnant," will come to serve as an inspiring model and catalyst for the formation of other groups. Silvoso says, "in expanding the perimeter, you must plan for and hope that everybody will eventually join in."[94] Of course, not everyone will; participants will thus need to guard against the temptation toward arrogance and superiority.

Once these groups are established, various modes of outreach can be used within the community. Silvoso mentions a few examples, but the most important factor is that the foundation of prayer and unity for undertaking the mission has been laid. The growth of the existing churches and the establishment of new churches should be the primary aim and result.

The one point where I take exception to Silvoso's approach is the first part of "Step 5: Attack and Destroy Satan's Perimeter." Ironically, in the book Silvoso does not develop this part of the strategy, which appears to be on the periphery for him. As I have already discussed earlier, I do not think that believers have the responsibility of confronting, binding, and casting down the spiritual powers ruling over the region. We do have the responsibility to pray for the people in the area with the full recognition that there is powerful demonic activity blinding these people to the truth of the gospel. We are also called to "proclaim the message" and "disciple the new believers." All of these activities represent frontal attacks on Satan's kingdom. As Paul said, the gospel is "the power of God for the salvation of everyone who believes" (Rom. 1:16). We don't have to be overly concerned about the territorial rulers. The reality of their presence should only drive us to God. He will deal with them.

A Final Word: An Appeal for Unity in the Church

What we have been discussing in this chapter is an issue that does not strike at the heart of the Christian faith. It is not a debate centering on the identity of Christ, the meaning of salvation, or the reliability of the Scriptures. This is a strategy issue, dealing with the authority of believers as they engage in the mission of the church. It is a doctrinal issue, and we need to search the Bible for perspective on it. But it is what I would call a peripheral doctrinal concern—so peripheral that a position on it will probably not make it into any official doctrinal statement of a church. It is certainly not something that should divide believers as they seek to reach the lost with the gospel of Christ.

Nevertheless, it is a divisive issue. It affects mission boards as they consider strategies for reaching villages and cities for Christ. It also affects churches as they endeavor to further the impact of the gospel in their own communities. As David Bryant recently said, "If Satan is able to 'hijack' the worldwide movement of prayer and discredit it by causing it to be consumed with less than the whole counsel and purpose of God for this generation, he will have won one of his most stunning coups!"[95]

My prayer is that mission boards and churches will keep this issue in proper perspective and not sever relationships over this issue. My hope would also be that the overzealous would recognize that there is little biblical, theological, or historical support for direct engagement with the so-called territorial spirits and that they would modify their practices accordingly. I would also hope that skeptical and complacent believers would recognize that the Christian life is a supernatural struggle that can only be lived by the power of the Spirit of God. This is particularly true when we endeavor to obey Christ by reaching out to the lost.[96]

Summary

1. There is a hierarchy among the demons and angels in the evil spiritual domain. Some evil angels have assignments over empires, people groups, countries, regions, territories, or cities.
2. There is struggle and warfare between the angels of God and the angels of Satan in the supernatural realm that has an impact on the unfolding of events on earth.
3. Through biblical revelation, God has heightened our awareness of the angelic realm. The knowledge he has given us is for the purpose of prompting our dependence on him through prayer.
4. Although God has given us the responsibility of exercising our authority in Christ over unclean spirits that afflict individuals, there is no biblical evidence that God has given us responsibility to bind, expel, or thwart the territorial rulers.
5. Although we do not have the authority to directly engage territorial spirits, we certainly have the right to appeal to God to hinder and obstruct the grip of a demonic ruler over an area so that the

gospel can be proclaimed and the darkness may be lifted from the eyes of the unbelieving.

6. "Spiritual mapping," or, as I would prefer to call it, creating a "spiritual profile" of people in a city or country, is a useful way to help the people of God pray more specifically. It is also beneficial for informing the teaching and discipling of new believers.

7. "Identificational repentance" is an appropriate way of leading the people of God in dealing with issues of corporate sin. It does not, however, enable Christians to "remit" the sins of the nonbelieving population of a city, remove the curse of God's judgment on them, or result in the weakening of the grip of the territorial spirits over the unbelieving population.

8. Christians do not need to feel a responsibility or a call to engage in a direct confrontation with the principalities and powers over a city, region, or a country. We appeal directly to God, who will direct his angels to fight the battles against the high-ranking powers.

Recommended Reading

Books Affirming Some Form of SLSW

Silvoso, Ed. *That None Should Perish: How to Reach Entire Cities for Christ through Prayer Evangelism.* Ventura, Calif.: Regal, 1994. Silvoso, an Argentinian evangelist and founder of Harvest Evangelism, implements some SLSW principles and practices in his evangelistic strategy for reaching a city with the gospel. He says little, however, about directly engaging the ruling powers. The book contains many practical and valuable insights in mobilizing Christian leaders in a city to pray and coordinate evangelistic efforts.

Wagner, C. Peter. *Confronting the Powers: How the New Testament Church Experienced the Power of Strategic-Level Spiritual Warfare.* Prayer Warrior Series. Ventura, Calif.: Regal, 1996. This book is the most recent of Wagner's many books on spiritual warfare and the most important on this topic. This is the first and only serious attempt to provide biblical, theological, and historical evidence for the practice of directly engaging territorial spirits.

————. *Warfare Prayer: How to Seek God's Power and Protection in the Battle to Build His Kingdom.* Prayer Warrior Series. Ventura, Calif.: Regal, 1992. This book is the best overall presentation of what "Strategic-Level Spiritual Warfare" is all about. The book is somewhat dated in that it represents the infancy of the warfare prayer movement.

Wagner, C. Peter, ed. *Breaking Strongholds in Your City: How to Use Spiritual Mapping to Make Your Prayers More Strategic, Effective, and Targeted.* Ventura, Calif.: Regal, 1993. This book is a collection of essays by evangelists, pastors, and people involved in prayer ministry. The emphasis of this volume falls on dealing with demonic strongholds over cities. The contributors—Wagner, George Otis Jr., Cindy Jacobs, and others—describe their strategies for spiritual mapping and confronting demonic strongholds over cities.

——. *Engaging the Enemy: How to Fight and Defeat Territorial Spirits.* Ventura, Calif.: Regal, 1991. This book is a collection of essays by evangelists and pastors on dealing with territorial spirits. The contributors include Wagner, Larry Lea, David Yonggi Cho, Dick Bernal, and John Dawson.

Other Books

Anderson, Neil T., and Charles Mylander. *Setting Your Church Free: A Biblical Plan to Help Your Church.* Ventura, Calif.: Regal, 1994. This book is an attempt to present spiritual warfare principles in a relevant way to help churches deal with issues of corporate sin.

Rommen, Edward, ed. *Spiritual Power and Missions: Raising the Issues.* Evangelical Missiological Society Series 3. Pasadena, Calif.: William Carey Library, 1995. This volume contains an important essay by three professors from Columbia International University—Robert J. Priest, Thomas Campbell, and Bradford A. Mullen—challenging much of what is said in the modern spiritual warfare movement. The essay, titled "Missiological Syncretism: The New Animistic Paradigm," suggests that there are many aspects of the beliefs and practices of the Christian leaders involved in SLSW and deliverance ministry that reflect more of an animistic worldview than a biblical understanding of reality. The volume also contains a lively response by Charles Kraft and an excellent essay by Patrick Johnstone on biblical intercession and missions.

Notes

Chapter 1: What Is Spiritual Warfare?

1. Mark Arax, "Hmong's Sacrifice of Puppy Reopens Cultural Wounds," *Los Angeles Times,* 16 December 1995, 1.

2. "Five Women Held in Fatal Anti-Demonic Ritual," *The Orange County Register,* 17 March 1995.

3. Eddie Pells (AP), "Father Feared Possession by the Devil," *The Orange County Register,* 24 July 1995.

4. Bob Drogin, "Witch Hunts: The Fatal Price of Fear," *Los Angeles Times,* 28 December 1994, p. 1 col. 1, p. 8.

5. Ethelbert Stauffer, *Theology of the New Testament,* 5th ed. (New York: Macmillan, 1955), 124.

6. Heiko A. Oberman, *Luther: Man between God and the Devil* (New York: Doubleday, 1992), 104–5.

7. Clinton E. Arnold, *Powers of Darkness: Principalities and Powers in Paul's Letters* (Downers Grove, Ill.: InterVarsity, 1992).

8. Sydney H. T. Page, *Powers of Evil: A Biblical Study of Satan and Demons* (Grand Rapids: Baker, 1995).

9. Harvey Cox, "Overview of Pentecostal Spiritual Healing Practices" (address presented at the "Spirituality and Healing in Medicine" conference sponsored by Harvard Medical School and the Mind/Body Institute, Boston, Mass., 4 December 1995).

10. There is, of course, a real danger in overstressing or misusing the battle imagery. In a recent statement on spiritual warfare, the Lausanne Committee on World Evangelization expressed the following concern: "We heard with concern of situations where warfare language was pushing Christians into adversarial attitudes with people and where people of other faiths were interpreting this as the language of violence and political involvement. We saw that the language of peace, penitence and reconciliation must be as prominent in our speech and practice as any talk of warfare." See "Statement on Spiritual Warfare: The Intercession Working Group Report, Lausanne Committee on World Evangelization," *Urban Mission* 13.2 (1995): 52 (originally published in *World Evangelization* 18.65 [December 1993]).

11. For these statistics, see G. Gallup Jr., *Religion in America: 1990* (Princeton, N.J.: Princeton Religious Research Center, 1990). The figure remained at 94 percent in the 1992–93 report (see G. Gallup Jr., *Religion in America 1992–1993* [Princeton, N.J.: Princeton Religion Research Center, 1993]).

12. Diana Eck, "Hindu and Buddhistic Spiritual Healing Practices" (address presented at the "Spirituality and Healing in Medicine" conference sponsored by Harvard Medical School and the Mind/Body Institute, Boston, Mass., 4 December 1995).

13. *Religion in America 1992–1993*, 30–33.

14. Phillip E. Johnson, *Reason in the Balance: The Case against Naturalism in Science, Law, and Education* (Downers Grove, Ill.: InterVarsity, 1995).

15. Ibid., 197.

16. Charles H. Kraft, *Christianity with Power: Your Worldview and Your Experience of the Supernatural* (Ann Arbor: Servant, Vine Books, 1989), 3–4.

17. Jeffrey Burton Russell, *Mephistopheles: The Devil in the Modern World* (Ithaca, N.Y., and London: Cornell University Press, 1986), 301.

18. Frank Peretti, *This Present Darkness* (Westchester, Ill.: Crossway, 1986).

19. Sherwood Lingenfelter, *Transforming Culture: A Challenge for Christian Mission* (Grand Rapids: Baker, 1992), 17. He notes, "Members of every society hold something of a collective worldview and participate in a structured social environment. They are socialized by parents and peers to accept these values, beliefs, and procedures for action, and to live within them, creating their collective conceptualization of 'this-worldliness.' Yet these social systems and worldviews become prisons of disobedience, entangling those who hold them in a life of conformity to social images that at their roots are in conflict with God's purpose for humanity as expressed in Jesus Christ."

20. See his popular book, *The Bondage Breaker* (Eugene, Ore.: Harvest House, 1990).

21. For a detailed academic treatment of the passage in its first-century cultural and historical context, see my *Power and Magic: The Concept of Power in Ephesians* (Grand Rapids: Baker, 1997), chap. 5: "The Conflict with the Powers," 103–22. For a more popular presentation of the passage, see my *Powers of Darkness,* chap. 11: "Spiritual Warfare," 148–60.

22. The passage does speak of "blood and flesh," but flesh is here used literally, not in the ethical sense of the evil inclination.

23. H. Engelmann, D. Knibbe, and R. Merkelbach, *Die Inschriften von Ephesos* (Bonn: Rudolph Habelt, 1984), no. 1123 (English translation mine).

24. See, for example, 1 Enoch 61.10; 2 Enoch 20.1; Testament of Levi 3.8.

25. Testament of Solomon 18.2. Although this document was written well after the New Testament, the traditions it contains (especially in chap. 18) are best traced to the Jewish demonology of the first century A.D. and before.

26. The first occurrence of "you" in the passage ("Satan has asked to sift *you* as wheat") is in the plural in Greek, perhaps indicating that Satan was intending to test all the apostles.

27. For more information, contact

Moms in Touch
P.O. Box 1120
Poway, CA 92074
Phone: (1-800) 949-MOMS

28. In November 1995, a number of prayer conferences and prayer events were held in the Los Angeles area to lift the city up in prayer. Conferences were sponsored by Har-

vest Evangelism and Global Harvest Ministries ("First Global Conference on Prayer Evangelism"), Campus Crusade for Christ ("Fasting and Prayer '95"), Women's Aglow Fellowship ("Be a Shining Light to the Nations"), and Pastor Jack Hayford of the Church on the Way ("Prayer's Dynamic and God's Visitation"), March for Jesus, and Love L.A. Shepherds' Prayer Gathering.

29. For more information about the Concerts of Prayer team and resources, contact

> Concerts of Prayer International
> P.O. Box 1399
> Wheaton, IL 60189
> Phone: (708) 690-8441; Fax: (708) 690-0160

See also the recent book by David Bryant, *The Hope at Hand: National and World Revival for the Twenty-First Century* (Grand Rapids: Baker, 1995).

30. See the plan outlined by Ed Silvoso in his recent book, *That None Should Perish: How to Reach Entire Cities for Christ through Prayer Evangelism* (Ventura, Calif.: Regal, 1994).

31. The Lausanne Committee for World Evangelization has attempted to link Christian leaders and organizations with a passion for praying for our nation and working toward the spread of the gospel through a ministry called "Mission America." For further information, contact

> Paul Cedar, Chairman
> Mission America
> 901 East 78th Street
> Minneapolis, MN 55420
> Phone: (612) 853-1762; Fax: (612) 853-1745

Another organization, "Intercessors for America," publishes a monthly newsletter designed to help people pray about key issues and events facing our nation. For further information, contact

> Intercessors for America
> P.O. Box 4477
> Leesburg, VA 22075
> Phone: (703) 777-0003; Fax: (703) 777-2324
> E-mail: USAPray@aol.com

32. For more information on praying through the 10/40 Window, contact

> Christian Information Network
> 11025 State Highway 83
> Colorado Springs, CO 80921
> Phone: (719) 522-1040
> E-mail: 73422.3471@compuserve.com

The Christian Information Network is a ministry of the New Life Church (Pastor Ted Haggard). The church is in the process of completing a massive "World Prayer Center" whereby prayer for the nations can be encouraged and greatly facilitated.

Additional information on praying for the unreached countries of the 10/40 Window can be obtained from the AD 2000 & Beyond Movement. This organization was established to encourage, motivate, and network concerned Christians by inspiring them with the vision of reaching the unreached by the year 2000 through consultations, prayer efforts, and written materials. For information, contact

> AD 2000 & Beyond Movement
> 2860 South Circle Drive, Suite 2112
> Colorado Springs, CO 80906
> Phone: (719) 576-2000

33. C. Peter Wagner, *Prayer Shield: How to Intercede for Pastors, Christian Leaders, and Others on the Spiritual Frontlines,* Prayer Warrior Series (Ventura, Calif.: Regal, 1992), 47–49.

34. Another first-century Jewish writer spoke of "demolishing strongholds." Philo attacked the Sophists and orators of his day saying, "For the stronghold which was built through persuasiveness of argument was built solely for the purpose of diverting and deflecting the mind from honoring God." He goes on to say, "But there stands ready armed for the destruction of this stronghold the robber who despoils injustice" (*The Confusion of Tongues* 129). He uses precisely the same terms Paul does for the "destruction" of the "stronghold."

35. Taken from John H. Leith, ed., *Creeds of the Churches* (Louisville: John Knox, 1982), 28–33. See also Philip Schaff, *The Creeds of Christendom* (New York: Harper & Row, 1931; reprint, Grand Rapids: Baker, 1990), 1:24–29.

36. For a defense of this interpretation of *stoicheia,* see my article, "Returning to the Domain of the Powers: *Stoicheia* as Evil Spirits in Gal 4:3, 9," *Novum Testamentum* 38 (1996): 55–76.

37. For a detailed description of the so-called Colossian philosophy set within its first-century historical context, see my monograph devoted to this topic: *The Colossian Syncretism: The Interface between Christianity and Folk Belief at Colossae,* Wissenschaftliche Untersuchungen zum Neuen Testament 77, 2d series (Tübingen: J. C. B. Mohr [Paul Siebeck], 1995; North American edition by Baker, 1996).

38. For a concise presentation of the beliefs of these and other cults coupled with a biblical response and evaluation, see the new sixteen-volume Zondervan Guide to Cults and Religious Movements, ed. Alan W. Gomes (Grand Rapids: Zondervan, 1995–). On Mormonism, Jehovah's Witnesses, and Christian Science, see the volumes by Kurt Van Gorden, Robert M. Bowman Jr., and Todd Ehrenborg, respectively.

39. On the New Age Movement, see Ron Rhodes, *The Counterfeit Christ of the New Age Movement* (Grand Rapids: Baker, 1990) and his *New Age Movement,* Zondervan Guide to Cults and Religious Movements (Grand Rapids: Zondervan, 1995).

40. Bultmann's overall conclusion is often quoted by New Testament scholars: "I do indeed think that we can now know almost nothing concerning the life and personality of Jesus, since the early Christian sources show no interest in either, are moreover fragmentary and often legendary; and other sources about Jesus do not exist" (*Jesus and the Word* [New York: Scribner's, 1934], 14).

41. Robert W. Funk and Roy W. Hoover, eds., *The Five Gospels: The Search for the Authentic Words of Jesus* (New York: Macmillan, 1993).

42. Ben Witherington III, *The Jesus Quest: The Third Search for the Jew of Nazareth* (Downers Grove, Ill.: InterVarsity, 1995), 57.

43. Michael J. Wilkins and J. P. Moreland, eds., *Jesus under Fire: Modern Scholarship Reinvents the Historical Jesus* (Grand Rapids: Zondervan, 1995).

Chapter 2: Can a Christian Be Demon-Possessed?

1. The three anecdotes are fictional, but the essence of each of the stories is based on the actual experiences of people I have ministered to or that were reported to me.

2. For a concise popular presentation of this theme, see Paul Thigpen, "Spiritual Warfare in the Early Church," *Discipleship Journal* 81 (1994): 29.

3. L. G. McClung Jr. states, "A review of the literature, history, and oral 'stories' of Pentecostalism reveals the centrality of the practice of exorcism in the expansion of the Pentecostal and charismatic movements" (in *Dictionary of Pentecostal and Charismatic Movements,* ed. Stanley M. Burgess and Gary B. McGee [Grand Rapids: Zondervan, 1988], s.v. "exorcism," 290).

4. Merrill F. Unger, *Biblical Demonology: A Study of the Spiritual Forces behind the Present World Unrest* (Wheaton, Ill.: Scripture Press, 1952), 100.

5. Merrill F. Unger, *Demons in the World Today: A Study of Occultism in the Light of God's Word* (Wheaton, Ill.: Tyndale House, 1971) and *What Demons Can Do to Saints* (Chicago: Moody, 1977).

6. C. Fred Dickason, *Demon Possession and the Christian* (Chicago: Moody, 1987; reprint, Westchester, Ill.: Crossway, 1989).

7. Ibid., 187.

8. See especially John Wimber, *Power Healing* (San Francisco: Harper & Row, 1987), where he notes: "I believe that believers and nonbelievers alike can be demonized" (p. 114).

9. *Oxford English Dictionary,* 2d ed. (Oxford: Clarendon, 1991), s.v. "possession."

10. The expression "he has a demon" *(echei daimonion)* does appear in the Gospels (e.g., Luke 4:33; 8:27), but the inverse, "a demon has him," never occurs.

11. The tradition of translating *daimonizomai* as "demon-possessed" did not originate with the Authorized Version of 1611. The rendering goes back at least as far as Tyndale's version of 1534, which translated Matthew 8:16 as "They brought unto him many that were possessed with devyllis." "Possessed" is also used by other English translations that predate the KJV, namely, Cranmer (1539), Geneva (1557), and Anglo-Rhemish (1582). The earliest English translation (Wiclif [1380]), however, does not use "possession" to translate Matthew 8:16: "thei brouyten to hym many that hadden deuelis." These translations were taken from *The English Hexapla* (London: Samuel Bagster and Sons, 1841).

12. *Oxford English Dictionary,* 2d ed., s.v. "possession," reports that possession could be used to express "the holding or having something as one's own, or in one's control" in the sense of "actual holding or occupancy, as distinct from ownership."

13. David Peterson, *Possessed by God: A New Testament Theology of Sanctification and Holiness,* New Studies in Biblical Theology (Grand Rapids: Eerdmans, 1995), 143, italics mine.

14. There is a segment of evangelicals who believe that Christians can apostatize, resulting in the loss of their salvation; thereby they cease to be Christians. They would contend that in such a situation demonic ownership by Satan is possible. This is a large and complex issue that the church has struggled with for years. Ultimately the answer depends on one's decision regarding what the Scriptures teach about eternal security.

15. Unger, *What Demons Can Do to Saints,* 72–73.

16. See Anthony A. Hoekema, *Created in God's Image: The Christian Doctrine of Man* (Grand Rapids: Eerdmans, 1986), 83–85.

17. See George E. Ladd, *A Theology of the New Testament,* rev. ed. (Grand Rapids: Eerdmans, 1993), 499, who notes, "Recent scholarship has recognized that such terms as

body, soul, and spirit are not different, separable faculties of each individual but different ways of viewing the whole person." See also Hoekema, *Image,* 204–10.

18. Peterson, *Possessed by God,* 108, aptly notes, "The Christian does not any longer live a life fundamentally determined and controlled by the flesh. Nevertheless, 'flesh' continues to be a powerful force in our experience."

19. Ladd, *Theology,* 514, aptly comments, "A person belongs either to one realm or to the other; and one's status is determined by whether or not he or she is indwelt by the Spirit of God."

20. Robert Boyd Munger, *My Heart–Christ's Home,* rev. ed. (Downers Grove, Ill.: Inter-Varsity, 1986).

21. Peterson, *Possessed by God,* 100.

22. See my entry, "Centers of Early Christianity," in *Dictionary of the Later New Testament and Its Developments,* ed. Ralph P. Martin and Peter H. Davids (Downers Grove, Ill.: InterVarsity, forthcoming).

23. See my *Power and Magic: The Concept of Power in Ephesians* (Grand Rapids: Baker, 1997), 14–20, for a description of the prevalence of magic and occultic practices in western Asia Minor, especially in Ephesus.

24. I follow the commonly used understanding of occultism as reflected in the major entry in *Encyclopaedia Britannica:* "Occultism encompasses a wide range of theories and practices involving a belief in and knowledge or use of supernatural forces or beings. Such beliefs and practices [are] principally magical or divinatory" (see *The New Encyclopaedia Britannica: Macropaedia,* 15th ed. [Chicago, 1993], 15:76–98, esp. 76).

25. *Papyri Graecae Magicae* 1.1–2. For further discussion, see my *Powers of Darkness: Principalities and Powers in Paul's Letters* (Downers Grove, Ill.: InterVarsity, 1992), 28–30.

26. See Gordon D. Fee, *1 and 2 Timothy,* New International Bible Commentary (Peabody, Mass.: Hendrickson, 1988), 98, 101.

27. George W. Knight, *Commentary on the Pastoral Epistles,* New International Greek Testament Commentary (Grand Rapids: Eerdmans, 1992), 426.

28. See W. Bauer, W. F. Arndt, F. W. Gingrich, and F. W. Danker, *Greek-English Lexicon of the New Testament and Other Early Christian Literature,* 2d ed. (Chicago: University of Chicago Press, 1979), 416.

29. J. Ramsey Michaels, *1 Peter,* Word Biblical Commentary 49 (Waco: Word, 1988), 299.

30. I have devoted an entire monograph to the background of Colossians; see *The Colossian Syncretism: The Interface between Christianity and Folk Belief at Colossae,* Wissenschaftliche Untersuchungen zum Neuen Testament 77, 2d series (Tübingen: J. C. B. Mohr [Paul Siebeck], 1995; North American edition by Baker, 1996).

31. Some have interpreted the *stoicheia* as "elemental principles" of some sort, such as basic principles common to all religion, foundational cosmological principles, or the domain of flesh, sin, and death. This interpretation is reflected in the NIV and NASB versions of the Bible. The term itself has a broad range of usage in the literature, where it has been used for the letters of the alphabet, the actual physical elements, the foundational principles of something, planets and stars, and even spirits and demons. The context of the usage in Colossians, however, suggests the demonic spirit interpretation, as reflected in the RSV and NRSV translations. Paul claims that the false teaching was inspired by the *stoicheia,* not Christ.

32. For a full discussion of this passage, see my treatment of it in "Returning to the Domain of the Powers: *Stoicheia* as Evil Spirits in Gal 4:3, 9," *Novum Testamentum* 38 (1996): 55–76.

33. Parts of this section are heavily dependent on my article, "Satan, Devil," in *Dic-*

tionary of the Later New Testament and Its Developments, ed. Ralph P. Martin and Peter H. Davids (Downers Grove, Ill.: InterVarsity, forthcoming).

34. Elaine Pagels, *The Origin of Satan* (New York: Random House, 1995). For Pagels, as for many scholars in the Western historical-critical tradition, the devil and his demons are the remnant of a primitive apocalyptic worldview—mythological accretions that have failed to go away in much of Christianity today.

35. See Colin Ross, *Multiple Personality Disorder: Diagnosis, Clinical Features, and Treatment,* Wiley Series in General and Clinical Psychology (New York: John Wiley & Sons, 1989), 60–61.

36. There is no officially recognized diagnostic category for this kind of altered consciousness attributed to a spirit presence—at least in the United States. The recently published 4th edition of the *Diagnostic and Statistical Manual of Mental Disorders (DSM-IV)* (Washington, D.C.: American Psychiatric Association, 1994), 484–87 (= §300.14)—the official psychiatric nosology of the American Psychiatric Association—subsumes these symptoms under the rubric of "dissociative disorders" or to the physiological effects of a general medical condition (e.g., seizure disorder) or to the effects of a substance (e.g., drug abuse or medications). As preparations were being made for the creation of the *DSM-IV,* a group of psychologists proposed the inclusion of a new diagnostic category called "Trance and Possession Disorder" (TPD) (see the *DSM-IV Options Book: Work in Progress* [Washington, D.C.: American Psychiatric Association, 1991], K:3 [= §F44.3 "Trance and Possession Disorder"]). After significant debate, the new disorder was not included in the revised diagnostic manual.

37. The disorder is now officially recognized by the important international medical/psychological diagnostic manual known as *The International Classification of Diseases (ICD-10),* prepared by the World Health Organization. The *ICD-10* describes the disorder as "a temporary loss of both the sense of personal identity and full awareness of the surroundings." The afflicted individual "acts as if taken over by another personality, spirit, deity, or 'force.' " The diagnostic category appears in the new 10th edition of the manual, *The ICD-10 Classification of Mental and Behavioral Disorders: Clinical Descriptions and Diagnostic Guidelines* (Geneva: World Health Organization, 1992), 156–57 (= §F44.3, "Trance and Possession Disorder").

38. Etzel Cardena, "Trance and Possession as Dissociative Disorders," *Transcultural Psychiatric Research Review* 29.4 (1992): 300.

39. Why did Jesus restrict the Twelve from taking anything on their journey? A variety of suggestions have been put forth, all or a combination of some of which may be right: (1) this was a prophetic sign of eschatological urgency to the people of Israel; (2) this was a means of identification with the poor; and (3) this was a sign of their utter dependence on God.

40. I. Howard Marshall, *Luke,* New International Greek Testament Commentary (Grand Rapids: Eerdmans, 1978), 351, correctly observes that "their preservation [i.e., the three accounts of the sending of the Twelve] by Mark and the other Evangelists indicates that the basic principles in them were regarded as of lasting value for the church."

41. See Robert Stein, *Luke,* New American Commentary 24 (Nashville: Broadman, 1992), 310: "This passage continues the theme of the mission of the seventy(-two) and thus, by extension, the future mission of the church." Marshall (*Luke,* 413) suggests that the passage prefigures the church's mission to the Gentiles.

42. Note what each of the following writers say about the authority of the believer in the name of Christ to command demonic spirits to leave afflicted individuals:

Justin Martyr: Justin believes that Jesus' promise to the Seventy—that they would have "authority to trample on snakes and scorpions" (Luke 10:19)—applied to Christians of his day. Commenting on this verse, he notes, "And now we, who believe on our Lord Jesus, who was crucified under Pontius Pilate, when we exorcise all demons and evil spirits, have them subjected to us" (*Dialogue with Trypho* 65).

"For numberless demoniacs throughout the whole world, and in your city [Rome], many of our Christian men exorcising them in the name of Jesus Christ, who was crucified under Pontius Pilate, have healed and do heal, rendering helpless and driving the possessing devils out of the men, though they could not be cured by all the other exorcists, and those who used incantations and drugs" (*Second Apology of Justin* 6).

Tatian: "Being smitten by the word of God, they [demons] depart in terror, and the sick man is healed" (*Address to the Greeks* 16).

Tertullian: "Let a person be brought before your tribunals, who is plainly under demoniacal possession. The wicked spirit, bidden to speak by a follower of Christ, will as readily make the truthful confession that he is a demon, as elsewhere he has falsely asserted that he is a god. . . . Fearing Christ in God, and God in Christ, they become subject to the servants of God and Christ. So at our touch and breathing, overwhelmed by the thought and realization of those judgment fires, they leave at our command the bodies they have entered, unwilling, and distressed, and before your very eyes put to an open shame" (*Apology* 23).

Origen: "For it is not by incantations that Christians seem to prevail (over evil spirits), but by the name of Jesus, accompanied by the announcement of the narratives which relate to Him; for the repetition of these has frequently been the means of driving demons out of men, especially when those who repeated them did so in a sound and genuinely believing spirit" (*Contra Celsus* 1.6).

Minucius Felix: "A great many, even some of your own people, know all those things that the demons themselves confess concerning themselves, as often as they are driven by us from bodies by the torments of our words and by the fires of our prayers . . . for when abjured by the only and true God, unwillingly the wretched beings shudder in their bodies, and either at once leap forth, or vanish by degrees, as the faith of the sufferer assists or the grace of the healer inspires" (*Octavius* 27).

43. Gregory Dix, ed., *The Treatise on the Apostolic Tradition of St. Hippolytus of Rome,* reissued with corrections, preface, and bibliography by H. Chadwick (London: Alban; Ridgefield, Conn.: Morehouse Publishing, 1991 [first published 1937]).
44. Philip Schaff, *History of the Christian Church* (1910; reprint, Grand Rapids: Eerdmans, 1994), 2:758–59.
45. Dix, *Apostolic Tradition,* ix.
46. Ibid., xxxix–xl.
47. For good discussions of the history and nature of the catechumenate, see Michael Dujarer, *A History of the Catechumenate: The First Six Centuries* (New York: Sadlier, 1979); Thomas M. Finn, *Early Christian Baptism and the Catechumenate: West and East Syria,* Messages of the Fathers of the Church 5 (Collegeville, Minn.: Glazier, 1992) and his *Early*

Christian Baptism and the Catechumenate: Italy, North Africa, and Egypt, Messages of the Fathers of the Church 6 (Collegeville, Minn.: Glazier, 1992). See also the collection of essays in the volume edited by Everett Ferguson, David M. Scholer, and Paul C. Finney, *Conversion, Catechumenate, and Baptism in the Early Church,* Studies in Early Christianity 12 (New York: Garland, 1993).

48. Tertullian, *De pudicitia* 19.19–20, as cited in Henry A. Kelly, *The Devil at Baptism: Ritual, Theology, and Drama* (Ithaca, N.Y.: Cornell University Press, 1985), 107.

49. Pseudo-Clement, *Recognitions* 2.71, as cited in Kelly, *The Devil at Baptism,* 124.

50. Origen, *Homily on Joshua* 15.5, as quoted in Everett Ferguson, *Demonology of the Early Christian World,* Symposium Series 12 (Lewiston/Queenston: Edwin Mellen, 1984), 128.

51. Pseudo-Clement, *On Virginity* 1.12. See the discussion in Ferguson, *Demonology,* 132–33.

52. The *Apostolic Canons* form the concluding chapter (8.47) of the *Apostolic Constitutions.*

53. On Byzantine demonology, see Richard P. H. Greenfield, *Traditions of Belief in Late Byzantine Demonology* (Amsterdam: Adolf M. Hakkert, 1988).

54. Calvin strongly and properly emphasized the sovereignty of God with respect to the demons, but envisioned a high level of influence evil spirits could have on Christians. He said that demons "exercise believers in combat, ambush them, invade their peace, beset them in combat, and also often weary them, rout them, terrify them, and sometimes wound them; yet they never vanquish or crush them" (*Institutes of the Christian Religion,* ed. J. T. McNeill [Philadelphia: Westminster, 1960], 1:176 [= bk. 1, chap. 14, sec. 18]).

55. On this issue, see the excellent discussion in Wayne Grudem, *Systematic Theology* (Grand Rapids: Zondervan, 1994), 494–97.

56. David Powlison, *Power Encounters: Reclaiming Spiritual Warfare* (Grand Rapids: Baker, 1995).

57. Ibid., 100.

58. Eanna Einhorne, "Tarot Therapy: Reaching Our Inner Allies and Spiritual Guides," *Information Press* 2.7 (March 1993): 21.

59. Duane Garrett, *Angels and the New Spirituality* (Nashville: Broadman and Holman, 1995).

60. Ibid., 140.

61. See, for example, Page's critique of this aspect of Neil Anderson and Tom White's approach in his *Powers of Evil,* 169 n. 91, 179 n. 154.

62. Jim Logan, *Reclaiming Surrendered Ground: Protecting Your Family from Spiritual Attacks* (Chicago: Moody, 1995), 35.

63. Neil T. Anderson, *The Bondage Breaker* (Eugene, Ore.: Harvest House, 1990) and *Victory over the Darkness: Realizing the Power of Your Identity in Christ* (Ventura, Calif.: Regal, 1990).

64. Gordon Fee has recently written a thorough biblical-theological study of the theme of the Holy Spirit in Paul's letters: *God's Empowering Presence: The Holy Spirit in the Letters of Paul* (Peabody, Mass.: Hendrickson, 1994).

65. Charles H. Kraft, *Christianity with Power: Your Worldview and Your Experience of the Supernatural* (Ann Arbor: Servant, 1989), 84. See also his essay, "What Kind of Encounters Do We Need in Our Christian Witness?" *Evangelical Missions Quarterly* 27.3 (1991): 258–65.

66. Kraft, *Christianity with Power,* 4–5.

67. Rodger K. Bufford, "Demonic Influence and Mental Disorders," *Journal of Psy-*

chology and Christianity 8 (1989): 35–48, has compiled a list of symptoms (see p. 36) that many people involved in deliverance ministry look for. The difficulty of diagnosing demonic influence solely on the basis of such symptoms is that each of the symptoms is associated with at least one of the mental disorders in the standard diagnostic manuals used by psychologists.

68. See the excellent article by Marguerite Shuster, "Giving the Devil More Than His Due: Sometimes Exorcism Causes Damage Not Deliverance," *Leadership* 12.3 (summer 1991): 64–67.

69. The seven steps may be summarized as follows:

1. *Counterfeit versus Real:* renounce your previous or current involvements with satanically inspired occult practices.
2. *Deception versus Truth:* announce and internalize the truth of who you are in Christ.
3. *Bitterness versus Forgiveness:* forgive others who have offended or hurt you so Satan does not take advantage of you.
4. *Rebellion versus Submission:* ask God to forgive you for a spirit of rebelliousness and the times you have not been submissive to those in authority over you.
5. *Pride versus Humility:* confess areas of pridefulness to the Lord and ask for his forgiveness.
6. *Bondage versus Freedom:* admit and confess patterns of habitual sin. Renounce these and ask God to break the bondage that has resulted from this behavior.
7. *Acquiescence versus Renunciation:* renounce the sins of your ancestors and any curses that may have been placed on you.

70. Marvin Meyer and Richard Smith, eds., *Ancient Christian Magic: Coptic Texts of Ritual Power* (San Francisco: Harper San Francisco, 1994).

71. Michael Warnke, *The Satan Seller* (Plainfield, N.J.: Logos International, 1972).

72. Michael Warnke, *Schemes of Satan* (Tulsa: Victory House, 1991).

73. John Trott and Mike Hertenstein, "Selling Satan," *Cornerstone* 21.98 (June–July 1992): 7–38.

74. Mike Hertenstein and John Trott, *Selling Satan: The Tragic History of Mike Warnke* (Chicago: Cornerstone, 1993).

75. Perucci Ferraiuolo, "Warnke Calls Critics Satanists," *Christianity Today,* 9 November 1992, 49, 52.

76. Perucci Ferraiuolo, "Warnke Admits Failure," *Christianity Today,* 17 May 1993, 88–89.

77. Tim Stafford, "Absence of Truth," *Christianity Today,* 14 September 1992, 18.

78. See the *Diagnostic and Statistical Manual of Mental Disorders (DSM-IV),* 4th ed. (Washington, D.C.: American Psychiatric Association, 1994), 484–87 (= §300.14).

79. On the topic of Satanic Ritual Abuse (SRA), see the excellent article by Robin D. Perrin and Les Parrott III, "Memories of Satanic Ritual Abuse: The Truth behind the Panic," *Christianity Today,* 21 June 1993, 18–23.

80. This could be said to characterize the general approach of the False Memory Syndrome Foundation, 3401 Market Street, Suite 130, Philadelphia, PA 19104.

81. Kenneth V. Lanning, "Ritual Abuse: A Law Enforcement View or Perspective," *Child Abuse and Neglect* 15 (1991): 173.

82. James T. Richardson, Joel Best, and David G. Bromley, *The Satanism Scare* (New

York: Aldine de Gruyter, 1991); Robert D. Hicks, *In Pursuit of Satan: The Police and the Occult* (Buffalo: Prometheus, 1991); Jeffrey S. Victor, *Satanic Panic: The Creation of a Contemporary Legend* (Chicago: Open Court, 1993); Debbie Nathan, *Satan's Silence: Ritual Abuse and the Making of a Modern American Witch Hunt* (New York: HarperCollins, Basic Books, 1995).

83. Colin A. Ross, *Satanic Ritual Abuse: Principles of Treatment* (Toronto: University of Toronto Press, 1995), 70–71.

84. Ibid., vii.

85. Ibid., 61–72.

86. Ibid., ix.

87. Ibid., x.

88. This is also the plea made by Martha Rogers in her introductory essay for a special issue of the *Journal of Psychology and Theology* focusing on Satanic Ritual Abuse. Her essay is entitled "A Call for Discernment—Natural and Spiritual," *Journal of Psychology and Theology* 20.3 (1992): 175–86.

89. Ralph Frammolino and K. Connie Kang, "Exorcism Ritual Ends in Death, Police Say," *Los Angeles Times,* 6 July 1996, sec. B3.

Chapter 3: Are We Called to Engage Territorial Spirits?

1. A portion of this chapter was presented at the annual meeting of the Evangelical Theological Society, Philadelphia, Pa., 18 November 1995. Portions have also been read by various members of the Spiritual Warfare Network. I am grateful for the comments I received that helped improve this chapter.

2. Mario R. Morales, "La Quiebra de Maximón," *Crónica Semanal,* 24 June 1994, 17–20, as cited by C. Peter Wagner in a 17 October 1994 memorandum distributed to members of the Spiritual Warfare Network. The account is also mentioned by Cindy Jacobs in her book, *The Voice of God: How God Speaks Personally and Corporately to His Children Today* (Ventura, Calif.: Regal, 1995), 250–51, and in Wagner's, *Confronting the Powers: How the New Testament Church Experienced the Power of Strategic-Level Spiritual Warfare,* Prayer Warrior Series (Ventura, Calif.: Regal, 1996), 217–20.

3. Beckett has now written the story in "Practical Steps toward Community Deliverance," in *Breaking Strongholds in Your City: How to Use Spiritual Mapping to Make Your Prayers More Strategic, Effective, and Targeted,* ed. C. Peter Wagner (Ventura, Calif.: Regal, 1993), 147–70.

4. See Edgardo Silvoso, "A Layman Challenges Demon Powers in Argentina," *Charisma and Christian Life,* January 1994, 70–75.

5. Edgardo Silvoso, "Prayer Power in Argentina," in *Engaging the Enemy: How to Fight and Defeat Territorial Spirits,* ed. C. Peter Wagner (Ventura, Calif.: Regal, 1991), 113.

6. The statement is included as an appendix in Wagner's, *Confronting the Powers,* 249–62.

7. C. Peter Wagner, *Warfare Prayer: How to Seek God's Power and Protection in the Battle to Build His Kingdom,* Prayer Warrior Series (Ventura, Calif.: Regal, 1992), 156.

8. C. Peter Wagner, "Twenty-One Questions," in *Behind Enemy Lines: An Advanced Guide to Spiritual Warfare,* ed. Charles H. Kraft and others (Ann Arbor: Servant, Vine Books, 1994), 135.

9. Larry Lea, "Binding the Strongman," in *Engaging the Enemy: How to Fight and Defeat Territorial Spirits,* ed. C. Peter Wagner (Ventura, Calif.: Regal, 1991), 88.

10. John Dawson, in the foreword to *Engaging the Enemy: How to Fight and Defeat Territorial Spirits,* ed. C. Peter Wagner (Ventura, Calif.: Regal, 1991), xi.

11. Dawson, in *Engaging the Enemy,* xii.

12. Wagner, *Warfare Prayer,* 176.

13. Wagner, *Confronting the Powers,* 200.

14. George Otis Jr., *The Last of the Giants: Lifting the Veil on Islam and the End Times* (Grand Rapids: Chosen, 1991), 85, and "An Overview of Spiritual Mapping," in *Breaking Strongholds in Your City,* ed. C. Peter Wagner (Ventura, Calif.: Regal, 1993), 32.

15. George Otis Jr. and Mark Brockman, eds., *Strongholds of the 10/40 Window: Intercessor's Guide to the World's Least Evangelized Nations* (Seattle, Wash.: YWAM, 1995).

16. Wagner, *Warfare Prayer,* 177–78.

17. John Dawson, *Taking Our Cities for God: How to Break Spiritual Strongholds* (Lake Mary, Fla.: Creation House, 1989), 183–89 (= chap. 19: "Identifying with the Sins of the City").

18. John Dawson, *Healing America's Wounds* (Ventura, Calif.: Regal, 1994), 276.

19. C. Peter Wagner, "The Philosophy of Prayer for World Evangelization Adopted by the AD 2000 United Prayer Track" (16 November 1994), statement no. 22, p. 7. The statement is now included in Wagner, *Confronting the Powers,* 249–62.

20. Wagner, *Confronting the Powers,* 158–59.

21. Wagner, *Warfare Prayer,* 156–57.

22. Ibid., 158.

23. Cindy Jacobs, *Possessing the Gates of the Enemy: A Training Manual for Militant Intercession,* 2d ed. (Grand Rapids: Chosen, 1994), 245–46.

24. Ibid., 232.

25. Victor Lorenzo, "Evangelizing a City Dedicated to Darkness," in *Breaking Strongholds in Your City,* 177.

26. Larry Lea, *Could You Not Tarry One Hour?* (Altamonte Springs, Fla.: Creation House, 1987), 93, as cited in Wagner, *Warfare Prayer,* 150.

27. Peter C. Craigie, *The Book of Deuteronomy,* New International Commentary on the Old Testament (Grand Rapids: Eerdmans, 1976), 379.

28. Sydney H. T. Page correctly summarizes the course of scholarship on this psalm when he observes that a consensus exists among contemporary scholars on understanding the gods in Psalm 82 as suprahuman beings rather than human rulers (*Powers of Evil: A Biblical Study of Satan and Demons* [Grand Rapids: Baker, 1995], 58).

29. The Hebrew Masoretic Text reads: "For all the gods of the nations are idols."

30. On Canaanite religion, see Peter C. Craigie and Gerald H. Wilson, "Religions of the Biblical World: Canaanite," in *International Standard Bible Encyclopedia,* ed. Geoffrey W. Bromiley and others, rev. ed. (Grand Rapids: Eerdmans, 1979–88), 4:95–101.

31. Ibid., 96.

32. James A. Montgomery comments, "The bk. of Dan. presents a full-fledged doctrine of the Princes of the nations, i.e., their celestial patrons" (*The Book of Daniel,* International Critical Commentary [Edinburgh: T. & T. Clark, 1927], 419).

33. See, for example, Stephen R. Miller, *Daniel,* New American Commentary 18 (Nashville: Broadman and Holman, 1994), 284–85; Page, *Powers of Evil,* 63–65; but compare Robert J. Priest, Thomas Campbell, and Bradford A. Mullen, "Missiological Syncretism: The New Animistic Paradigm," in *Spiritual Power and Missions: Raising the Issues,* ed. Edward Rommen, Evangelical Missiological Society Series 3 (Pasadena, Calif.: William Carey Library, 1995), 73.

34. See Miller, *Daniel,* 279–82.

35. There are some scholars who think the *archontes* of this passage refer strictly to the human rulers. The evidence points more strongly to the demonic rulers that instigated the death of Christ. See D. Aune, "Archon" in *Dictionary of Deities and Demons in*

the Bible (Leiden: Brill, 1995), 153–59, esp. 158.

36. See "Statement on Spiritual Warfare: The Intercession Working Group Report, Lausanne Committee on World Evangelization," *Urban Mission* 13.2 (1995): 52 (originally published in *World Evangelization* 18.65 [December 1993]).

37. Wagner, *Warfare Prayer,* 20.

38. Others have also noted this misapplication of Daniel 10; see Gerry Breshears, "The Body of Christ: Prophet, Priest, or King?" *Journal of the Evangelical Theological Society* 37.1 (1994): 13–14; Page, *Powers of Evil,* 65; Priest, Campbell, and Mullen, "Missiological Syncretism," 73.

39. See Henry A. Kelly, *The Devil at Baptism: Ritual, Theology, and Drama* (Ithaca, N.Y.: Cornell University Press, 1985).

40. *Firmicus Maternus: The Error of the Pagan Religions,* trans. and annotated by C. A. Forbes, Ancient Christian Writers 37 (New York: Newman, 1970), 71–72.

41. Wagner, *Warfare Prayer,* 147.

42. See my *Power and Magic: The Concept of Power in Ephesians* (Grand Rapids: Baker, 1997), 54–55.

43. Point 3 of "The Philosophy of Prayer for World Evangelization Adopted by the AD 2000 United Prayer Track" (cited in Wagner, *Confronting the Powers,* 252).

44. This is also the opinion of C. Peter Wagner, based on a discussion with him 11 January 1996.

45. This is also the conclusion of Overseas Missionary Fellowship (OMF) missionary Chuck Lowe, who has just completed a comprehensive analysis of SLSW in a manuscript tentatively titled *Defeating Demons: A Critique of Strategic Level Spiritual Warfare.*

46. Some interpreters think that they were reviling the good angels who functioned as angelic guardians of the Old Testament Law (Torah) or that they were, as Gnostics, railing on the creator god and his angels. R. Bauckham (*Jude, 2 Peter,* Word Biblical Commentary 50 [Dallas: Word, 1983], 262–63) characterizes the opponents as rationalists who may have doubted the very existence of supernatural powers and thus spoke of the powers of evil in skeptical, mocking terms. Their reviling appears to be more direct than this, based on how Peter clarifies that the good angels never directly revile them.

47. See my *Power and Magic,* 62–64.

48. Geoffrey W. Bromiley, "Keys, Power of the," in *International Standard Bible Encyclopedia,* ed. Geoffrey W. Bromiley and others, rev. ed. (Grand Rapids: Eerdmans, 1979–88), 3:12.

49. Wagner, *Confronting the Powers,* 104–12, 220–22.

50. For an English translation, see Knut Schäferdiek, "The Acts of John," in *New Testament Apocrypha,* vol. 2, *Writings Related to the Apostles; Apocalypses and Related Subjects,* ed. Wilhelm Schneemelcher, rev. ed. (Louisville: Westminster/John Knox, 1989), 152–209.

51. See Schäferdiek, "Acts of John," 207–8 n. 55. See also Richard E. Oster, "Ephesus as a Religious Center under the Principate, I. Paganism before Constantine," in *Aufstieg und Niedergang der römischen Welt* 2.18.2 (Berlin: Walter de Gruyter, 1993), 1713–14. The pertinent ancient texts recording the destruction of the temple are collected and printed in *Forschungen in Ephesos veröffentlicht vom Österreichischen Archäologischen Instituts* (Vienna: Alfred Holder, 1906), 1:262–72.

52. Cited in Schäferdiek, "Acts of John," 156.

53. Cited in Philip Schaff, *History of the Christian Church,* vol. 3, *Nicene and Post-Nicene Christianity* (1910; reprint, Grand Rapids: Eerdmans, 1994), 66.

54. Wagner, *Confronting the Powers,* 104.

55. R. van Dam, "Hagiography and History: The Life of Gregory Thaumaturgus," *Classical Antiquity* 1 (1982): 302.

56. See the extensive discussion of this theme in ibid., 272–308. See also Alban Butler, who comments regarding many of the stories, "there is little doubt that a good deal of it is legendary" (*Butler's Lives of the Saints,* edited, revised, and supplemented by H. Thurston and D. Attwater [London: Burns and Oates, 1956], 4:362).

57. Lowe, *Defeating Demons,* chap. 13, points this out as well.

58. Mike Wakely, "A Critical Look at a New 'Key' to Evangelization," *Evangelical Missions Quarterly* (1995): 159.

59. Oster, "Ephesus as a Religious Center," 1700–1706.

60. Duane A. Garrett, *Angels and the New Spirituality* (Nashville: Broadman and Holman, 1995), 216.

61. The word itself has a history of usage in British English for "the supposed line of a prehistoric track in a straight line usually from hilltop to hilltop with identifying points such as ponds, mounds, etc., marking its route" (*Oxford English Dictionary,* 8:876–77). The concept of a gridwork of ley lines has become quite popular in contemporary occultism, but plotted from sites that are thought to contain psychic or occultic power. In fact, a new magazine entitled *The Ley Hunter* was launched in Great Britain and is devoted to the study of leys, ancient wisdom, sacred sites, and cosmic energy.

62. Neville Drury, *Dictionary of Mysticism and the Occult* (San Francisco: Harper & Row, 1985), s.v. Drury reports that psychical researchers and mediums claim that "patterns of psychic energy emanate from the leys." He also notes that some UFO researchers "believe that the ley-lines are power grids used to guide extraterrestrial visitors who have allegedly contacted human civilization since earliest times and profoundly influenced myths and legends." See also "Leys," in *Encyclopedia of Occultism and Parapsychology,* 2d ed., 3 vols. (Detroit: Gale Research, 1984).

63. The Lausanne Committee on World Evangelization also expressed concern about a reversion to pagan worldviews. Their recent statement on spiritual warfare warned, "There is a danger that we revert to think and operate on pagan worldviews. . . . The antidote to this is the rigorous study of the whole of Scripture" ("Statement on Spiritual Warfare," 52).

64. Otis is currently writing a book titled *Spiritual Mapping Today: A Practical Guide to Identifying Obstacles to Revival in Your Community.* He has just completed another book, *The Twilight Labyrinth: A Revealing Journey into the Spiritual Dimension,* in which he attempts to reveal the workings of spiritual powers in the religious and occultic practices in a variety of cultures that militate against the spread of the gospel. Part of his objective is to demonstrate that there is indeed a real devil and demonic activity that lies behind human suffering, worldviews, mythological motifs, and religious systems.

65. This was confirmed in a telephone conversation with George Otis Jr., 7 November 1995.

66. Especially the book edited by C. Peter Wagner and Mark Wilson, *Praying through the 100 Gateway Cities of the 10/40 Window* (Seattle, Wash.: YWAM, 1995).

67. This remark comes from an endorsement on the inside front cover of the book.

68. Dawson, *Engaging the Enemy,* ix. In the study guide for his book *Taking Our Cities for God* (Lake Mary, Fla.: Creation House, 1989) Dawson similarly downplays any need to name and cast down territorial spirits: "It is important to note that there are no stories [in *Taking Our Cities*] that depict an individual identifying principalities and powers and then singlehandedly overcoming them" (*Taking Our Cities for God Study Guide* [Altamonte Springs, Fla.: CharismaLife Learning Resources, 1990], 5).

69. Cited in Wagner, *Confronting the Powers,* 260, italics mine.

70. Kjell Sjöberg, "Spiritual Mapping for Prophetic Actions," in *Breaking Strongholds in Your City,* 109.

71. Ibid., 118.

72. Personal conversation with Peter Wagner at the Global Harvest Ministries offices, 11 January 1996.

73. Lorenzo, "Evangelizing," 190.

74. See *Oxford English Dictionary,* 13:591.

75. Dawson, *Healing America's Wounds,* 45–47.

76. Joe Hellerman, "Some Additional Thoughts about Building a Theological Foundation for Racial Reconciliation," unpublished paper written for the Promise Keepers organization, 1996.

77. Dawson, *Healing America's Wounds,* 230.

78. Hellerman, "Racial Reconciliation," 3.

79. Personal correspondence, 14 June 1996.

80. Sherwood Lingenfelter, *Transforming Culture: A Challenge for Christian Mission* (Grand Rapids: Baker, 1992).

81. Walter Wink, *Engaging the Powers: Discernment and Resistance in a World of Domination* (Minneapolis: Fortress, 1992), 75.

82. John Wimber notes, "When I prayed about Australia I asked *God* to come against the spirit of rejection. If he chose to deploy angels or send his Spirit to bind the territorial spirit, that was his business. My trust is in God and his strategy, not my ideas and efforts" (*Power Points* [San Francisco: HarperCollins, 1991], 183).

83. Michael Ebert, ed., *WindoWatchman* (Colorado Springs, Colo.: Christian Information Network, 1994); George Otis Jr. and Mark Brockman, eds., *Strongholds of the 10/40 Window: Intercessor's Guide to the World's Least Evangelized Nations* (Seattle, Wash.: YWAM, 1995); Patrick J. Johnstone, *Operation World: The Day-by-Day Guide to Praying for the World,* 5th ed. (Carlisle, England: OM Publishing; Grand Rapids: Zondervan, 1993).

84. David Bryant, *The Hope at Hand: National and World Revival for the Twenty-First Century* (Grand Rapids: Baker, 1995).

85. Neil T. Anderson and Charles Mylander, *Setting Your Church Free: A Biblical Plan to Help Your Church* (Ventura, Calif.: Regal, 1994).

86. Ibid., 228.

87. See the list of renunciations and announcements, ibid., 307–9.

88. Ibid., 313–14.

89. Ibid., 317–18.

90. Ed Silvoso, *That None Should Perish: How to Reach Entire Cities for Christ through Prayer Evangelism* (Ventura, Calif.: Regal, 1994).

91. Victor Lorenzo, a co-worker of Ed Silvoso with Harvest Evangelism, has written a description of how the strategy was applied to both Resistencia and La Plata. See Victor Lorenzo, "Evangelizing a City Dedicated to Darkness," in *Breaking Strongholds,* 171–93.

92. Silvoso, *That None Should Perish,* 73.

93. Ibid.

94. Ibid., 250.

95. Letter to me dated 14 June 1996.

96. The concern to find unity in the midst of the present divisiveness about spiritual warfare issues is also a concern of the Lausanne Committee on World Evangelization. In their recent statement on spiritual warfare, they note: "We are concerned that the subject and practice of spiritual warfare is proving divisive to evangelical Christians and pray that these thoughts of ours will help us to combat this tendency. It is our deep prayer that the force for evangelization should not be fragmented and that our love should be strong enough to overcome these incipient divisions among us" ("Statement on Spiritual Warfare," 53).

General Index

Scripture Index

221

6:6–13 105
9:21 113, 119
10:45 64

Luke

2:7 88
4:1–13 104
4:6 20
4:18 22
4:33 205 n. 10
4:37 88
8:27 205 n. 10
9:1–6 105
10:1–11 105
10:17 51, 105, 116, 164
10:17–20 105
10:18 51
10:19 105, 161, 164,
  208 n. 42
11:14–23 106
11:20 20, 105
11:21 22, 81
11:22 22, 49
11:24 88
14:9 88
22:3 113
22:31 120
22:31–32 45
22:32 125

John

1:1 62
8:32 121
8:44 97
12:31 20, 154
14:2–3 88
14:16 188
14:17 42
14:18 42
14:26 188
14:30 20
15:26 188
16:11 20
17:3 21
19:11 113
20:23 169
21:15–21 45

Acts

2:38 180
4:18 52
4:29 52
4:31 52
5:1–11 113
5:3 97
13:4–12 187
13:6–12 166
16:16–18 106, 166
19 132, 167, 172
19:10 91
19:11 91
19:11–12 106, 167
19:12 91
19:13–16 91
19:18 91

Romans

1:16 188, 196
5:1 80
5:12–21 113
6 122
6:6 40
6:12 89
6:12–13 82
6:12–14 113
6:13 23
8:13 122
8:16–17 81
8:38–39 81
11:32 187
12:19 89
13:12 23

1 Corinthians

2:6 154, 156
2:6–8 168
2:8 154, 156
4:9 168
6:19 81
10:20 153
11:1 106
13:12 11
15:24 38

2 Corinthians

1:22 56
2:1 56

2:4 56
2:11 27, 69
3 182
3:3 56
3:6 56
3:8 56
3:17 56
3:18 56, 182
4:4 20, 97, 189
5:5 56
5:7 55
5:11 184
5:13 184
5:17 83, 84
5:18–20 51, 55
5:18–21 56
5:19 184
5:20 184
5:21 55, 184
6:2 56
6:4–10 55
6:7 23, 55
7:2 55
10 55
10:1–3 54
10:3–5 54
10:4 23
10:5 65
10:13–15 54
10:14 55
11:3 54
11:4 54, 55
11:10 55
11:14 54
11:17 55
11:23–33 55
12:6 55
12:7 100, 120
12:7–10 125
12:8 125
13:7 56
13:8 55
13:9 56
13:10 56
13:14 56

Galatians

4:3 59, 204 n. 36, 206
  n. 32

Clinton E. Arnold (Ph.D., University of Aberdeen) is professor of New Testament language and literature and director of the Th.M. program at Talbot School of Theology. A noted authority on New Testament backgrounds and spiritual warfare, he has written and lectured on these topics for both academic and general audiences. His books include *Power and Magic: The Concept of Power in Ephesians*, *Powers of Darkness: Principalities and Powers in Paul's Letters*, and *The Colossian Syncretism: The Interface between Christianity and Folk Belief at Colossae*.